Penguin   Arkana

ASTROLOGY: A KEY TO PERSONALITY

Born in London, Jeff Mayo served with the Royal Engineers during the Second World War helping to make the maps for the invasion of Europe; he later saw active service in Normandy and Germany. For several years after the war he farmed in Devon with his brother and they were among the pioneersof organic farming.

Jeff Mayo was Head Tutor and then Principal of the Faculty of Astrological Studies before starting the Mayo School of Astrology in 1973, of which he is still Principal-Emeritus. He is the author of *Teach Yourself Astrology*, now in its thirtieth continuous year in print, and also *The Astrologer's Astronomical Handbook, How to Read the Ephemeris, How to Cast a Natal Chart* and *The Planets and Human Behaviour*. He has also contributed numerous articles to a wide range of magazines in the UK and abroad. His internationally acclaimed research studies with Professor Hans Eysenck of The Institute of Psychiatry in London appeared in the American *Journal of Social Psychology*. He is a Fellow of the Royal Meteorological Society and lives in Combe Martin in devon.

JEFF MAYO

Astrology: A Key to Personality

ARKANA
PENGUIN BOOKS

ARKANA

Published by the Penguin Group
Penguin Books Ltd, 27 Wrights Lane, London w8 5tz, England
Penguin Books USA Inc., 375 Hudson Street, New York, New York 10014, USA
Penguin Books Australia Ltd, Ringwood, Victoria, Australia
Penguin Books Canada Ltd, 10 Alcorn Avenue, Toronto, Ontario, Canada m4v 3b2
Penguin Books (NZ) Ltd, 182–190 Wairau Road, Auckland 10, New Zealand

Penguin Books Ltd, Registered Offices: Harmondsworth, Middlesex, England

First published in 1995
10 9 8 7 6 5 4 3 2 1

Copyright © Jeff Mayo, 1995
All rights reserved

The moral right of the author has been asserted

Set in 10.25/13pt Monotype Garamond
Set by Datix International Limited, Bungay, Suffolk
Printed in England by Clays Ltd, St Ives plc

To all those who have inspired me
to look for a spiritual reality in all
things, and to seek the best in
other people

Contents

Illustrations

Preface

The quest for identity

When I first planned this book I provisionally chose the title *The Quest for Identity* because, whether we are aware of it or not, there is a basic need within each one of us to seek to discover our true identity: to find out who we really are, why we behave as we do, whether we would behave differently in many ways if we understood our true selves. Is it possible to see ourselves as others see us and if so, would we realize that our own image of ourselves may well be rather surprisingly different and may need a little revision?

One part of maturity is having a firm sense of identity and this is essential to any enduring, meaningful endeavour or relationship. Identity should correspond to one's self-concept, and although it is constantly developing and changing, its fundamental structure remains the same. It is this structure (or 'blueprint' at birth) that astrology reveals so distinctly. Development and growth depends largely on the individual's capacity to realize this structure's *potentialities*.

We know that parental influence, educational opportunities and the relationships we form can either encourage or retard the development of potentially beneficial qualities. But whatever influence our childhood or adult environments may have had upon us, our *choice* of behaviour and response can only have stemmed from the root being that is unique to each of us. We may try, but we cannot be anyone else.

It is because each of us is a unique human being, different from anyone else, that we each have an identity of our own, an individual personality. Inevitably our true identities will be difficult to distinguish clearly because part of the process of growing up and developing personality is to identify or associate ourselves with what is considered 'normal' behaviour and conduct within current conventions and the sector of society we find ourselves in. This may have a subtly stressful effect because unnatural demands and pressures are put upon the psyche, resulting in suppression of other, more natural desires for self-expression. There is also identification with particular successful individuals or those we admire and respect. In this sense we seek to model ourselves on other people, to incorporate their attributes and thus to display similar behaviour. I know of no method of psychological diagnosis other than astrology that can see through these guises and imitations to an individual's basic structure of potentialities.

Following healthy and positive examples set by others is praiseworthy, but this is distinctly different from trying to ape someone. We need other people not only for the benefits and pleasures we can share, for sexual satisfaction and experience, for building a home and begetting children; we need others for *comparison* with ourselves, so that we can learn to recognize our strengths and weaknesses and identify our own unique features.

It is hoped this book will launch you on an exciting adventure through which you will learn to use your own time, date and place of birth to help you understand more clearly the dynamic structure of your personality and identity.

A unique system of personality interpretation

Traditionally, astrological textbooks have dealt solely with the interpretation of behaviour with no reference to how behaviour might be determined. I have always felt that the reasons for an individual's behaviour cannot be properly understood without relating it to environment, potential stress reactions, the subtle yet powerful undercurrents of survival instincts and the basic human need for fulfilment of the psyche's potentialities. This is what I have done in this textbook, with a unique system based essentially on what I have classified as *survival needs* and *functional needs*. It presents the essence of my personal research, involving thousands of birth charts and case histories, and of experience gained during forty years' study and practice as an astrological consultant and teacher.

To bring even greater clarity to the understanding of behaviour the planets, signs, angles and aspects within a birth chart are shown to relate separately to dynamic psychological features and, when seen interrelated in an individual chart, these present a vivid description of the personality.

The origins of astrology in antiquity

The understanding and presentation of astrology has undergone dramatic changes since the basic concepts of the subject were initiated at the same time the foundations of civilization were being laid in that area of the Middle East known as Mesopotamia. Here, enthusiastically and industriously, the fundamental ideas about orientation and correspondences were developed, particularly by those two great races, the Chaldeans and the Babylonians.

Astrology was developed by all of the early civilizations many centuries before the birth of Christ. The concept of a divine correspondence between planetary deities and human life appeared perfectly natural and purposeful. Observation of the heavenly bodies was an inevitable extension of man's awareness of his environment and his detection of their cyclic motions told him of the passage of time and the seasons from which he was able to construct calendars. Astrology, chronology and navigation were the primary forms of scientific endeavour in the cultures of prehistory. Knowledge of the motions of the celestial phenomena was also deemed important for the timing of sacrifices and the celebration of religious ceremonies, as well as such knowledge helping to elevate the soul.

It seems to be a basic need within man to recognize patterns and rhythms in nature. Astrology was developed through celestial observation, enabling man to understand and foresee planetary patterns. This encouraged another basic need: the imposition of order, a form of mastery over his environment.

Astrology: the basis for a reconstructed discipline of psychology

It can only be a matter of time before astrology is accepted by the majority of psychologists as the basis for a new and reconstructed discipline and study of human psychology. It may preferably not be called 'psychology'. Perhaps biocosmology would be an apt title:

> bio: life, course or way of living – but in modern scientific words, extended to mean 'organic life'
> cosmology: the theory of the universe as an ordered whole, and of the general laws which govern it

Many pages in this book could be filled with quotations from scientific writings that would appear to confirm the validity of astrological concepts. Let just one suffice here, from *ISA Transactions*, Vol. 8, No. 4, 1969, published by the Instrument Society of America, Pittsburgh, Pennsylvania:

The human living on the planet Earth is governed more by the motion of celestial bodies than scientists think ... Intermediate between the two extremes of heavy, slow celestial bodies governed by gravitational forces and electrons in atoms, humans are both made of, and have to live in, electromagnetic forces, fields, and waves.

The late Dr Carl Jung, the eminent Swiss psychologist, who, for the last thirty years of his life often employed astrology 'in cases of difficult psychological diagnosis', wrote in *The Secret of the Golden Flower*:

Astrology is assured of recognition from psychology without further restrictions, because astrology represents the summation of all the psychological knowledge of antiquity.

One doesn't need to believe in a Creator or the continuation of one's spirit after the death of the body to be a good astrologer, but without that belief an exhilarating awareness of that vitally important dimension of experience must be lacking. A sense of the eternal reality and survival of the spirit within the limited physical body and the belief that there *is* a reason for pain, suffering and death in the midst of life and the seeking-for-happiness can inspire the astrological counsellor in his comfort and guidance of the distressed or depressed client.

Astrology, as presented in this book, provides the means by which anyone can realize the profound and exciting truth that the psychological patterns of behaviour which represent their own unique personality correspond to patterns created by planetary interrelationships.

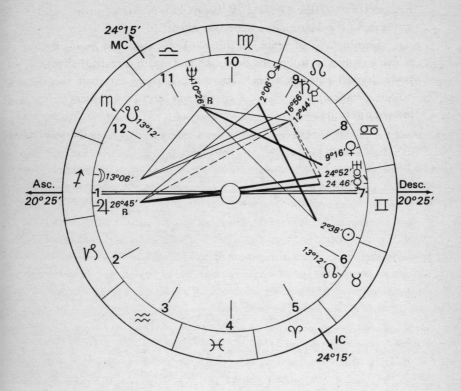

Figure 1

Janet's birth chart

CHAPTER I

Introducing Astrology

This book is about astrology and how, with a little serious study, you could apply it to yourself and others with considerable benefit. You may know nothing about the subject or perhaps think that it is to do with 'the stars' and is an amusing form of 'fortune-telling' as suggested by astrological predictions given in some newspapers and most women's magazines.

Forget all of those newspaper and magazine columns, because the astrology you are about to learn and to test the authenticity of for yourself is something quite different. The astrology taught in this book is *a unique system of predicting potential human behaviour through the interpretation of planetary motions and their angular relationship to the Earth.* All will be explained in detail, step by step.

Birth data: the starting-point

To astrologically predict a person's potential psychological make-up, the astrologer will need that person's *date, time and place of birth.* The time should be as exact as possible. A birth chart can then be calculated and erected, as has been done for our example case, Janet (see figure 1).

The astronomical components

The birth chart is composed of symbols, presented as a 'pattern' unique to the person upon whose birth data it is based. Each symbol, astronomical by origin, is correlated with psychological features from which human behaviour can be interpreted.

The planets and moon's nodes

☉	Sun	♄	Saturn
☽	Moon	♅	Uranus
☿	Mercury	♆	Neptune
♀	Venus	♇	Pluto
♂	Mars	☊	North node
♃	Jupiter	☋	South node

The Moon's nodes (☊ ☋) will not be used for interpretation. I know of no research that has yet presented these nodes as valid psychological features but as astronomically they represent very significant points in the Moon's motions, they are entered in Janet's chart and the reader may wish to include these for examination in his or her subsequent collection of charts.

The signs of the zodiac

♈	Aries	♎	Libra
♉	Taurus	♏	Scorpio
♊	Gemini	♐	Sagittarius
♋	Cancer	♑	Capricorn
♌	Leo	♒	Aquarius
♍	Virgo	♓	Pisces

Aspects between planets and planet-angles

♂	conjunction
∟	semi-square
✳	sextile
☐	square
△	trine
⬓	sesquiquadrate
♂°	opposition

The angles, or sectors, of environmental relationships

Me Sector: 8° either side of the Ascendant angle (Asc.).
Us Sector: 8° either side of the Imum Coeli angle (IC).
You Sector: 8° either side of the Descendant angle (Desc.).
Them Sector: 8° either side of the Midheaven angle (MC).

The Distinctive Zones:

Zone 1: extending 8° *before* an angle.
Zone 2: extending 8° *after* an angle.

The houses

Traditionally there are twelve so-called houses. Although these will be shown according to the Equal House System in very brief lines in Janet's chart, the houses will not be employed in the interpretation of psychological features or with regard to her potential activities.

The calculation of a birth chart

This book is planned to deal essentially with the interpretation of a birth chart and not with the calculation of the chart, which would entail a number of very detailed chapters. It is expected that a large percentage of readers will already know how to calculate charts and that others (an increasing number each year) will have a calculator or computer programme for doing this work. For those wishing to learn how to calculate charts, step-by-step teaching with examples is given in my *How to Cast a Natal Chart*. For those wishing to have computer-calculated charts for birth data they supply, I would highly recommend contacting Astrocalc, 67 Peascroft Road, Hemel Hempstead, Herts HP3 8ER, England. However, in Appendix II a very brief account is given of the procedure for the calculation of a birth chart, purely as a guide for those who have never done these calculations before.

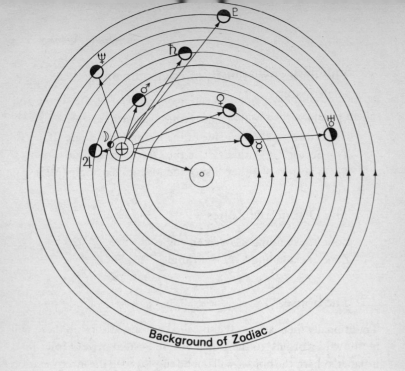

Background of Zodiac

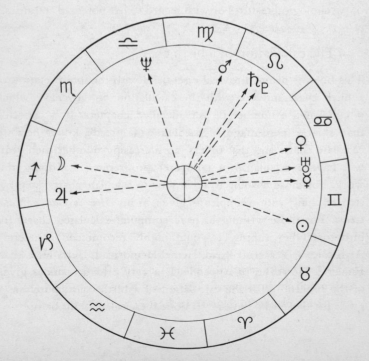

Summary of chapters

At the end of most chapters a summary is given of the theme and
salient points of the chapter.

Figure 2

Bottom Positions of the planets relative to the Earth
symbolized in the birth chart. *Top* Same positions of
the planets in their orbits relative to the Earth

CHAPTER 2

The Cosmos within Man

Life: the orderly design

The human organism as we know it today is the product of millions of years of evolution. There are scientists who would have us believe that it was sheer chance that certain basic chemicals came together to produce the primeval stirring of organic life, that all forms of organic life on Earth including man-in-the-making originated accidentally. They believe that the coming together of certain chemicals was a fortuitous occurrence, not necessarily intended or planned.

This is one way of saying that there is no Creator who had a conception of life and generated the necessary energy for its development. Or, if there were a Creator, He had no distinct plan for there to be life on Earth. It seems that this type of scientist believes that the evolution of man followed no certain pattern; that each momentous step forward – from a single cell to multiple cells to a nervous system and awakening consciousness – was only one possibility among thousands of other possibilities, as distinct from certainty.

That all forms of life on Earth are necessary features of an orderly design may not be apparent to most of us. There seems to be so much chaos and injustice; human existence is mostly a struggle from birth to death against unexpected accidents and worries, adversity, stress and sickness. Frequently many may feel justified in questioning what kind of a God would allow these things to happen. We think so much that happens in life just doesn't make sense or appears unfair.

And yet to those of us who do recognize an orderly design to life, despite the apparent chaos within social and political structures, the seemingly unjust contrasts of the wealthy and the poverty-stricken and the sudden traumatic upsets in our individual lives, the question is not 'what kind of a God would allow these things to happen?' but, 'in what *way* are these things a part of life?'

One of the most exciting explorations for the human spirit is the discovery of the basic orderly design which is the 'blueprint' for the unfolding patterns of life in all its milliard interdependent forms.

Astrology is one method of exploration.

Man's interaction with the environment

Man is the most advanced species of all the thousands of different organisms living on Earth. Man is also an organism and as such he too is subject to natural laws from conception and throughout his life, just like any other life form.

From the very moment of his conception, when he is but a single, fertilized, microscopically-small cell, this embryo-man must begin to interact with his environment. The saga has commenced – another unique story of heroic achievement and miraculous adventure. His cell multiplies and multiplies, always evolving strictly to basic primitive instructions. The instructions express orderly patterns. These patterns already contain the potential structure and individuality of the child-man who will at his proper time be born into a new and more demanding environment.

Always there must be an environment, an outside-himself-otherness, for man to engage with, to relate himself to. In his primitive germ-state as a single cell and as a fully-grown man, it is this *interplay of opposing forces* that will determine what he becomes, how he lives and when he dies.

Life is not possible without an environment for any organism. No growth can take place without environmental stimulus and nourishment. From conception until death the human organism is dependent upon its environment. Adaptation to its surroundings is necessary for survival.

Astrology shows how the individual man or woman interacts

with his or her environment, will seek to adapt to exterior pressures and situations and relate to other people.

The cosmic environment

You and I each have our own environment. Most particularly this consists of everything immediately around us – the people, the places we live and work and whatever we may ourselves contribute to influencing our surroundings. There is also the environment of our community and of the systems of the society and country we are born into or happen to reside in. Each order of environment provides its own stimulus for the development of our unique behaviour potential.

Astrology teaches us that we also interact through our behaviour and, biologically, through the fluids, nervous system and every cell in our body, with a much, much wider environment: our planet Earth and the cosmos beyond.

What is astrology that it can reveal so much about individual human behaviour? As we read in chapter 1, astrology is a unique system of predicting potential human behaviour through the interpretation of planetary motions and their angular relationship to the Earth. In short, the interrelated planetary pattern at any given moment correlates with the psychological pattern of potential behaviour in a child born at that same moment.

Indeed, there is no other method by which one can quickly and accurately understand the psychological make-up of an individual. The study of astrology and unbiased research into its basic theories will help to establish the general laws or principles underlying behaviour. Astrology provides an insight into man's interrelationship with the Earth and cosmic environments.

It is understandable that somebody who has never studied astrology and does not know about the subject's basic theories would find it impossible to believe that the Sun, Moon and distant planets have a psychological and biological link with us here on Earth. Very simply, the astrological theory is that the interrelated positions of the Sun, Moon and eight planets of the solar system at the moment of a child's birth, and relative to the point on the Earth's surface where birth occurs, correlate with potential behaviour patterns and dominant drives in that child. Thus, for an astrologer to plot an accurate chart for someone in order that its interpretation is distinct from the thousands of other individuals born on the same date, their time and place (as well as date) of birth must be supplied. The word 'astrology' derives from the Greek *astron*, meaning 'star' and *legein*, meaning 'speak'.

Man is not an isolated creature. He forms an interdependent part of his environment – which extends from his own being to the cosmos beyond planet Earth.

Origins of astrology

The word 'astrology' is derived from the Greek language, but astrology was not invented or discovered by the Greeks. Development to its present form as the most valid basis to psychology has been a continuous process extending over thousands of years. We can only surmise how the concept of astrology formed in the minds of men. Primitive man's initial observation of the heavens and his accompanying wonder would eventually have developed into an indispensable means of timing festivals and regulating cultivation of crops for survival. The earliest traces of astrology are found among the Sumerians, the early inhabitants of Mesopotamia, about 4,000 years before the birth of Christ. Geographically, ancient Mesopotamia refers to the southern portion of present-day Iraq.

However, the growth of astrology was not confined to Mesopotamia. Wherever ancient civilizations flourished, so was there awareness of the seasonal rhythms observed in nature and eventual deification of the 'wandering stars' – the planets – in the heavens.

Archetypal patterns

Who can say what inner sense prompted or compelled these early observers to associate the planets with the powers and qualities of *particular* gods? 'This early, groping stage in man's identification of a god-force outside himself with potential qualities within himself was no chance happening. This may be seen as a natural stage of awakening consciousness, an impulse derived from man's elementary experiences of living, forged and projected by his own psychic energies from within the dark unconscious depths of his being.'[1]

In other words, the names and characteristics given to the cosmic bodies (Sun, Moon, planets) were not determined by chance, but were appropriate projections of man's own archetypal or instinctive impulses that were (and still are) basic to his survival. These drives which seek to direct his life from within his psyche, man embodied in the gods represented physically by the visible planets in the heavens. This was not done by one nation or civilization alone, but by different nations throughout the ancient world. This may be taken as evidence of the common origins of all races in the dark mists of primeval time; evidence that the psychic roots of all men share the energies and influences of the *collective unconscious*; and perhaps evidence that humanity's collective unconscious or matrix of evolving psychological patterns might also share common roots with the solar and planetary environment outside the planet Earth.

The deities, for instance, identified with the planet Mars, were associated with war, carnage and storms and were the slayers of dragons: the Greek Ares, the Hindu Indra, the Euphratean Nergal, the Germanic Tiwaz. One of the basic survival needs in man, as in all organisms, is *to stay alive*: to resist threats from the environment by aggressive attack and annihilation by alien, menacing forces. Since man was first placed within an environment and encountered an outside-himself-otherness, this will have been a principal need or archetype to help him survive. These similar Martian deities personified this archetype and vital survival need and this one planet was chosen and worshipped not just by one civilization or nation, but universally.

If the term 'archetype' is unfamiliar to you and you find the concept difficult to grasp, all will be clearly explained to you and your interpretation of astrological charts will be much benefited. It is a major concept indicated by Dr Carl Jung, as is the collective unconscious. I have felt it necessary to introduce these concepts in this chapter because I know of no other terms that can so clearly describe the source of man's many powerful psychological drives, the evolution of his awakening consciousness and the inherited instincts common to all mankind.

By 'archetypes' we mean primordial patterns or impulses which pre-exist human consciousness and from which spring all meaningful drives, desires, instinctive survival reactions to the environment and familiar patterns of behaviour. By the 'collective unconscious' we mean a source of dynamic energy, accessible and vital to all humanity since man was first conceived by the Creator. We could not exist as humans if we did not share this common, universal source of life-energy with the rest of humanity. We are each a separate entity and yet we have common roots. Through these roots we learn to develop instinctive patterns of behaviour, patterns that are basic to survival and to the purpose of our being.

The circle of the astrological chart containing the Sun, Moon, planets and the twelve zodiacal signs that are shared by all men and women symbolizes our common roots and the potential for survival and growth.

Each powerful drive or desire in man has its archetypal pattern. Our reaction to danger, our need to gamble perhaps, to achieve power, to make love, to exchange ideas or to study a new subject as you may now be doing – each is a product of one or more archetypal functions. Our bodies are programmed with the accumulated experiences of our ancestors over thousands of generations. The essence of their experiences of the day-to-day challenges of life is built into the billions of cells in our bodies.

Each one of us is 'linked to the very first life-striving of the primeval organism that has evolved into what we now call man and woman. We have inherited this built-up symbolic formula in a biological sense through our brain structure, which has evolved out of the whole drama of human life experienced individually by our ancestors in an unbroken line from the beginnings of organic life itself.'²

Through astrology, the dominant archetypes that are likely to significantly motivate us can be predicted, as can their contribution to the shaping of our individual personalities.

The cosmos within man

You are now completing the second chapter in this study of astrology. You have set foot on an adventure full of romance and the wonder of exciting discoveries. This adventure, once experienced, will inevitably be pursued further by most because, mysteriously, to be guided by astrology along the route we will take is to many like going home and remembering familiar words of wisdom from a long, long time ago; from a time when we *knew* that the cosmos was at the centre of man, just as man looks out from the centre of the cosmos.

Summary of chapter

1 The theme of this chapter is that the cosmos is within man, in the sense that the interrelated planetary pattern at any given moment and for any given place on Earth correlates with the psychological pattern of potential behaviour in a child born at that moment.

2 This picture of man's destiny being linked with the cosmos beyond and including planet Earth can also be viewed as the cosmos being at the centre of man, as man looks out from the centre of the cosmos.

3 Thus, astrology can be defined as a unique system of predicting potential human behaviour through the interpretation

of planetary motions and their angular relationship to the Earth.

4 Despite the apparent chaos and injustices of life, there is a basic orderly design that is the 'blueprint' for the unfolding patterns of human evolution and behaviour. Astrology is one method of exploring these patterns.

5 There must always be an environment, an outside-himself-otherness, for man to engage with, to relate himself to. Astrology can show how an individual interacts with his environment and will seek to adapt to exterior influences and relate to other people.

6 Each powerful drive or desire in man has its archetypal pattern. Through astrology the dominant archetypes or drives likely to be significantly active in an individual can be predicted, as can their contribution to the shaping of that individual's personality.

7 The collective unconscious is a source of dynamic energy shared in common by all men and women, and in which all of humanity has its psychic roots.

Notes

1 Jeff Mayo: *The Planets and Human Behaviour*, p. 20 (L. N. Fowler & Co. Ltd, 1982)
2 Ibid, pp. 139–140

CHAPTER 3

The Dynamic Image of Creation

The mystery of life's purpose

Winston Churchill's remark about Soviet history might well be applied to a description of life's purpose: 'a riddle wrapped in a mystery, inside an enigma'. We can only speculate as to why we and everything around us exists. Why should we be born only to die? Why should we live on this planet we call Earth and for what purpose do the Earth and other planets revolve about the Sun? Why the Sun? Why the distant stars and galaxies? Why were we intended to have eyes to see these milliard different forms, and why should the human race evolve a brain and senses to be able to think and reason about life and its purpose?

Possibly ten thousand years from now man will still not be certain that he understands God's purpose in creating life. Perhaps that ultimate knowledge must always elude human understanding. But what is certain, man must always go on seeking answers to life's mysteries and wonders. He must know why things are, what they consist of, and how each thing relates to its environment.

The dynamic image of creation

Man's capacity to create must surely be the manifestation of a 'divine spark' – a little bit of the Creator within man. In Genesis 1:27 we read 'So God created man in his own image'. Until I began to study astrology way back in 1947 I was not sure how to think about this biblical revelation. The theological interpretations did not satisfy me. It was through astrology that I began to find an explanation that seemed to give sense and reason to how man could possibly be made in God's image. As my studies and researches widened to embrace the cellular structure of the human body I realized the perfect and wholly satisfying interpretation of these magical eight words from Genesis.

I realized that there is more than just the fact that the planetary pattern at birth synchronizes with the potential pattern of psychological behaviour within a child. Here we link only the whole man with the planetary pattern. The, shall we say, thread of purposeful energy links not just man and the planets but continues in 'both directions', deeper within the human body to infinitesimal proportions within the cells and beyond our Solar System to the infinite known and unknown expanses of the universe. I have coined a name for this 'thread' of purposeful energy that links all energy systems from microscopically small human cells to the distant billions of immense galaxies: the energy flow of the *dynamic image of Creation*.

The phrase 'So God created man in His own image' symbolizes the most profound and exciting of all realities. The ancient Hermetics were aware of this, although they could not have known of the miniature world of the human cell when they spoke of the macrocosm or great world being repeated in the microcosm or little world . . . 'as above, so below'. Dr Carl Jung wrote that 'Our psyche is set up in accord with the structure of the universe, and what happens in the macrocosm likewise happens in the infinitesimal and most subjective reaches of the psyche,'[1] and in St Luke 17:21 we are shown that we each possess what we may think of as the *essence* of our Creator, when Jesus says '. . . behold, the kingdom of God is within you.'

The basic unit of life

Believers in a Creator of life will for centuries have understood for themselves personally what may be meant by 'the kingdom of God is within you'. But I feel that one needs the further insight of astrological knowledge to illuminate this concept. While it is incarnated on Earth, one's psyche needs the whole structure of the physical body through which to express and develop the individual's potential. Therefore, despite its incredible smallness, each one of the billions of cells in our body would seem to be the physical mediator between God and man. In computer language, this is where our Creator has programmed the instructions for our growth.

Initially the single fertilized egg or cell from which each human being begins at conception is programmed with its instructions, with the dynamic image of creation. Even before this cell begins to divide and to multiply by continual division into billions of new cells, it knows exactly what it must do. It knows which cells to create for the thousands of different processes needed to construct and maintain the foetus and the eventual child-to-be-born. It knows the exact time-table for each process. However powerful future electron micrographs may be in magnifying a single human cell for the discovery of previously unknown mechanisms, no machine will ever be able to read the instructions that cell has been given, just as no instrument will ever see or read a thought as it is experienced in the brain of a man or woman.

The supreme role of the cell has been dramatically described, for example: 'Whatever its form, however it behaves, the cell is the basic unit of all living matter. In the cell, nature has enclosed in a microscopic package all the parts of processes necessary to the survival of life in an ever-changing world;'[2] 'The cell represents the body in miniature. It may be looked upon as a working model in which we can study on a smaller scale the activities that take place in the body as a whole;'[3] in the body 'the functional unit, the arena in which the forces of life do battle, is the cell'.[4]

Life means activity, and the human organism is a dynamic system of complex energy exchanges motivating continual changes, inspired and directed by that spark of divine creativity at the very centre and nucleus of each of the billions of cells. 'The very framework of the body is always changing: the pattern alone remains.'[5]

Interdependence of all life

I have said that one needs the further insight of astrological knowledge to illuminate the concept that 'the kingdom of God is within'. Astrology demonstrates that there is *order* in life and that chaos is a natural feature in the continuous and vital process of achieving *equilibrium* or *harmony* within and between living organisms. Astrology teaches us that, however stupidly man may fight and destroy in his attempt to dominate his natural environment and be arrogantly autonomous, he is not an isolated being and is dependent for survival upon all other organisms – animal, vegetable and cosmic. Astrology focuses one's awareness on the *interdependence* of all life, from cells to man to planets, the Sun and distant galaxies.

Astrology, or the interpretation of human behaviour through its correlation with planetary patterns, was not invented by man; the correlation always existed and this fact of nature has simply been discovered. We are only on the threshold of discovering the significance of interrelationships between organisms, human and otherwise, on all levels of experience.

It is important to understand how the whole of the universe is literally held together by a system of cells. Each cell has its central nucleus or 'brain': extract this and the cell dies. The brain of man corresponds to the cell's nucleus: extract this and man dies. To expand further:

'The Sun is the heart or nucleus of the Solar System: obliterate the Sun and the planetary system would disintegrate. The galactic centre is the nucleus for our galaxy. And so with all stars and galaxies of stars. Life is one great energy system. Within this energy system are infinite aggregations of lesser energy systems. Each is concerned with maintaining itself, yet is dependent upon its environment and other energy systems, each giving and taking, creating and maintaining the vital equilibrium.'[6]

Equilibrium: the harmonizing principle

The natural laws directing the cell's dynamic processes correspond to the laws governing the human body's physiological and psychological activities. The cell 'is a being with a life of its own, equipped with organs that supply nourishment, and handle metabolism and excretion.'[7]

The following activities are but a few of the thousand or so taking place at any one moment in the human cell. These correspond to major processes in the whole human body and to important functions underlying the behaviour of the psyche:

Ability to reproduce.

Reaction to stimuli.

Transformation of simple materials into complex substances.

Assimilation of nourishment to replenish the system's energy.

Decomposition and excretion of unwanted material.

Internal generation of energy.

Maintenance of energy balance and an efficient system of economy.

Works towards a highly integrated community life with other cells.

Is necessarily self-centred yet co-operates with other cells.

Its behaviour is restrained from excesses by other cells.

Adjustment and plasticity are essential conditions.

Is in constant commerce and needs a balanced interaction with its environment.

Constructs, builds and plans.

Has an inherent tendency towards change.

Seeks growth and extension of its system.

These are necessary organic activities for a cell's survival and you will learn how similar these are to basic drives and processes of behaviour within the psyche that can be interpreted through astrology. It is known that 'the cell is a dynamic equilibrium . . . From and to the world around it takes and gives energy. It is an eddy in a stream of energy.'[8]

One of the principal laws in nature, which surprisingly psychologists seem rarely to give any special attention where human behaviour is concerned, is that of achieving and maintaining equilibrium, or harmony, stability. We will say more about this in subsequent chapters. In the physical body probably the most striking feature is the organism's instinctive endeavour to maintain a 'constant internal environment'; this is called *homeostasis*. Maintaining a regular temperature within the body, however hot or cold the exterior environment may be, is a typical example.

That immortal part deep within man that we have seen was made in the image of the Creator manifests itself in the fundamental need to attain perfection and wholeness: to be godlike. Astrology provides a unique means of seeing an individual man or woman in their potential wholeness of being – through the complex patterns of the chart viewed as a whole. The fully trained and caring astrological consultant seeks accuracy in interpretation of the strengths and weaknesses indicated in a birth chart by analysing the chart and its human subject *holistically*. 'Holism' (or 'wholism') from the Greek *holos*, meaning 'whole', is defined as 'the creation by creative evolution of wholes that are greater than the sum of the parts.'[9] Isolated features in the chart – Sun or Moon by sign placing, the Ascendant, a close major aspect, an angular planet – have their special individual significance, but the astrologer can only successfully interpret how best and most naturally the subject may achieve equilibrium or a balanced personality by relating the varied parts to the *whole* chart pattern.

The interdependence of separate organisms, the adaptation of these individual features to a harmonious community to achieve equilibrium and the quest for wholeness of being . . . here we have three key factors for the interpretation of the astrological chart.

Summary of chapter

1 The aim of this chapter is to show how the Genesis account of man being made in God's image would seem to be confirmed by the creative potential impregnated in every human cell that manifests itself in man's fundamental and powerful need for perfection and wholeness.

2 The same structural pattern of dynamic energy exchanges

and equilibrium between all parts is repeated in the organisms of the infinitesimally small human cell, man, human societies, the Solar System and distant galactic formations.

3 The mysterious 'thread' of energy-flow carrying instructions for recreation and growth and linking the human cells with the planets and the billions of remote galaxies can be thought of as conveying the divine image of creation.

4 Jesus said, 'the kingdom of God is within'. We may correlate this with the single fertilized cell at conception knowing exactly what it must do to construct from its creation of billions of other cells a complete human body, for incarnated flesh to interpret the Word of the Creator.

5 The cell is the basic unit of life and represents the whole body in miniature.

6 A thousand or so different activities for its own and the whole organism's survival take place in the cell at any moment. Many of these are similar to physiological processes occurring in the larger physical body and to processes of behaviour within the psyche.

7 The trained astrological consultant interprets the birth chart and its human subject holistically, relating each isolated feature to the whole chart pattern to determine how equilibrium or a balanced personality may be achieved most naturally.

Notes

1 Dr Carl Jung: *Memories, Dreams, Reflections*, p. 309 (Collins & Routledge & Kegan Paul, 1963)

2 John Pfeiffer: *The Cell*, p. 8 (Time-Life Books, 1969)

3 Kenneth Walker: *Human Physiology*, p. 9 (Pelican Books, 1962)

4 C. U. M. Smith: *The Architecture of the Body*, p. 122 (Faber & Faber, 1964)

5 Ibid, p. 122

6 Jeff Mayo: *Teach Yourself Astrology*, p. 11 (The English Universities Press Ltd, 1983)

7 Lennart Nilsson & Jan Lindberg: *Behold Man*, p. 10 (Harrap, 1974)

8 Sir Charles Sherrington: *Man on his Nature*, p. 81 (Pelican Books, 1955)

9 *Everyman's English Dictionary* (J. M. Dent & Sons Ltd)

CHAPTER 4

The Uses of Astrology

Value to parents

Since I first began to study astrology at the end of World War II, my own personal experience of this subject's practical application has proved to me in thousands of cases the tremendous value of astrology. There is no other method by which an individual's potentialities and type of personality can be predicted.

Many of my female astrology students have waited for the birth of their baby – with watch, ephemeris, pen and blank chart-form for that miracle moment of new life to occur! Then shortly after the birth, if physically able to do so, the mother has plotted her baby's 'blueprint of unique personality' and begun to see this taking shape, feature by feature. Before her child is one hour old she can already have a vivid picture of the potential qualities and temperament it should have developed by the time it is attending infant school, entering its 'teens' or blossoming into adulthood.

It can be of inestimable value for parents to know in advance, even well before their child is capable of expressing obvious individual features, how it is likely to cope with the demands and pitfalls of growing up; whether it will tend to over-react emotionally and temperamentally to well-intentioned parental discipline; be very much a noisy extrovert; or maybe a sensitive and shy introvert. 'Being forewarned is being forearmed': what a lot of tears and tantrums and misunderstandings can be avoided if the parents know just what is likely to be 'going on inside' their child at moments of difficulty, uncertainty or apprehension, and can guide and encourage so that (for the child) the most natural and constructive reactions are expressed.

Astrology has been called, with justification, a science of

relationships. How important it is that each parent has a harmonious and loving relationship with each of their children during the critical formative years. A branch of astrology called *synastry* compares the charts of any two persons with a view to understanding the potentially strongest or weakest links between their personalities. Much of benefit can be gleaned from the comparison of a child's birth chart with the charts of each parent. This can be a particularly exciting and moving experience for a parent – to be able to assess the potential future relationship with their child who is, perhaps, as yet only a few hours old.

Value to oneself

We speak of *potentialities* being interpreted from a birth chart because no trained astrologer would rigidly state that what the chart indicates will be expressed *exactly* in a particular way, with no variations. As humans we thankfully have the power of choice, even if the measure of free will is restricted to the limitations of our own mini-world as shown by our birth chart. Parental influence and environmental circumstances will also govern the opportunities for developing our innate qualities and talents.

What is exciting is that each of us does have potentialities, special qualities and talents. Whether any of these are ever fully or even partially realized depends not just on beneficial parental or environmental contributions and encouragement, but mostly on *how we choose* to develop and apply them.

Firstly, of course, it is necessary to recognize our potentialities, to know they exist: to know, perhaps, that the fund of emotional energy we possess need not always be an embarrassment or a source of confusion or conflict with others, but is just the type of energy which, when combined, for example, with a sensitive, feeling nature, is needed for a creative and artistic leaning we might never have been aware of but for our birth chart.

Of equal importance to knowing our potential qualities is knowing our limitations, so that we do not waste time (even many years) chasing particular goals in the least fruitful direction, unsuccessfully, and with increasing frustration. It is of immense value also to understand where we are potentially vulnerable physiologically and psychologically to stress.

Value to teachers and educational authorities

Over the years a high percentage of students enrolling for my school of astrology's correspondence courses have been teachers. I see this as a very encouraging trend in society, that men and women whose profession is concerned with educating young minds are keen to study a subject which will enable them to better understand these youngsters as individuals.

Time and again teachers have told me how much the teacher–pupil relationship has improved because they know – even if based only on date and not time of birth – the strengths and weaknesses of each pupil. Without astrological knowledge they would scarcely or never have been aware of these. In addition, the teachers have felt stronger, more confident and better suited for their responsible task through increased and deeper knowledge of their own strengths and weaknesses.

One of my personal astrological students was an Area Educational Psychologist employed by the County Psychological Service. It was not until he was near retirement that he came upon my *Teach Yourself Astrology* in the local library and for the first time became aware of astrology's value. He took up its study 'to improve professional psychology in the educational and child-guidance field'.

Traditional prejudices against astrology by those ignorant of its truths are slowly breaking down in the various fields of medicine, psychology, education and science. But future historians will surely look back at the twentieth century in astonishment that a subject that has been practised for over 6,000 years and been shown to be the basis and starting-point for psychology is not yet (in 1995) taught in every university.

Early recognition of antisocial tendencies

Occasionally one hears about a teenage girl or boy, possibly well-educated, who suddenly shocks and distresses their family by committing a serious offence 'completely out of accord with their character'.

Prior knowledge of the youngster's birth chart would have given some warning to parents of a potential rebellious or delinquent tendency. The chart would show the most vulnerable areas in the psychological make-up through which antisocial behaviour could be triggered off.

It must, however, be emphasized that not a single birth chart is without areas of potential discord and stress. Most of us might well have the seeds of delinquency and antisocial behaviour in our personality; probably circumstances of birth and environment have prevented these seeds from being nurtured in destructive directions. Many individuals, even if born into loving and caring families, are abnormally vulnerable to antisocial reactions to stress and frustration. An astrologer must take the utmost care not to overreact to difficult psychological patterns indicated in a chart that may give an exaggerated and negative diagnosis.

Before presenting oneself as a consultant to others it is imperative that a thorough training is received in astrology.

Each year astronomical amounts of public money and thousands of hours of magistrates', social welfare officers', probation officers' and prison authorities' time could be saved if astrology were accepted and constructively practised by parents and those responsible for the training of young people into wholesome citizenship.

The value of astrological training for social workers and the probationary service will now be clearer to the reader. Rehabilitation programmes and therapeutic treatment for criminals and all types of offenders could be geared more certainly to the personalities of individuals.

Value to psychologists and psychiatrists

'The lack of an adequate coherent theoretical structure has limited the advance of social psychology'.[1] And not only of social psychology but of *all* areas of human activity in which psychologists and psychiatrists work. This is not only my opinion, having searched fruitlessly through scores of psychological textbooks, but is surely the opinion shared by most psychologists.

The truth is that the psychologists (lacking astrological knowledge) can never satisfactorily realize a sound structure to describe the complexity of human emotions and needs on which to build their understanding of individual behaviour. Astrology has a beautifully ordered astronomical basis. The psychologist can only hazard hopeful guesses about a patient, dependent on observed answers and reactions from that patient to tests and groping questions, whereas the astrologer, if challenged concerning a particular interpretation of a client's personality, can point to distinct mathematically-based factors in the birth chart.

This book is essentially about psychology from an astrological viewpoint and so you will read much concerning the traditional concepts of psychologists. We need only state here that the value of astrology to psychologists and psychiatrists is inestimable and that in the not-too-distant future astrology must be universally accepted as the starting-point for psychological diagnosis.

The successful fulfilment of relationships

To successfully and pleasingly develop our individual potentialities and to satisfy the constant needs of our psyche, we must each learn to harmonize and integrate with our environment. We cannot achieve growth – mentally, emotionally, spiritually – without forming relationships with other people. This can be a tricky and hazardous venture even when all seems to be going well! We cannot always be sure how the other person – even our closest friend or relative – will react to the way we behave towards them.

Knowing the other person's chart pattern and therefore their dominant and sensitive personality features, can make a successful relationship so much more likely. The comparison of individual charts (synastry) can be particularly helpful for a couple planning to get married. Potential strengths and weaknesses in the relationship can be frankly discussed and the couple can look into the charts for ways of resolving possible conflicts or stresses stemming from weak and inharmonious features.

Vocational potential

Looking back at your life, can you truthfully say that you have fully expressed your talents in a job that would have been your first choice? It is true that probably most of us would never have the opportunity to follow the vocation we most desired. But then, do you really know how you could best employ yourself? Perhaps you could be a considerably different person if you were self-employed. Yet can you be sure whether it would be wise to throw in the security of your present job and suddenly be responsible in every sense for the survival and living standard of yourself and your family?

This is the kind of information and guideline that can be gleaned from a chart.

A classic example of one area in which astrology can help is that of the son following in the father's line of business. Let us say the father has an engineering business that he founded himself. Especially with past generations it would be expected that the first-born son, at least, would 'go into the family business' and ultimately inherit it (Tom Bloggs & Son). In our example case the first-born son is put into the engineering business on leaving school but – horrors! – as he is given more responsibility, he makes one heck of a mess of things. If only the parents had consulted a reputable astrologer whilst the lad was still in his early school years . . . they would have been advised that engineering for wee Harold would spell disaster, whereas if they had directed his education so that his potential creative and musical talents could be developed and encouraged, he might now be Sir Harold

Bloggs conducting his world-famous symphony orchestra – instead of the frustrated Harold at the helm of an almost bankrupt engineering business.

The promotion of health

Health is soundness of body and mind. It derives from the Old English *haelan*, to heal, become sound. To be healthy is to have good health, to be vigorous, to be *whole*some.

The astrologer is trained to see the birth chart not just as a circle containing a variety of separate parts but as a whole person, the totality of whom is greater than the sum of the parts. If, for instance, we wish to interpret an individual's Sun according to the sign it is in, the Sun's true function in psychological and health-related terms could only be accurately known when the Sun is seen in relation to the whole pattern of the chart, and not as an isolated feature based only on the sign and the aspects directly involved.

Regrettably, very little research has been attempted on the correlation of astrological factors with specific diseases. This is a field of research full of potential, where the medical profession should co-operate with astrologers. The planets, signs and aspects have been connected since ancient times with specific organs and bodily functions and their affinity with certain ailments and diseases. However, especially if they have had no medical training, my students have always been warned to be extremely careful if predicting possible ill-health conditions for a client.

Astrology, responsibly practised, may be used to promote awareness of the need for a wholistic lifestyle and attitude to one's place within the environment. It has somewhere been stated that possibly ninety-five per cent of our illnesses and diseases are self-induced. The astrological chart can indicate the potential imbalances, stresses and exaggerated forms of behaviour an individual can produce within his psyche that will inevitably aggravate specific ill-health conditions. The chart can also indicate the most natural (for the person concerned) ways in which a healthy and wholesome balance can be restored psychically and physically.

A psychologist has said of counselling or psychotherapy that it has 'the aim of promoting self-understanding and resolution of personality conflicts'.[2] This is precisely one of the aims of the astrological chart where there is maladjustment and imbalance in the personality and its physical vehicle.

Is astrology a science?

The word 'science' derives from the Latin word *scire*, meaning 'to know'. A generally applied definition is 'knowledge systematically arranged.'

Astrology clearly fits the above but this is no proof of astrology's validity, because the above definitions are too loose. Astrology is much more than just 'knowledge systematically arranged'. It is a *philosophy*, a 'study of ultimate reality'[3], a 'body of laws and principles belonging to a branch of knowledge'[4], or the 'knowledge or study of the principles of human action or conduct'[5].

It is possible that various astrological theories may never be proven under strict scientific analysis, but thousands of sincere and non-gullible workers in the field of astrology will know the theories for facts: 'A great deal of human thought and knowledge cannot, by its very nature, be included in the body of knowledge we call science.'[6]

Several astrological theories have already been demonstrated as truths under strict research controls. This has been achieved most notably through the published works of Michel Gauquelin and of myself in co-operation with Professor Hans Eysenck. Further research will inevitably confirm the validity of astrology as a system of predicting human behaviour. Astrology would appear therefore to already fit the definition of science as 'a body of tested objective knowledge, obtained and united in principle by inductive methods.'[7]

If we were to confine our acceptance of *truth* to only those phenomena that can be proven to exist because they can be weighed, measured or counted, are obliging enough to fit conveniently into a scientific boffin's pigeon-hole or achieve a statistically significant level, how void of feeling and sense of values and inspiration life would be!

The scientist and zoologist already quoted, Dr Stanley D. Beck, is a rare breed of scientist when he admits: 'It is quite obvious that not all meaningful human knowledge can be reduced to scientific terms. Interpretation of ultimate meaning and value in human terms will, in the final analysis, be made more on the basis of spiritual awareness than on scientific acuity.'[8]

The beautiful, exciting, dynamic structure that we can find no better name for than astrology is quite real. As real as the Sun and the Moon and the planets and you and I, even if the dynamic yet mysterious energies that link all these things cannot be seen and may never fully be revealed to man. Astrology can open new avenues of investigation for scientists, providing a deeper understanding of countless human activities and other phenomena with its predictable mathematical basis.

What astrology is not

Astrology is not a doctrine of fatalism. An astrologer may predict the most likely ways in which a baby will develop psychologically, and only in terms of potential behaviour. The birth chart will show potentialities and, within the limitations of the chart's framework, the subject will have free will to choose, consciously or not, how his potentialities are developed and whether particular reactions to the environment or to his own inner drives are constructive or destructive. How, or to what degree the subject chooses, the astrologer cannot say with certainty, but he can predict the options open to the subject.

Astrology is not a cult, nor is it aligned with any particular religion. The true believer in the orderly patterns and cycles of growth that astrology reveals and describes will believe in a divine Creator. He will see all forms of religious belief as different ways of seeking this Being and of understanding why men and women have life and must die. He will see true religion as the seeking for a quality in living to be shared with others and will believe in the 'brotherhood of all mankind'.

Astrology is not fortune-telling, neither does the astrology you are now studying have anything to do with the generalized star columns in daily newspapers and women's magazines.

Summary of chapter

1 The theme of this chapter is the inestimable value of astrology to the individual and to society, and its varied and important uses.

2 Astrology can be of obvious value for parents who want to know their child's psychological and vocational potential during the early, formative years.

3 Astrology has been called a science of relationships.

4 Of equal importance to knowing one's potential qualities and talents is knowing one's limitations.

5 Astrology can be of immense value to teachers and educational authorities and improve teacher–pupil relationships.

6 Astrology can enable the early recognition of potential anti-social tendencies in a child and thus direct right action not only by parents but by the social welfare and probationary services.

7 Astrology, with its predictable mathematical/astronomical basis, needs to be recognized and universally accepted as the starting-point for psychological interpretation.

8 Astrology can promote awareness of the need for a wholistic lifestyle and attitude to one's place within the environment, and the maintenance of sound mental and physical health.

9 Astrology is a philosophy, the knowledge or study of the

principles of human action or conduct; and already fits the definition of science.

10 Astrology is not a doctrine of fatalism, a cult or a means of fortune-telling; nor is it aligned with any particular religion. It proclaims true religion to be the search for a quality of living that may be shared with others.

Notes

1 David Krech, Richard S. Crutchfield & Egerton L. Ballachey: *Individual in Society*, p. 3 (McGraw-Hill Book Co. Inc., 1962)

2 P. E. Vernon: *Personality Assessment*, p. 3 (Methuen & Co Ltd, 1964)

3 *Everyman's English Dictionary* (J. M. Dent & Sons Ltd)

4 Ibid

5 *Shorter Oxford English Dictionary* (Oxford University Press)

6 Stanley D. Beck: *The Simplicity of Science*, p. 134 (Penguin Books, 1962)

7 Ibid, p. 134

8 Ibid, p. 229

CHAPTER 5

Stress: Threat or Challenge

To enable you to interpret a birth chart as accurately as possible, the emphasis in this book is on the prediction of potential stress-related behaviour. When counselling a client it is of the utmost importance to gain as much information as you can about stress in the client's life. Their chart will reveal their most likely reactions to problems and conflicts encountered in their environment and personal relationships, and the harmful stress they are capable of generating.

At the end of this chapter you will be shown the two types of stress reactions to circumstances and to other people that each one of us can experience. But first, before we consider what stress is and how it can activate behaviour, let us be quite clear what we mean by behaviour and the psyche.

The psyche and behaviour

The unique value of astrology in aiding an individual's quest for identity is its ability to predict potential behaviour.

To clearly understand what we are attributing to astrology, we must be certain of the concepts we are using. 'Behaviour' is the way one acts – it is the body and psyche in action. It is the way one reacts to the environment, both internal and external. Used in this context, 'body' refers to one's physical and physiological features and their contribution to the way one behaves. The *psyche*, however, is that inner part of oneself which feels, thinks, worries, laughs, dreams and is all too aware of its own self. The psyche's (or psychic) structure comprises both conscious and unconscious processes and therefore all mental, emotional and feeling activity. 'Mental' activity is of the mind, and when we speak of the 'mind' we are referring to the source of *conscious psychological activity*, the expression of thought, ideas, intellect and intelligence.

There is one very important statement made above with reference to behaviour: behaviour is the way one reacts to the environment. Neither you nor I could exist without an environment. Our survival depends upon our obtaining continuous nourishment and sustenance from the environment; this requires an ability to successfully cope with the external world. Life is a continuous interaction between an organism and its environment. Thus, we each contribute to the environment of others, demonstrating the inescapable law of interdependence.

A vital application of astrology is its prediction of the potentially characteristic way a subject will interact with his or her environment – in short, the prediction of his or her behaviour. To generate activity for an interaction to occur at all, the subject must respond to the exterior environment's stimulus or to the internal environment's demands, such as hunger, sexual desire and frustration.

The key factor is stress.

What is stress?

'Stress' is generally mentioned in terms of excessive tension, nervous and emotional strain experienced as a result of pressure of circumstances that make life difficult to cope with. One thinks of a keyed-up feeling, of being 'uptight', highly-strung, depressed, anxiety-prone. This kind of stress is the response experienced by one any physical or psychological demands made by the environment that can unbalance one's equilibrium. But stress is not all bad. It is nature's way of activating the psyche and its body so that it will seek some form of tension-relaxing behaviour. It is, therefore, a principle determinant of all human behaviour.

Fear is at the root of stress associated with anxiety, uneasiness and all forms of strain and restriction. But stress is not something 'out there' in the environment or in the situation we find ourselves in. We are not mere victims of stress in the way that we cannot avoid getting wet in the rain if we have to go out unsuitably dressed. Stress depends on one's response to potentially stress-inducing events or environmental influences. We can think of the environment and oneself engaged in a dynamic relationship, a transaction that determines what is potentially stressful; but it is oneself who chooses to register stress a lot, a little, or not at all.

Thus, we could define stress as the way we feel about an environmental stimulus, the way we react to its happening to us. Our reaction may not necessarily be an active response; it may simply be the way we feel about the stimulus or view it.

Stress is adaptation

On page 18 we have said that to understand human behaviour we must recognize that one of the principal laws in nature is that of achieving and maintaining equilibrium, harmony and stability. In physiological terms, the organism's instinctive and ceaseless endeavour to achieve this state is called homeostasis. Psychologically, this drive manifests itself in man's fundamental need to attain perfection and wholeness. These vital needs will be achieved neither physiologically nor psychologically, even in the small measure we may hope for in our present stage in evolution, unless we learn to adapt to our constantly changing and complicated environment.

Stress is the result of how we choose (consciously or unconsciously) to respond to our environment. This response is our choice of adaptation or maladaptation. Stress, therefore, is a vital activating feature in the psychic process of adaptation. Indeed, we can truthfully say that stress *is* adaptation.

You and I, in our individual quest for identity, need to recognize that stress makes life and growth possible. To survive, man must continually adapt to life and its inevitable changes. Everything in life, especially the crisis points and major changes, is potentially stressful. But a life without stress would be static, non-existent, impossible.

The fight or flight stress response

The stress response has primeval origins as an instinctual reaction by the organism to a life-threatening situation. Prehistoric man was the hunter or the hunted and in either role he would have experienced stress as a requisite for success and survival.

Under the stress of fear, anger and excitement, secretions pour into the bloodstream from the adrenals, known as the 'fight or flight' glands of the endocrine system. This adrenalin has a major role in stimulating and preparing the organism to cope with threats to its well-being or survival.

Even though man has evolved to his present 'civilized' state, equipped with an incredibly complex brain and a choice of life-styles and activities, his primitive stress response mechanism is still a powerful expression of his whole organism. With the development of consciousness, man may think he is now far removed from the dominating influence of bygone animal-like instincts. But these instincts remain with him. The fight or flight stress response is stimulated in countless ways, mostly very subtly, in his daily self-preservation and competitive encounters with his fellows. Indeed, the control of stress and related pressures is now probably far more hazardous and complicated than it ever was for his primitive ancestors. Their stress responses would barely have been triggered by anything other than direct physical encounter with an adversary or prey; certainly not by such sophisticated stimulations to the senses as ideas, memories, nostalgia, anticipation, mathematical theorizing, religious beliefs, emotional intimacy, craved-for drugs and alcohol.

Too little stress

Adverse and harmful stress can also develop through too little challenging and stimulating stress being present in one's life.

Stress then becomes frustration, boredom, dissatisfaction or discontentment. When stress levels in one's life fall too low, one may seek positive readjustment and stress is then the excitement one seeks and finds, or the pre-excitement of the search.

We need to have sufficient stress in our day-to-day interests and activities to make life exciting, interesting and comfortable, for our lifestyle and self-expression to be at least reasonably balanced in terms of exertion and relaxation; but not to have so much stress as to cause distress. Too little stress can result in a monotonous and meaningless existence.

We choose our own stress

Positively or negatively, we choose our own measure of stress by the way we view events and situations and endeavour to cope with them or just let them happen to us. We have already emphasized this point but it can be said again, because you will learn that through the practice and application of astrology, life is not seen as fatalistic simply because potential behaviour can be predicted through one's birth chart. The basic pattern of potential strengths and weaknesses, areas for most useful growth as well as those of limitation, is a framework within which we can, with free choice, develop and realize our unique identity. However hard the knocks and shocks we receive, the stress we register as our reaction to these arises from within our psyche.

We may not choose many of the stress-inducing incidents that happen to us, nor even have had any influence over their occurrence – such as the car that reverses into our own vehicle in a car park. But the stress is not the negligent-other-driver nor the accident his negligence caused. The stress is the way we feel about the incident, the way we react to its happening to us.

Our bodies learn to respond to similar situations in a similar stressful manner. These responses are programmed as habits. We need to identify any particularly harmful stress-habits and thus choose to try and change these fixed responses to specific situations so that any damage to ourselves is lessened or eliminated.

Stress as a valuable human response

Stress becomes a creative force when it can be usefully adapted and transmitted to work for ourselves and others, not against us. We need to discover how to manage and use it to advantage, to thrive on its stimulus and energy, to achieve personal fulfilment through the stretching of one's responses to physical and mental limits in active stress seeking – as with successful athletes, artists, creative geniuses, mountaineers or test pilots. In our own way, by challenging the limits indicated in our chart we can achieve some satisfaction and growth through deliberate exposure to stressful conditions, pressure and competition, reaching into the unknown and uncharted areas of the physical or mental environment.

It is vitally important that the astrological-consultant, when counselling a client, understands the benefits that stress can bring, especially as a response to challenge and change. To attain a reasonably balanced and healthy lifestyle stress is an essential and stimulating ingredient. Our energies and emotions that create the stress we feel must be constructively harnessed and controlled. If they are, then stress will provide the challenge and the stimulus to enable us to cope successfully with many crises which otherwise would cause us great distress.

The intentional wooing of stress can bring the feeling of being intensely alive and different from anyone else.

When stress becomes distress

When we cannot cope with the demands of life and the environment, we are failing to adapt successfully or comfortably to circumstances. There will be personal reasons for our faulty, inadequate or inappropriate responses and through our individual birth chart there will be indications of the areas of our psyche in which we are likely to be most susceptible or vulnerable to imbalance and maladjustment and hence to adverse stress.

Typical circumstances that may make the stimulation and exhilaration of normal and potentially beneficial stress through personal relationships and activities become distress are: emotional insecurity, friction with others, loss of a loved one, loss of one's job, accumulating frustrations, mounting pressure of work and commitments, harassment, oppression, loneliness, drastic and unexpected change, commuting, job dissatisfaction. We can all add other stress-inducing circumstances to this list. One of the most evident signs of stress becoming distress is one's experience of a 'draining emotional tiredness'.

We can also make ourselves physiologically vulnerable to stress, dis-ease and varying degrees of distress through faulty nutritional patterns, excessive consumption of sugar, salt and synthetic food additives, mineral and vitamin deficiencies, overeating, sluggish metabolism and consequent accumulation of toxic wastes, tobacco poisoning, excessive alcohol, environmental poisons and lack of exercise.

Thus, we have seen that stress can be invigorating and challenging and is a natural response of the psyche to the environment and to the demands of life, but when tension and strain become too uncomfortable or the psyche feels inadequate to produce the appropriate responses, adverse stress or distress results. This is an experience related purely to the psyche and is usually an expression or effect of one or more of the following conditions:

a psychological imbalance;
a physiological imbalance;
maladjustment with the environment;
inadequacy of understanding particular stress-inducing
     situations through inexperience or ignorance;
overpowering pressure of some adverse force or influence.

Adverse stress symptoms

We all recognize the tell-tale and all-too-familiar symptoms of stress response to environment and nervous/mental/emotional pressures, tensions and conflicts. To list but a few commonplace symptoms:

feeling anxiety-prone, depressed, that nothing will ever go
   right;
being still tired on awakening in the morning;
feeling bad-tempered, irritable; shouting at one's children;
life feels like one long monotonous slog;
often very near to tears, and frequently sighing;
feeling uptight, highly-strung, 'out of control';
impaired concentration and memory;
increased cigarette or alcohol consumption;
craving for the stimulus of spicy and sweetened foods;
over-reaction to every minor problem.

Stress-related physical afflictions

In order to maintain a steady and satisfying level of stress the human organism, controlled by a 'master' mechanism deep in the brain, constantly regulates the amount of stimulation the psyche receives from the environment or that is generated within oneself. Evolution has equipped us to react to stressful situations and emergencies physically, as we have seen with the 'fight or flight response', but every organism has its limits of endurance.

It is probable that every illness and disease has developed largely as a result of aggravating stress responses. Just a few of the significantly stress-related physical afflictions recognized by the medical profession are: allergies; skin disorders; arthritis; asthma; headaches and migraine; cancer; muscle cramps and spasms; colitis; sexual dysfunction; immunological system breakdown; hypertension; coronary heart disease; and peptic ulcers.

Astrology and the two basic types of stress reaction

As we have seen, stress is most commonly associated with adverse strain and tension, but it can also be used as a valuable and constructive response. For birth chart interpretation, we will distinguish between the two opposing stress reactions as follows:

(+) Stimulus reaction (comfortable): Any stress registered is responded to with an absence of discomfort and uneasiness, utilizing the stress-energy constructively/creatively, enjoyably. This class of response allows equilibrium and satisfaction in the relationship with the environment (i.e. other person/persons, situation). Helpful and tolerable in promoting stress-relief. This class of reaction will embrace traits characteristic of normal self-expression.

(−) Stress reaction (uncomfortable): Any stress registered is responded to with discomfort, uneasiness or strain. This class of response is unlikely to achieve equilibrium or satisfaction in the relationship with the environment (i.e. other person/persons, situation), even if an apparent personal/material gain is made. Unhelpful for the promotion of stress-relief.

As you will learn when you read the respective chapters, each planet, sign, angle and aspect is associated with particular traits or features of behaviour. These traits will be helpfully classified for you under one of the two stress reactions above. Because psychologists vary considerably in their definition of a trait this would be an apt moment to give you our definition of a trait: it is a form of behaviour that is reasonably characteristic and distinctive.

Summary of chapter

1 The theme of this chapter is to show that stress is a principal determinant of behaviour since stress is the way we *feel* about an environmental stimulus and the way we react to its happening to us. Stress and behaviour are therefore the way one reacts to the environment.

2 Stress is nature's way of activating the psyche so that it will seek tension-relaxing behaviour.

3 Failure to adapt successfully or comfortably to the demands of life and our environment makes the psyche vulnerable to distress, anxieties, emotional insecurity and ill-health.

Further reading

For further understanding of stress, refer to chapter 23 and the section headed 'Stressmanship' on page 264.

CHAPTER 6

The Astronomical Framework for a Birth Chart

To understand and to visualize the planets and signs more clearly as they appear in the birth chart, it is necessary to understand the astronomical framework that is the basis for all astrological theories. Those readers who are conversant with these astronomical factors may skip this chapter, though it will be useful to know they are here for quick reference.

If there were no astronomical framework, no celestial points and circles of reference, a birth chart could never be known. The main circles of reference that are used to locate a planet's position relative to any place on Earth and form the basic structure of the birth chart are the *horizon*, the *equator* and the *ecliptic*. We will show concisely where these are around us and in relation to you and me, and how they interrelate. We will refer mostly to figures 3 and 4, with a brief look at figures 1 and 2.

What is a birth chart?

A *birth chart* is a circular diagram or map derived from the three great circles of horizon, equator and ecliptic in which the Sun, Moon and planets are plotted in their positions at a given time, relative to a given location on Earth. This is usually for a human birth, though it may refer to the moment and place when anything begins, such as the start of a business venture or a marriage. In figure 1 (page xvi) you will see the birth chart calculated for Janet, the young woman whose chart and case history we shall be studying and working on.

The daily positions of the planets are given in an ephemeris, calculated and compiled by astronomers. Many astrologers now use computers programmed to calculate exact positions for a given time and place. But whether one uses a computer programme or an ephemeris, these positions have to be calculated with reference to a basic framework. At the end of this chapter we will bring together what you have read in this chapter by describing the symbolism of the birth chart as illustrated in figure 4.

The geocentric framework

From our *viewpoint on Earth* we look out at the rest of the universe. This must be our starting-point and our central reference point for understanding the geocentric framework used by astronomers and astrologers. The Sun, Moon and planets, and even the distant constellations, *appear* to revolve about us. This is not really what is happening except, in a sense, for the Moon (Earth's satellite). The Sun, not the Earth, is of course the common centre of gravity for all the planets in the Solar System.

However, because the astrologer is concerned with the angular relationship of the Sun, Moon and planets as seen from the Earth, he is perfectly correct in symbolizing the Earth as a kind of axis around which the rest of the cosmic bodies revolve. Thus, in the lower diagram in figure 2 the small circle containing a cross in the centre of the astrological chart symbolizes the Earth as the central point of reference.

The celestial sphere and the Meridian

At night when we gaze at the stars, it is easy to imagine them as points of light speckling the inside of a spherical dome – the visible top half of a whole sphere, the lower half being beneath the level of our feet – and that we are at the dome's centre. And so we speak of the celestial sphere.

In figure 3 you will see a number of circles contained within an outer circle. We call the outer circle *the Meridian*. This diagram shows the basic astronomical framework, composed of all the

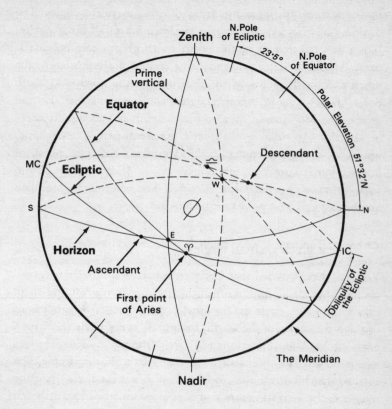

Figure 3

The Celestial Sphere (described for Polar Elevation
51°32′N, the latitude for London)

circles of reference necessary for plotting the positions of the Sun, Moon and planets relative to the Earth. This great circle is called *the* Meridian to distinguish it from all other meridian circles. The distinction is obvious because its circle embraces all other circles. It is often referred to as the north–south great circle because it passes through the zenith and nadir (poles of the horizon), the north and south points of the horizon and the north and south poles of the equator. Another significant feature is that the Sun crosses the Meridian at midday (i.e. when it is midday anywhere on Earth). At midday the Sun's apparent path (the ecliptic) intersects the great circle of the Meridian, and this point of intersection is known to astrologers as the *Midheaven* (MC, from Latin, *Medium Coeli*) or *Upper Meridian*. The poles of the Meridian are the east and west points of the horizon.

Great circles, small circles

You may have noticed that we refer to particular circles as 'great' circles. There is an important distinction between great and small circles. A great circle is any circle, the plane of which passes through the centre of the Earth. In figure 3 every circle shown is a great circle. A small circle is any circle, the plane of which does not pass through the centre of the Earth. For example, the equator which corresponds to latitude 0° is a great circle. Its plane intersects the Earth's centre and is equidistant from its north and south poles. All other parallels of latitude are small circles because their planes do not intersect the Earth's centre.

The horizon and its intersections with ecliptic and equator

The *horizon* is the great circle shown in figure 3 that can be traced through the four cardinal points from N to E to S to W and back to N. Its poles are the *zenith* (directly above the observer) and the *nadir* (directly beneath the observer). A line drawn between zenith and nadir would flow in the direction of gravity, as with a plumbline. The horizon is defined as a great circle, parallel to the observer's visible horizon.

The horizon's most significant role in the birth chart is determining the *Ascendant* or *rising degree* for any given time and place. This occurs where its east point intersects the ecliptic. For any specified place on Earth the horizon remains constant. But the Earth continuously rotates on its axis and so a different degree of the ecliptic rises above the eastern horizon roughly every four minutes. On average, a new zodiacal sign will reach the Ascendant once every two hours.

The *Prime Vertical* is shown in figure 3 because it is a vertical circle passing through the zenith and nadir, and through the east and west points of the horizon. Its plane corresponds to the points of intersection of the horizon and equator.

Terrestrial and celestial equators and their co-ordinates of measurement

The *terrestrial equator* is a great circle corresponding to the Earth's largest circumference, midway between its north and south poles. *Polar elevation* (figure 3) is the height of the north pole of the equator above the horizon at a given place and is equal to that place's latitude or angular distance from the equator.

If we imagine the plane of the terrestrial equator projected beyond the Earth, this 'extended' plane is called the *celestial equator*.

The terrestrial equator is a great circle known as a *parallel of latitude*, corresponding to latitude 0°. On the terrestrial sphere, parallels of latitude and *meridians of longitude* are the well-known co-ordinates for locating a place on a map. With reference to the celestial equator, we use similar co-ordinates for fixing the position of a heavenly body. These are *parallels of declination* (which correspond to similar measurements in terrestrial latitude) and *meridians of right ascension*. A planet exactly on the plane of the equator has no declination (0°). Measurement in declination is either north or south of the equator according to a planet's position.

For either terrestrial longitude or right ascension, which are measured around the equator, there is no natural zero, so an arbitrary choice is made. The great circle passing through the poles of the equator and the position of Greenwich (England) is where measurement in terrestrial longitude begins. Thus, the longitude of Athens is 23°46′ east, which means it is situated 23°46′ east of the Greenwich meridian (0°).

The First Point of Aries and measurement through the twelve signs

The term 'right ascension' is not normally used by the astrologer, but it is useful to know what it is, as from this co-ordinate the positions of the Sun, Moon and planets are converted into *celestial longitude* for the annual ephemerides. We can define right ascension as measurement eastwards in the plane of the equator in degrees of arc, or in hours of time, from the First Point of Aries.

The *First Point of Aries* is where the ecliptic and equator intersect at the vernal equinox. There is another point of intersection of the ecliptic and equator and this is known as the *First Point of Libra*, which occurs at the autumnal equinox. Both intersections are called equinoctial points. At the First Point of Aries the Sun is crossing the equator from south to north, and this, at the vernal equinox, is where the cycle of the twelve zodiacal signs begins each year around 21 March with Aries 0°. At the First Point of Libra the Sun is crossing the equator from north to south.

The Sun and planets appear to go round the Earth from east to west because of the diurnal motion or rotation of the Earth on its axis, whereas in reality they, like the Earth, move from west to east. As the Earth is the central point of reference and we see the planets move from east to west, this is the direction in which celestial longitude is measured. Astrologers convert longitudinal measurement into the twelve signs of equal 30° length.

Due to the Earth's rotating motion, the complete 360° circle of the ecliptic (and hence the twelve signs) passes any part of the

Earth's surface within the period of about twenty-four hours. But the Sun, of course, takes a full year to travel these 360°.

The ecliptic and the zodiac

The great circle the Sun appears to follow in its journey around the Earth, taking a year to complete one cycle, is called the *ecliptic* (figure 3). The ecliptic, or Sun's path as seen from the Earth, corresponds very closely to the orbits of the other planets.

This apparent path of the Sun and the planets in the sky was recognized by the ancient priest-astrologers and plotted against the background of constellations of fixed stars – so called because, due to their vast distances from the Earth, they appear to stay in the same positions relative to the Earth for several centuries and seem fixed in space. Certain patterns of grouped stars or constellations 'through which the Sun and planets moved' were associated by these early priest-astrologers with mythological figures significant to their primitive stellar religion. In due course these very special constellations came to be known as the *zodiac* (Greek: *zōon*, living thing). It is important to remember that these twelve constellations have only a mythological connection with the twelve signs of the zodiac we use today, even though they have identical names.

The zodiac is thought of as a belt of the sky with the ecliptic as its centre, extending about 8° north and south of the ecliptic, within which the Sun, Moon and planets always remain. Pluto is the exception, its inclination to the ecliptic reaching as much as 17° measured in celestial latitude. The ecliptic is so named because eclipses can only occur when the Moon is in or very near to it.

Declination

We will not be using parallels of declination with the interpretational system taught in this book, but it is well that you understand what is meant by declination, especially if at some time you wish to experiment with parallels.

We have already seen that the Sun's path along the ecliptic crosses the equator from south to north at the vernal equinox, around 21 March. In the Northern Hemisphere this is the first day of spring. Each successive day the noon Sun appears higher in the heavens because the angle of the Earth's plane of the equator to the plane of the ecliptic increases.

This angle is measured in declination, which, as you will recall, is measurement north or south of the equator. The Sun reaches maximum declination north (about 23.5°) around 21 June. This tells us that, measured along a declination circle and northwards from the equator, the angle between the plane of the equator and the plane of the ecliptic is 23.5°. The Sun's maximum declination north marks the summer solstice. Increase in declination is halted; the Sun, as it were, stands still (Latin: *sistere*, to cause to stand still); and then declination begins to decrease. Around 21 September the Sun and the plane of the equator are in line (Sun has declination 0°) as it crosses from north to south of the equator. This is the autumnal equinox. Throughout the world day and night are again of equal length, as they were at the vernal equinox. Around 21 December the Sun reaches maximum declination south (about 23.5°), marking the winter solstice.

Celestial longitude for plotting a planet's position

The plane of the Earth's orbit around the Sun determines where the ecliptic lies in relation to the Earth's equator. In what is known as the Ecliptic System we use the co-ordinates of celestial longitude and celestial latitude to plot the position of a planet. Celestial latitude is rarely used by astrologers: it is measurement in degrees, minutes and seconds north or south of the ecliptic.

Celestial longitude is of prime importance to astrologers. It is measurement in degrees, minutes and seconds of arc eastwards in the plane of the ecliptic from the First Point of Aries to the meridian of longitude which passes through both the planet and the poles of the ecliptic. As an example, when Mars is in Aries 21°, Mars has travelled a distance of 21° eastwards from where the ecliptic intersects the equator.

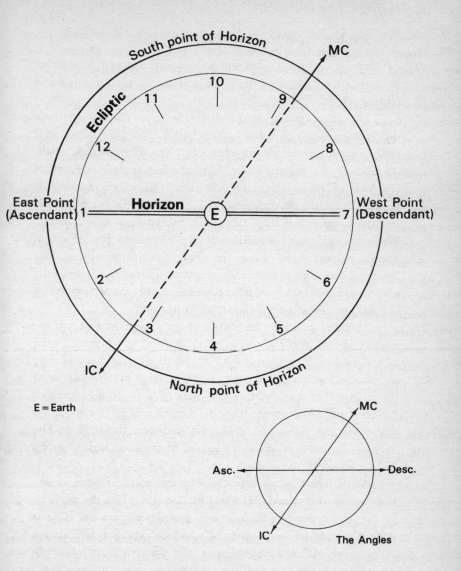

Figure 4

The birth chart symbolizes the birth locality's
relationship to the ecliptic

Symbolism of the birth chart

Let us refer to figure 4. This will help you get a clearer perspective of the birth chart and how it relates to the astronomical framework.

The basic framework of the birth chart consists of three different sized circles forming what appears to be a wheel with twelve equally-spaced incomplete spokes. The innermost and smallest circle containing the letter 'E' symbolizes the planet Earth as the focal or central point of reference. It is where man stands looking out at the universe around him. The middle circle symbolizes the ecliptic; it is the circle of the twelve signs of the zodiac. The outer circle conveniently encloses the symbolic picture and in a sense we may think of it as the distant boundaries of our Solar System. So as not to confuse the diagram with too much detail the planets and the signs have not been entered. The planets would be entered just inside the middle circle, the 'ecliptic'.

As the chart would be calculated for a specified place on the Earth's surface, that place must have a horizon, symbolized by the horizontal line. The chart would be calculated to a specified time and so the horizon is extended (as the celestial horizon) as far as the ecliptic. The specified time and place of birth would mean that the chart has an ascending sign or *Ascendant*. This is symbolized where the east point of the horizon intersects the ecliptic. The opposite sign will be at the west point intersection and is known as the *Descendant*.

As the chart is calculated to time and place of birth, it will also have a Midheaven (MC) and its opposite point the IC. The MC is where the ecliptic intersects the upper meridian. This is symbolized by the arrow directed upwards. The Sun will always be near the MC at midday but at any moment in the cycle of twenty-four hours there will be a *culminating degree* of the ecliptic, another term for the MC. Its opposite point, the IC (*Imum Coeli*) or lower meridian, is symbolized by the arrow directed downwards.

The twelve incomplete 'spokes' of the 'chart wheel' are

known as the *cusps* (divisions) of the twelve houses. These are
shown as the twelve numbered, equal sections in figure 4. For our
system of charting, the house cusps are shown incomplete or by
only a small line. This is preferred to the traditional cusps that cut
right through the chart and can be confused with aspect-lines. The
Ascendant determines the point where the system of houses
begins.

In figure 4 you will see a similar diagram entitled *the angles*.
These will be described to you later as indicative of major psycho-
logical features. The angles are symbolized by the Ascendant–
Descendant axis and the MC–IC axis.

These are the major astronomical factors necessary to construct an astrological chart based on a given time, date and place
of birth. At this stage we cannot incorporate the all-important
aspects – sensitive angular contacts between planets – without
which a chart's interpretation would be grossly incomplete.

You may have wondered why the south point is shown at
the top of the chart and the north point at the bottom. The
moment a celestial body crosses the upper meridian of a place it
is said to be *southing* that meridian. The Sun always souths a
meridian around noon. The name derives from the fact that this
transit occurs at the south point of the horizon. But why south
at the top, where one would expect to find north? We have to
think of ourselves as the observer standing facing south. East
(Ascendant) is on our left where the Sun rises over the horizon.
In *correct sequence* the Sun moves in an arc to the south (high in
the sky), then disappears below the horizon in the west (Descendant) on our right. It reaches the north point of horizon around
midnight.

Summary of chapter

1 The aim of this chapter is (a) to show how the symbolism of
  the birth chart relates to the major features of the basic
  astronomical framework and (b) to describe these features
  and how their functions interrelate.

2 Because we look out at the rest of the universe from our standpoint of Earth, a geocentric viewpoint, our planet must be the central or focal point of reference for measuring the Earth's relationship to the motions of the Sun, Moon and planets.

3 The three major circles of reference for determining the Ascendant and Midheaven, or plotting the positions of the celestial bodies relative to the Earth, are the horizon, the equator and the ecliptic.

4 The astronomical definition of the Ascendant is the point where the east point of the horizon intersects the ecliptic that determines where the system of houses begins. It also signifies the rising sign and is where the planets rise.

5 The intersection of the ecliptic and the equator at the vernal equinox determines the First Point of Aries, the reference point of prime importance in astronomy and the point where the cycle of the twelve signs of the zodiac begins.

CHAPTER 7

Time: A Key to Identity

What is time?

Time gives continuity and pattern to life. For astrological purposes time, in terms of date and moment (hour, minute) of a child's birth, together with co-ordinates of the birthplace, is a vital factor if an accurate chart is to be constructed for an individual.

But what do we mean by time?

The dictionary defines 'time' as 'a system of measuring and determining the duration of anything; finite duration as distinct from eternity.'[1] And yet we know that time is more than just a convenient system reckoned by our clocks and by the years that inevitably tick by at each birthday.

Time is one of the three fundamental measurements for the physicist – the other two being distance and mass – that can describe anything in the universe.

Psychologically one might see time as a feature of consciousness, the means by which we give order and structure to our experiences and to our observation of the continuity of life. Our reasoning tells us that we exist in time, and yet to try and explain what it *is* makes time seem such an intangible thing. But there is something so ordered, so concrete and inevitable about the 'time' to which our lives are regulated that it then seems such a tangible part of life! Especially when one realizes how much time can be manipulated through imagination, memory and foresight – deciding present action through knowledge of the past and anticipation of the future.

Astronomers are not concerned with defining the ultimate nature of time, only with measuring it, and their means for doing this we shall see presently. Time is a very, very intimate and pervasive feature of our lives. Not just because as civilized creatures we cannot avoid conforming to patterns of activity geared to clock time – convenient periods for working, playing and synchronizing our activities with other people's. It is because, in a sense, every living thing is a time mechanism and because 'we must be constructed out of time as certainly as we are constructed of bones and flesh.'[2]

It would be natural for an astrologer to believe that we must be 'constructed out of time' because over thousands of years the astrologers' knowledge and skill for interpreting individual human potential and behaviour has derived from the time of birth. The interplay of planetary cycles, the periods of which can be timed accurately, have been an essential feature of his philosophy and his understanding of the psychological mechanisms of behaviour. Now the astrologer is no longer alone in his belief that potential individual behaviour is related to time-cycles, that man grows and evolves in time. Scientists, biologists and increasing numbers of the medical and psychological professions believe that 'time governs not merely man's activities but his very being. Like every living organism, he exists by grace of thousands of intricately synchronized rhythms.'[3] They believe that we each have an internal or biological clock or clocks.

Man's cellular time structure

Biological clocks and their rhythms are not part of the structure for interpretation in this book but they are worthy of mention, albeit brief. Further research is needed to relate biological rhythms with planetary rhythms and cycles. Already much research has shown certain biological rhythms to be linked with a lunar periodicity.

Biological clocks are often referred to as physiological clocks because the detected rhythms in internal bodily activities are seen as physiological measurements in time. These are mostly brought about by means of oscillations with periods of approximately twenty-four hours, that is, by endogenous diurnal rhythms (endogenous: growing from within). This diurnal rhythm is, of course, the result of the approximate twenty-four hours rotation of the Earth on its axis relative to the Sun. The diurnal rhythms are now usually called *circadian* rhythms (*circa*: about; *dies*: day).

What is the source of these biological clocks? Where are they inside the body? It is generally agreed that the 'master clock' is located in the nucleus of the cell. Personally I believe that the cell *is* the 'clock'. This vital regulator of specific physiological time-cycles and rhythmic activity is not a portion of the cell but is the *whole* cell structure. We can no more exist without this 'unseen' time structure than we can exist without the physical structure of our being. We can speak of the temporal structure (anatomy in time) of living beings as well as the spatial structure (anatomy in space). Our own individual internal physiological clocks are products of the evolutionary process of natural selection, of adaptation to the environment for survival and realization of potential. Just as our entire being is dependent for wholeness of mind and body upon an integrated internal time structure, so is it equally dependent upon a balanced synchronization with the complex time structure and rhythms of the environment.

An individual's quest for unique identity can be helped considerably by recognition of his or her own time structure.

If it were not for the cyclic rotation of the Earth on its axis and the Earth's revolving about the Sun, which produce the day/ night cycle and the annual cycle of the seasons respectively, the concept of 'time' would not exist for us.

In *Cycles*, the journal of the *Foundation for the Study of Cycles*, a reprint appeared of a research paper by Dr S. W. Tromp, Ph.D. at Leiden (The Netherlands), entitled 'Possible Effects of Extra-terrestrial Stimuli on Colloidal Systems and Living Organisms'.[4] The concluding paragraph is worth quoting:

... there is little doubt that certain physical factors are active in our environment which are still not very well known ... Both the time of the day (circadian rhythms), the time of the year, the year itself and the location on Earth are factors to be considered. In other words the physiological phenomena in man and animals are a function of time and location on Earth, which may become a new concept in future scientific research.

Dr Tromp's research and reasoning are to be applauded. But to speak of 'time and location on Earth' as a 'new concept' is to be quite a few centuries out of date! He is merely giving scientific confirmation to a fact known to astrologers for aeons.

In a previous article Dr Tromp had written:

A study of the many observed cycles in nature, both in the living and non-living world ... supports the assumption that, apart from local terrestrial causes, all living processes on Earth and their evolution, and also human thinking and behaviour probably are controlled or seriously affected by extra-terrestrial forces or partly unknown energy fields in the universe.[5]

Time factors used in astrology

You have already seen that the two basic factors for plotting a birth chart are time and space. In other words, date and time of birth, and place of birth. In chapter 6 you were shown the framework of circles and reference points by which the astronomer plots the exact location of a celestial body. This framework derives entirely from the Earth–Sun relationship.

The Earth's angular relationship to the Sun is the source of the basic units of time employed in astrology. All time measurements derive from this relationship, which produces two cycles of motion: the *year*, derived from the Earth's orbit of the Sun; and the *day*, derived from the Earth's axial rotation. These are the two simple motions involving the Earth and Sun from which we can begin to understand measurement in time and space for the construction of astrological charts. There are, of course, subdivisions, such as the twelve months being subdivisions of the year and the twenty-four hours being subdivisions of the day. There are others which will now be explained.

Tropical year, sidereal year

There are several kinds of year, but the two of special importance for astrologers are the tropical year and the sidereal year.

The *tropical year* (Greek: *trope*, turning) is the time that elapses between the successive passages of the Sun through the vernal equinox, or First Point of Aries. This period, vernal equinox to vernal equinox, measures 365 days, 5 hours, 48 minutes and 46 seconds in mean solar time.

The stars provide a convenient and essentially fixed system of reference for man. Thus, we have the *sidereal year* (Latin: *sidus*, star) that is measured relative to the stars. The interval between the passage of the Sun across a secondary to the ecliptic (meridian of longitude intersecting the poles of the ecliptic) which passes through some fixed star and its return to that same star is called a sidereal year. In mean solar time this equals 365 days, 6 hours, 9 minutes and 10 seconds. In reality this is the true year, the period taken by the Sun to return to exactly the same position against the background of stars as seen from the Earth.

Calendar year or civil year

As a calendar for civil and chronological usage, neither the tropical nor the sidereal years would be of much practical value. And so a year having an exact number of days was invented and called the calendar or civil year. Thus our calendar year has 365 days, with 366 days in each leap year.

Month; week

The word 'month' derives from the Moon and refers to the Earth–Moon cycle, but this has no relationship to the familiar calendar month that is an approximate one-twelfth of our year, January through to December.

The *synodic month* is the interval between consecutive conjunctions of Sun and Moon as seen from the Earth. Its average length is twenty-nine days, twelve hours, forty-four minutes and three seconds. We call this a *lunation*, from New Moon to New Moon.

The *sidereal month* is the Moon's period of revolution relative to the stars. The mean length is twenty-seven days, seven hours, forty-three minutes and twelve seconds, which is more than two days shorter than the synodic month (see figure 5).

The *week* is a non-astronomical element of the calendar. Its origin goes back centuries before the Christian era to the great early astronomical period of the Babylonians.

The day; mean solar day

Each day we experience, familiarly divided into twenty-four equal hours, derives from the Earth's axial rotation. Our fixed twenty-four-hour day is geared to the mean Sun, hence it is a *mean solar day*. Its division into two twelve-hour periods comes to us from the Babylonian era of 5,000 years ago.

Sidereal day

The *sidereal day* is the exact period of rotation of the earth on its axis, measured in sidereal time between two successive transits of the First Point of Aries over the observer's upper meridian. The moment this Point crosses the meridian of any given place corresponds to zero hours, zero minutes, zero seconds. Sidereal time and the sidereal day for that given place begins.

A sidereal day of twenty-four hours of sidereal time equals only 23 hours, 56 minutes and 4.09 seconds of mean solar time. Thus, a sidereal day is completed three minutes and fifty-six seconds *faster* than a mean (solar) day.

Apparent solar day

Because the Earth is ceaselessly turning on its axis, the Sun appears to be the body that is moving. When we speak of this movement of the Sun, visible in daytime, we refer to the *true* Sun.

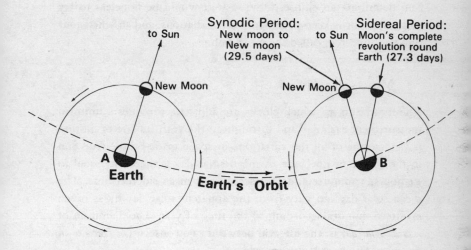

Synodic Period:
New moon to
New moon
(29.5 days)

to Sun

New Moon

to Sun

New Moon

Sidereal Period:
Moon's complete
revolution round
Earth (27.3 days)

A
Earth

Earth's Orbit

B

Figure 5

Difference between the Moon's synodic period
and sidereal period

This movement of the Sun is its *apparent* motion, because it is visible, evident. Because it is the apparent motion of the Sun, we call the interval between two successive passages of the Sun across the lower meridian of a given place the *apparent solar day*. The apparent speed of the Sun as seen from the Earth varies at different times of the year, due to the orbit of the Earth about the Sun describing an ellipse. Obviously it would be hopeless to try and make clocks keep pace with such variations, and so a fictitious Sun was invented, called the mean Sun.

Mean solar day

The mean Sun, to which clocks are adjusted, provides a uniform measurement each day and throughout the year. Its rate of motion is the average of all the variations in speed made by the true Sun in the course of one year. A mean solar day is therefore equal to 24 hours, 3 minutes and 56·5 seconds of mean sidereal time. The mean solar day can vary from the apparent solar day by as much as fifteen minutes according to the time of year. The definition of a *mean solar day* is: the interval between two consecutive transits of the mean Sun over a given meridian.

Sidereal time

Sidereal time is a direct measure of the diurnal rotation of the Earth. Astrologers must use sidereal time for determining the angles of a birth chart. Sidereal time is defined as measurement westwards in the plane of the equator from a given meridian to the First Point of Aries, as determined by the Earth's rotation.

Local sidereal time

Local sidereal time is sidereal time for a given instant for the observer's meridian. Most annual ephemerides give sidereal time for noon at Greenwich, England, for each day of the year. Because it is for Greenwich, this is also local sidereal time for

Greenwich (or for any other place worldwide that has the same meridian as Greenwich). The reason why we speak of a local sidereal time is because at any moment the sidereal time is different for different meridians. The calculation of the Ascendant and Midheaven for a given time and locality is determined by sidereal time, and one needs to know what the local sidereal time is for that particular time and locality.

Solar time; apparent solar time

Solar time or apparent solar time is time reckoned by the true apparent or visible Sun. Solar time measures the position of the Sun from zero to twenty-four hours as it appears to encircle the Earth between two successive transits of a given meridian. This is determined by the Earth's axial rotation.

Mean solar time; clock time

We have seen that, with regard to the mean solar day and the apparent solar day, it would be impossible to base our complex human activities upon the true Sun in terms of apparent solar time. Hence our clocks are synchronized to a fictitious Sun known as the mean Sun. It provides a uniform time called mean solar time or clock time.

Longitude equivalent in time

An important step in calculating local sidereal time for a given birth time is known as longitude equivalent in time. Its name is self-explanatory. It refers to the difference in time between the terrestrial longitude of a given birthplace and the terrestrial longitude for Greenwich (England). There are 360° in the full circle of terrestrial longitude. The mean Sun travels twenty-four hours in a complete mean solar day. If we divide 360 by 24 we will see that the distance travelled by the mean Sun in one hour of mean solar time is 15° of arc of terrestrial longitude, or 1° every four minutes.

Greenwich Mean Time (GMT)

In October 1884 the meridian of Greenwich (England) was internationally chosen as the prime meridian from which all terrestrial longitudes should be measured. A system of Standard Times was also recommended, differing by an integral number of hours from Greenwich (local) mean time. Not all countries immediately adopted those recommendations, but since then all clocks throughout the world have been synchronized with Greenwich Mean Time. GMT is, of course, the standard time for Great Britain.

Standard Time; Zone Time

As we have seen, all countries have now adopted a Standard Time based on Greenwich Mean Time. When calculating a birth chart for someone born outside the United Kingdom it is imperative to check whether the given time is in that country's Standard Time or in GMT. For large continents, such as the USA, or at sea, a system of *zones* is used to keep the time the same over specific ranges of longitude. These are known as time zones.

Summer Time; Daylight Saving Time

Summer Time was introduced into Great Britain in 1916 and has been used ever since. Clocks are advanced one hour for several months between spring and autumn. During certain years of the Second World War in Great Britain Double Summer Time (clocks advanced two hours) was used in summer and for the rest of the year ordinary Summer Time applied. Many other countries have adopted this system but refer to it as Daylight Saving Time (DST). During both world wars DST in the USA was called War Time.

Summary of chapter

1 This chapter shows that time is an intimate, inescapable

reality which determines an individual's birth potential and capacity to adapt to his or her environment.

2 Time is a vital key to an individual's identity. Understanding of psychological potential can be realized through the critical factors of time and place of birth.

3 Time gives continuity and pattern to life. In a sense every living thing is a time mechanism and man is constructed out of time as well as of flesh and bones.

4 Time would not exist for us but for the Earth's axial rotation and its revolving about the Sun.

Notes

1 *Shorter Oxford English Dictionary* (Clarendon Press, Oxford, 1950)

2 Gay Gaer Luce: *Body Time*, p. 13 (Temple Smith, 1972)

3 *Time*, p. 9 (Time-Life International (Nederland) N. V., 1970)

4 Dr S. W. Tromp: 'Possible Effects of Extra-terrestrial Stimuli on Colloidal Systems and Living Organisms' (*Cycles*, Vol. XXIV, No. 10, November 1973)

5 Dr S. W. Tromp: 'Research Project on Terrestrial, Biological, Medical and Biochemical Phenomena, Caused or Triggered by Possible Extra-terrestrial Physical Forces' (*Cycles*, Vol. XXI, No. 2, Foundation for the Study of Cycles, 1970)

CHAPTER 8

Planetary Rhythms

Rhythm: the manifestation of pattern

Life is in continual flux. Every moment of each day and of each night our individual psyche is dependent for survival upon the successful interactions of internal rhythms and energy exchanges with the external environment.

Rhythm is the manifestation of basic patterns in life that produce a measured flow and timing of energy. The study of rhythms reveals the correlation and interdependence of parts for the production of an harmonious whole.

Astrology is the interpretation of the rhythms underlying human behaviour. In this chapter we will look very briefly at the major planetary rhythms which produce the mathematical data the astrologer depends upon for plotting the planet's positions relative to the Earth for a given time.

Earth's axial rotation

The spinning or rotating of the Earth on its axis is from west to east, which means that if you stand facing south, the Earth beneath your feet turns eastwards, anticlockwise. The diurnal rotation of the Earth is one complete turn on its axis or a sidereal day. The Earth's rotation determines the angles of the birth chart.

Earth's orbital revolution

We call the orbital motion of the Earth about its centre of attraction (the Sun) its *orbital revolution*. All planets move in a direct motion eastwards around the Sun, following the eastward rotation of the

Sun on its own axis. A planet's orbit is elliptical in shape. From our standpoint on Earth, our planet's revolution of the Sun produces the appearance of the Sun moving through the zodiacal signs during the passage of a year. The Sun's, Moon's and planets' positions in longitude arise from the Earth's orbital revolution.

Gravitation and planetary motion

The planets move only because they are acted on by some force. That force we know to be gravitation. In 1665, when he was only about twenty-three, the English astronomer Sir Isaac Newton discovered the law of gravitation:

Every particle of matter in the universe attracts every other particle with a force varying directly as the product of their masses and inversely as the square of the distance between them.

Gravitation (Latin: *gravitas*, weight) acts upon objects to produce a force experienced as weight or pressure. Variable motion is the result of the matter in a body having mass. The Earth attracts the Sun; the Sun attracts the Earth. But the Sun has the greater attractive force because it has the greater mass. Thus, as we have said, the planets move only because they are acted on by some force. Our Earth's terrestrial globe attracts everything to itself, like a magnet. Gravity is an effect produced by attraction to a centre, and so weight is the tendency of bodies to fall towards the Earth.

Planetary perturbations

The Earth would constantly follow the same orbit around the Sun were it not for the gravitational attraction of the other planets, known as perturbations of the Earth's orbit. Thus, gravity is a controlling force in keeping a planet in its orbit with reference to a central body, but it is also a disturbing influence on other planets.

Precession of the Equinoxes

A rhythm of major importance to the evolution of life on Earth involves our planet with the Sun and Moon and is known as the *Precession of the Equinoxes*. It is caused by the gravitational action of the Sun and Moon on the equatorial bulge of the Earth. Precession is a slow swinging motion of the Earth's axis of rotation, rather like that of a toy top. The Earth's axis is tilted, and referring to figure 3 (page 45), we see that the angle thus produced between the plane of the equator and the plane of the ecliptic is called the *obliquity of the ecliptic*. This angle decreases by a mere 47″ a century. The Earth's tilt means that the northern extremity of the axis points towards a star we know as *Polaris* or the *Pole Star*.

Due to precession the Earth rotates obliquely upon itself, a gradual retrograde motion of the equinoctial points along the ecliptic against the background of stars. Thus, Polaris was not always near to the Earth's north pole. About 2,000 years ago, when the great observational astronomer, Hipparchus, discovered this displacement of the Earth's axis, the vernal equinox occurred against the background of the constellation Aries. Hence, the First Point of Aries. But at the present time, due to precession, the First Point of Aries occurs against the background of the constellation Pisces. The complete retrograde cycle of the equinoctial points, called a Great Year, takes about 25,800 years.

Moon's nodes and declination

The system for interpreting charts employed in this book does not take into consideration the *declinations* of the planets that produce parallel aspects. But it is as well to understand what is meant by declination in case you should wish to test the parallel aspects.

The combined movement of the Earth–Moon system is illustrated in figure 6. The Earth, by its gravitational hold on the Moon, appears to carry its satellite with it along the ecliptic. But the Moon's orbit, unlike the Earth's, is not in the ecliptic. It

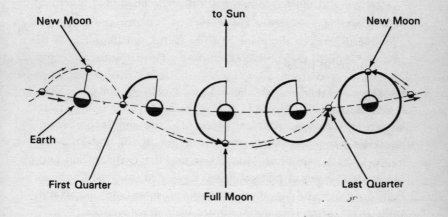

Figure 6

Combined motion of Earth and Moon

inclines at an average angle of 5°8' with it. The two points where the Moon's orbit intersects the plane of the ecliptic are called the *nodes*. The *north node* or *ascending node* (☊) is where the Moon's orbit intersects with the ecliptic from south to north. The ancients knew of this and called it the Dragon's Head. The *south node* or *descending node* (☋) is where the Moon crosses the ecliptic from north to south. The ancients called this the Dragon's Tail.

A full and illustrated explanation of declination is given in my *Astrologer's Astronomical Handbook*.

Lunation phases

Everyone is familiar with the Moon's cycle, beginning at New Moon, through Full Moon and on to the next New Moon. This is known as a *lunation*. At New Moon the Sun and Moon are in direct line, or *conjunction*, viewed from the Earth. Referring to figure 6 again, when the Moon is at its First Quarter, Sun and Moon are in *square* aspect (90° apart) as viewed from the Earth; at Full Moon Sun and Moon are in *opposition* aspect (180° apart); and at the Last Quarter Sun and Moon are again in *square* aspect.

Rhythmic cycle of the seasons

The two most obvious environmental rhythms affecting human life and growth are the diurnal (twenty-four hours) axial rotation of the Earth and the revolution of the Earth around the Sun (solar year). We are particularly aware of the latter cycle through the procession of the seasons – spring, summer, autumn, winter. The main cause of the differing nature of the seasons is the inclination of the Earth's axis and the changing direction of its axis of rotation relative to the Sun. This is illustrated in figure 7.

Thus, a principal cause of the seasons is the varying angle at which the Sun's rays strike different parts of the Earth's surface, creating variations in temperature. It is not only the height of the Sun in the noon sky that affects temperature, but the length of the period from sunrise to sunset.

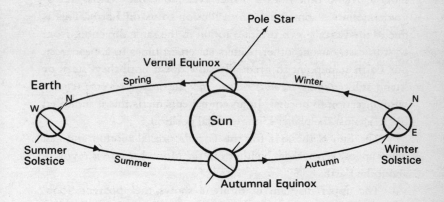

Figure 7

Inclination of the Earth's axis, the main cause
of the seasons

Retrograde motion

It may be puzzling that a planet will at some time move in a reverse direction to normal. This is known as *retrograde* motion. The reason for this is illustrated in figure 8.

Planets orbit the Sun from west to east. This is their direct motion. At no time does a planet ever move backwards. Retrograde motion is something of an illusion to us on Earth. This is due to the Earth's own orbital motion in the same direction, from west to east, causing other planets at certain times to appear from our Earth standpoint to gradually slow down until they 'stop' or 'stand still' (*stationary point*) before moving in the reverse (clockwise) direction to normal. In an annual ephemeris this is indicated by 'R' against the planet's longitudinal position.

The Sun is the axis for the Earth's orbital motion and can never appear retrograde. Neither can the Moon because it revolves about the Earth.

The upper diagram in figure 8 shows the apparent 'loop' described by a *superior* planet (i.e. a planet outside the Earth's orbit such as Mars, Jupiter, Saturn, Uranus, Neptune and Pluto) in its path between two stationary points that enclose between them the arc of retrogression (or retrogradation). Between the arc ABC the planet appears to move *eastwards* (direct). Its angular motion decreases as it approaches C (stationary point). Then the planet appears to move *westwards* (retrograde) along the arc CDE, until E (stationary point) is reached. The arc EFG traces its eastward and direct motion again.

In the lower diagram we can see the Earth's orbit inside the superior planet's orbit and, by following the direction of the arrows, realize how it is that a planet, as seen from the Earth, *appears* to 'go retrograde'. One can deduce from the positions of Sun, Earth and superior planet that a planet can only appear retrograde around the time of its opposition aspect with the Sun, the Earth being between the two bodies.

Mercury and Venus are known as the *inferior* planets because their orbits lie inside the Earth's orbit. Either of these two planets

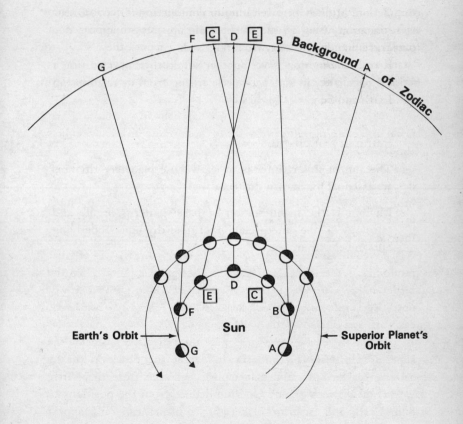

Figure 8

Retrograde motion

can only appear retrograde when directly between the Sun and the Earth. This is also when either is nearest to the Earth and is at *inferior conjunction*. *Superior conjunction* is when Mercury or Venus is on the other side of the Sun and furthest from the Earth. Midway between Greatest Elongation East (B) and inferior conjunction (D), these planets will appear to be stationary because for a brief while they are moving exactly towards the Earth. This explains why an inferior planet can only appear retrograde around inferior conjunction. Midway between inferior conjunction (D) and Greatest Elongation West (F) the planet again appears stationary, due to its travelling exactly away from the Earth.

Retrograde motion is yet another subtle rhythm, featuring a periodic peculiarity in a planet's cycle arising from its relationship with Earth and Sun.

Summary of chapter

1 The aim of this chapter is to show how planetary rhythms are essential for human existence.

2 Rhythm is the manifestation of basic patterns in life and astrology is the interpretation of the rhythms underlying human behaviour.

CHAPTER 9

The Astrological Components of Personality

We have reached a stage in this book when it would be appropriate to briefly review certain significant features that have been covered so far and to summarize in a concise and clear-cut manner the vitally important astrological components of personality that will be dealt with in detail in the next few chapters.

The cosmos within man

In chapter 2 we read that the cosmos is within man, in the sense that the interrelated planetary pattern at any given moment and for any given place on Earth correlates with the psychological pattern of potential behaviour in a child born at that moment. We can more easily understand this profound truth when we look at figure 1 (page xvi) and figure 4 (page 51) (illustrating the birth chart), and read on page 44 that the birth chart symbolizes man at the centre of the universe looking out at the Sun, Moon and planets that appear to revolve around him. The focal point for these heavenly bodies is man – each individual man or woman.

Just as we could not survive without our earthly environment, which we are dependent on for sustenance, stimulation and growth, so could we not even exist on this Earth plane without our vital link with the cosmic environment.

The cell: mediator between God and man?

Some astrologers may ask, 'What does it matter how the Sun, Moon and planets and zodiacal signs influence or correlate with individual human behaviour as long as we know this is true?' Fair enough, but there are others of us who must always seek further understanding of man's relationship with his environment and with the spiritual forces within life. I believe that, through its many creative functions and as the basic unit of life containing the pre-programmed processes necessary for an individual's survival and development of a unique personality, each cell is a mediator between God and man. Jesus said, 'the kingdom of God is within you.' The cell is man's link with God, through which the Word of God speaks, creates a miniature universe within each human being, and impregnates man with the potential to seek perfection and wholeness.

Astrologers have demonstrated that 'personality' and individual behavioural patterns can be correlated with the ever-changing patterns of interplanetary motions and relationships. The ancient Hermetics knew this: 'As above, so below', they taught. Anyone, sceptic or otherwise, can realize this if they put astrology to the test. The astrological components with which personality potential can be predicted that are employed in this book are briefly listed now and will be dealt with in detail in subsequent chapters.

The survival needs

For life to continue for any organism it must develop ways of surviving. By tracing the evolution of man from his most primitive driving force, the need to survive and to preserve his identity as an individual organism, it is possible to construct a coherent and unifying framework of the psyche's potential based on six classes of *survival needs*. This is the starting-point for the realization of a structure for interpreting the potential within the psyche. Never before in astrological literature has such an in-depth study been undertaken, enabling us to see more clearly the psychological function of each planet in a birth chart.

The planets: functional needs

A *functional need* is an activity vital to the fulfilment of the psyche's unfolding of potentialities. Each functional need – and therefore, for the purpose of astrological interpretation, each planet – is instrumental in the working of the human psyche in a useful, effective, specialized form, and for the greater purpose of wholeness of experience and expression.

The signs: disposition

The psychological make-up of each one of us contains a complex mixture of the qualities of all twelve zodiacal signs. But each of us has a particular sign or signs shown more prominently in our birth chart and their associated traits will, therefore, be more evident in our behaviour and self-expression. The signs represent twelve different directions of courses of action, interest and behaviour. We can see each sign as a *quality of differentiation*, a special feature within the psyche, vital for giving diversity of purpose and direction to the functional needs represented by the planets. The signs are best described concisely as expressive of *disposition* – a tendency to act in a certain necessary manner.

The angles: environmental relationships

The angles of a chart represent four basic forms of relationship we can make with our environment. They intensify and amplify the function associated with a planet aspecting them and provide a vitally important dimension of uniqueness to the individual concerned. Certain very sensitive areas produced by the angles are known as *Distinctive Zones*, and a planet placed in one of these zones indicates the potential for achieving some act or expression of distinction.

The aspects: focus on the satisfaction of special needs

An aspect – or specific angular relationship – between two planets stimulates and activates the functional needs associated with these planets, intensifying the necessity for achieving satisfaction through these particular needs. Focus on the satisfaction of these functional needs classifies them as 'special' needs for the individual concerned. They can be seen as significant areas of experience in one's striving to achieve self-fulfilment.

It is vital to distinguish between planet and sign

We will learn how a particular survival need influences the functions and traits of planets and aspects. We will learn that the signs have a different role to play in a chart to that of the planets because they give diversity of purpose and direction to the functional needs represented by the planets. Whereas each planet's functional need is a specialized form of activity and expression. For an accurate interpretation of a birth chart it is vital to recognize this distinction between planet and sign.

Summary

1 Survival needs are underlying powerful forces influencing the behaviour and drives of every man and woman. They can generate expressions of intensity of feeling, great determination and compulsion, fanaticism, obsession, selfishness, worthy dedication or fear of insecurity.

2 Functional needs, represented by the planets, are activities vital to the fulfilment of the psyche's unfolding.

3 Each psyche contains qualities of all twelve zodiacal signs, expressing a tendency to act in a certain manner.

4 Angles represent four basic forms of relationship we can

make with our environment and intensify a planet's function.

5 Aspects activate the functional needs (planets) and focus on the satisfying of these special needs.

CHAPTER 10

The Structure for Survival

In this book you are being shown a method of interpreting a birth chart that in several respects breaks with tradition in the employment and application of basic chart features. A framework has been constructed emphasizing the basic needs of the human psyche, using concepts universally accepted by psychologists.

This chapter briefly describes my search for this framework or 'structure for survival'. The gradual process of discovery over many years and the eventual piecing together of the details was an adventure tinged with excitement, frustration and periods of despair. Ever since I first began to study astrology at the end of World War II, I had sought to understand the driving forces behind human behaviour. Always I encountered the same stumbling block: the lack of cohesion with the generally accepted variety of theories.

The search for a starting-point

For more than thirty years I searched psychological, biological, anatomical and physiological literature for an understanding of man's functioning as an organism, and especially for information about the psyche with its feelings, thought processes and complex behaviour patterns, hoping to clearly unify all aspects of the psyche within one sound basic structure.

I searched in vain. Invaluable guidelines were given by Dr Carl Jung who, of course, was despised by the ever-increasing multitude of Behaviourists and the laboratory psychologists who still fanatically believe that the behaviour of distressed rats is the surest way to understanding the emotions of men and women. The more I read the more confused I could have grown had I not employed in my own teaching and counselling work the basic astrological structure for interpreting individual human behaviour and potential stemming from the relevant moment of birth. It was obvious that in no way could the orthodox psychologists construct a universally acceptable psychological structure without the knowledge of astrological principles to which standard psychological concepts could be adjusted.

While I was engaged in highly successful astrological/psychological research with Professor Hans Eysenck of the Institute of Psychiatry in London, I asked him in a letter of 9 February 1978 if he could advise me of a basic structure or framework to aid in the psyche's interpretation. His reply of 22 February 1978 was no surprise: 'The unified system of personality description you look for is still a long way in the future; for the time being you will have to make do with P, E and N!' (P, E and N: his measurements of psychoticism, extraversion and neuroticism).

Psychology began as a 'science' in 1879. So what went wrong over all these decades? Clearly, psychologists who did not use astrology were floundering in a sea of words and conflicting concepts like a ship without a rudder. Astrology was never considered, despite the fact that a brilliant thinker like Dr Carl Jung had written: 'Astrology is assured of recognition from psychology, without further restrictions, because astrology repre sents the summation of all the psychological knowledge of antiquity.'[1]

An increasing number of psychologists have published their own opinions regarding the static and confused state of orthodox psychology and of its practitioners: 'At the moment the views of professional psychologists still seem mainly to be in a state of bewildered confusion; and there is a crying need for an entirely fresh examination of the subject from top to bottom.'[2] There is Ludwig Wittgenstein's much-quoted aphorism that 'in psychology there are experimental methods and conceptual confusions' and Sigmund Koch's opinion that 'it is by this time utterly and finally clear that psychology cannot be a coherent science, or indeed a coherent field of scholarship, in any specifiable sense of coherence that can bear upon a field of inquiry.'[3] Another writer refers to 'the present state of relative chaos' that psychology is in[4] while R. B. Joynson writes that 'It is not unreasonable to suggest . . . that we are no better off than we were in the 1890s . . . There is nothing to provide a starting-point for interpretation.'[5]

I am not intent on bashing psychologists, even though many of their fraternity who are totally ignorant of astrological truths enjoying bashing astrologers. I am simply letting other enlightened psychologists and writers point to the chaos that exists, whilst feeling sad that the astrological chart is not universally the basis for personality interpretation as indeed it should be.

Psychology has been called the science of the human mind; the science of human behaviour; and, by the influential William James, 'the science of mental life'. Eysenck speaks for a large section of psychologists when he says that mind and soul 'are of little use in dealing with the observable world of living things.'[6] Anything that cannot be measured and statistically verified does not exist. Presumably the fact that I love my wife must never be taken into account should the reasons for my behaviour towards her be analysed! A typical example of the astronomical waste of energy, money, skills and precious time is given by Eysenck. He relates that the American psychologist, Harry Harlow, 'has spent more than twenty years investigating the importance of the phenomenon we call love in rhesus monkeys . . . He found that female adults usually make better mothers than male adults.'[7] !!!

There is a considerable lack of unity in the definitions of major concepts: 'the words used by psychologists are a constant source of anxiety to them and of rage to their readers'[8]; 'the lack of an adequate coherent theoretical structure has limited the advance of social psychology.'[9] P. E. Vernon has said that 'the primary aim of psychology has been to establish the general laws or principles underlying behaviour and thinking.'[10] Yes, that is the primary aim, but how much longer do psychologists have to fumble around with excellent concepts, yet remain unable to find a unifying and cohesive structure? Even today, basic concepts like 'personality' create confusion: 'thoughts on and investigations into the concept of personality have been bedevilled by a lack of agreement on what "it" really is'[11]; 'Psychology is not even quite sure what personality is.'[12]

Is it little wonder that I searched in vain for an established structure that would clearly unify all aspects of the psyche?

But all was not lost! I had always felt that the key or starting-point to the realization of a possible coherent and unified structure of the psyche would be very simple. It was. And one didn't need to be a qualified psychologist to realize this – indeed it seems it was preferable not to be.

Survival: the starting-point

Survival must surely be the key concept from which to start to realize the possible structure for interpreting the potential within man's psyche.

The basic primitive driving force for activity, the principle need for any living organism, is survival or self-preservation. All other needs stem from this or, as with the more cultural, creative and spiritual needs, cannot be realized until the primitive survival needs have been largely satisfied. Put in another way, the primitive survival need means the preservation of the organism's identity. As man has evolved, as his needs and tastes have become more sophisticated and involvement with his environment more complex, so has the search for individual identity become more of an urgency.

Survival and the environment

For life to continue for any organism it must develop ways of surviving. Each one of us is an organism and we depend utterly for survival upon our environment. As with our ancestors millions of years ago, so today we too are subject to a two-way interaction: our organism or self versus the environment. However attached we may feel to other people, we are each a separate organism – not just physically, but mentally, emotionally, spiritually. It is true that we share a vital link with our Creator and that we share the archetypes and the Collective Unconscious realms of energy. But, as for the situation we are born into, even before the umbilical cord connecting us to our mother is severed, we are very much on our own.

Very much on our own, especially for the purpose of experiencing ourselves and our environment, for being responsible for our unique contribution to the environment and for determining the development of our potentialities. In terms of survival and growth, life demands that man and the living features of his environment function interdependently.

To survive, man must form two major relationships with his environment: *to keep alive* – to engage with and resist threats from the environment, to control and master the environment as a defence; and *to obtain sustenance* (nutrition, organic needs) – to be sustained by, utilize and adapt to the environment. There is also a third relationship: *to perpetuate the species* (reproduction, sex) – to relate yourself to and unite with the environment for the sharing and re-creation of yourself and others.

Man's intricate patterns of relating to his fellows and of thought application did not just happen. It took aeons for even the simplest thought or feeling reaction to manifest itself and have meaning. Countless stages in the ceaseless struggle with the environment to avert extinction would have produced the further adaptive transformations necessary to evolve a nervous system, the brain, sight and speech, intelligence and the creative potential of mind.

From the first fearfully fragile life-form, and with each stage of its evolutionary unfolding to become present-day man and woman, surged the potent and increasingly complex energies needed for survival, unbroken threads linking millions of generations of our ancestors. Little wonder these energies are still powerfully registered within man's psyche and are clearly recognizable as forming the basic structure of his patterns of behaviour.

The complex emotions, thinking processes and traits of men and women can all be related to a few basic survival needs. Thus, from the simple starting-point of man's will to survive, the structure giving coherence and unification to his psyche's complex behaviour took on a solid and unquestionable shape with the foundation stones of these survival needs.

The survival needs

It is necessary to define what I mean by 'need'. Psychologists frequently make a vague or inadequate distinction between needs, drives and motives, or vary in their choice of definition, one giving the definition for 'drive' that another uses for 'need' and yet another uses for 'motive'. My definition of 'need' is a manifestation of a deficiency. Any organism must constantly strive to achieve and maintain an equilibrium on all levels, psychically and organically, for the organism to function efficiently and healthily. The pursuit of equilibrium is a universal characteristic of life, the restoration of balance. A need initiates an impulse that registers a deficiency and provides a stimulus or *motive*. The motive, to correct or satisfy the deficiency, conditions and determines which direction to take. We must be clear about this: the motive is not the actual resultant activity. The motive directs interest and behaviour towards a goal. This produces or motivates the necessary *drive*. This drive is the activity or active striving. Hunger, for instance, indicates an organic need. Thus, hunger provides a motive for determining a means of satisfying this need. The choice of motive activates the appropriate drive, and this is the actual behaviour or activity directed towards the satisfying of the hunger-need.

My *Structure for Survival* is based on *six classes of primary needs*, as follows:

SNA – to attack, master and control the environment.

SNB – to endure, be sustained by and utilize the environment.

SNC – to be safe and secure against the environment.

SND – to unite interdependently with the environment.

SNE – to yield to the environment.

SNF – to explore the environment for creative and inventive expediency.

Every human activity will be covered by at least one of the above. I shall make this clearer in the details that follow.

Survival Need A (SNA): *Self-preservation – to attack, master and control the environment*

To reach out to encounter the environment.

Survival through authority and control; increased autonomy.

The self supreme; the self coping alone.

To engage with the environment.

1 To keep alive
   (a) by force.
   (b) by being better, more competent, than others.
2 To engage with, encounter the environment
   (a) to approach.
   (b) to meet face to face; confrontation.
3 To resist threats from the environment
   (a) resist threats from the environment with force.
   (b) conflict with, oppose, be against.
   (c) if necessary, to destroy that which threatens or opposes.
4 To control the environment
   (a) to be in control of, coping with, manipulating.
   (b) to master, subjugate.

Major drives: achievement, activity, aggression, ascendance, autonomy, competitiveness, dominance/power, exhibition, independence, manipulative, objective, prestige/status, recognition, self-assertion, superiority, acquisitive, exposition.

Survival Need B (SNB): *Self-preservation – to endure and be sustained by the environment*

To utilize the environment.

Survival through endurance, adaptation.

Organic needs.

Dependence on the environment for renewal and sustenance.

1 To obtain nourishment from the environment
   (a) to keep alive.
   (b) to maintain fitness and efficiency, physically and mentally.
   (c) to revive and sustain activity.

2 To learn that the environment is the sole provider of sustenance
   (a) to work and interact with the environment productively.
   (b) to utilize the environment.
   (c) to adapt to the environment's rhythms.

3 To achieve growth through the environment
   (a) to cultivate growth through experience.
   (b) to sustain growth through endurance.

Major drives: acquisitive, affiliative, altruistic/sympathetic, conservation, construction, manipulative, order, retention.

Survival need C (SNC): *Self-preservation – safety and security*
To protect against the environment.
Survival through security.
Defence against the environment.

1 To protect against the environment
   (a) to build defences.

2 To achieve safety within the environment
   (a) to maintain security against adversity.
   (b) to have stability.
   (c) to feel free from danger.

Major drives: safety, security, conservation, defensiveness, maternal, affectional, affiliation.

Survival Need D (SND): *Preservation of the species.*
To unite with the environment and others of the same species.
Survival through interdependence.
To involve with the environment.
Sharing, recreating with the environment.

1 To perpetuate the species
   (a) sexual interaction.

(b) preservation of self-identity.

(c) to adapt to and utilize another person for reproduction of self.

2 To share self with others

(a) to interact socially.

(b) to involve with, unite with others.

(c) give to and share self with others.

Major drives: affectional, affiliation, altruistic/sympathetic, intra-ception, maternal, nurturing, objective, play, prestige, recognition, self-assertion, self-esteem/consistency, sex, social adaptability/socia-bility, social approval, status, exhibition.

Survival Need E (SNE): *Self-preservation – submission to the lead of others*

To yield to the environment.

Survival through dependence.

1 Yielding to, controlled by the environment.

2 To be protected by the environment.

3 To be used by others in return for shelter and guidance.

4 To submit to and be led by others.

5 To be dependent on others.

Major drives: affectional, affiliation, conformity, deference, depend-ency, self-consciousness, self-esteem/consistency, self-submission, social approval, succour.

Survival Need F (SNF): *Creative and inventive expediency*

Need for creativeness and self-exploration.

Survival through creativeness.

Self-actualization.

1 To explore the environment for advantage.

2 Development of creativeness, originality, inventiveness, experimentation.

3 Self-exploration.

4 To seek truth and understanding of life.

5 Awareness of an omnipotent Being, a Maker: worship, religion, spiritual growth.

Major drives: activity, affectional, autonomy, change, cognizance, contrariness, exploratory, independence, inquisitive, objective, manipulative, order, play, prestige, self-assertion, self-esteem/consistency, sex, sentience, understanding, creativity, curiosity.

Astrology and the survival needs

The survival needs are underlying powerful forces influencing the behaviour and drives of every man and woman. They are varied expressions of a deep-rooted compulsion that must be satisfied. When a particular SN is dominant in the psychological make-up of an individual, this will often be apparent through intense forms of self-expression and fixity of purpose and intent. The SNs seem related to the functions of the planets and their aspects because each planet represents a specialized form of psychic activity; whereas the signs essentially give diversity of purpose and direction to a planet's function. In the chapter on the planets, guidelines will be given concerning each planet's connection with particular SNs.

There is no necessity yet to incorporate the interpretation of SNs in a chart analysis. However, for those who are interested, after having read the chapters in this book on interpretation, some additional insight regarding a subject's motives for concentrating energies in certain directions may be gleaned and attributed significantly to a very primitive level of the psyche's activity. In the next chapter, concerning the planets as 'functional needs', you will see that no single planet's influence is associated significantly with all the SNs. The Sun's influence, for instance, is significant with SNs ABCDF but not E; Neptune's influence is significant with only SNs E and F. Thus, particularly interesting and deep-rooted subtle influences on a subject's behaviour will be pinpointed through a major aspect between two planets whose influence is considered significant with regard to the same SN.

Janet, for example, has ☉ □ ♂ (Sun square Mars). Both ☉ and ♂ are significantly related to SNA and will, therefore, be vital to the satisfaction of SNA: 'to attack, master and control the environment for self-preservation.' Thus, underlying Janet's ☉ □ ♂ is a powerful instinctive need for self-preservation through attacking, mastering, or controlling the environment, rather than through, say, SNB, 'self-preservation through endurance and sustenance.' The ☉ □ ♂ feature of her make-up instinctively fights, seeks direct confrontation with threats to her survival. That is the deep-rooted, primitive, instinctive reaction. In present-day terms we would see this as being prepared to engage and resist any efforts by others to force their demands or influence upon her. Through ☉ □ ♂, her instincts direct her to swiftly resist any attempt to weaken her self-control and ability to cope and if necessary to master and manipulate that which would threaten or subjugate her. In most instances ☉ □ ♂ will probably stimulate her to engage with the environment, pushing herself forward rather than holding back and waiting for others to take the initiative.

But, Janet also has ☽ △ ♄. Both ☽'s and ♄'s functions are vital to the satisfying of SNB, SNC and SNE – self-preservation or survival through endurance and the utilization of the environment (SNB), through security and protection against the environment (SNC) and through submission to the lead of others (SNE). Hence we see at least two opposing facets of Janet's personality: to resist any threats upon her by (a) fighting and (b) adapting through endurance, securing a defence against, or yielding to the lead of others (probably if they were stronger and more competent than herself).

If a beginner-student naturally puzzles over the existence of such contrasts in the same individual, it must be remembered that we all possess conflicting elements in our personality. The key to understanding why this is so in Janet's case is that the 'functional needs' (FNs) ☉ and ♂ are being expressed for the satisfaction of SNA, whilst for the satisfaction of SNB, SNC and SNE it is the two considerably different FNs of ☽ and ♄. You may notice when you read through and study chapter 11 that ☉ and ♂ also have a significant influence through the SNB and SNC mentioned above (concerning ☽ ♄), but the expressions of these FNs are different to those of ☽ △ ♄ (Moon trine Saturn). Similarly ♃ ♄ ♅ and ♇

can also be significantly involved in mutual aspects (and with ☉ ♂) vital to the satisfaction of SNA.

After studying the SNs related to several thousand birth charts where I have significant information or detailed case histories concerning the subjects of the charts, I see this as an area of tremendous importance for research. However, until computer programmes can be designed to improve upon the human brain and intelligence where chart interpretation is concerned, the SNs are likely to benefit each individual client (through these SNs being interpreted by an astrologer in terms of the client's unique chart pattern) far more evidentially than a computer study involving several thousand charts may satisfy a research team in terms of statistical significance. An SN cannot be wholly valued as an isolated factor, but must be seen and employed as one feature of a dynamic system that is identified as a unique human being and personality.

Summary of chapter

1 The aim of this chapter is to show that, by tracing the evolution of man from his most primitive driving force, the need to survive and to preserve his identity as an individual organism, it is possible to construct a coherent and unifying framework of the psyche's potential based on six classes of survival needs.

2 Every human activity is covered by at least one of the survival needs.

3 All other needs stem from the basic primitive driving force of survival. This is the starting-point for the realization of a structure for interpreting the potential within man's psyche.

Notes

1 Richard Wilhelm and Carl Jung: *The Secret of the Golden Flower*, p. 143 (Kegan Paul, Trench, Trubner & Co., Ltd, 1942)

2 Sir Cyril Burt, in Foreword to *The Act of Creation* by Arthur Koestler, p. xvi (Hutchinson of London, 1969)

3 Sigmund Koch: *Psychology as a Science*, p. 35 (Paper to the Royal Institute of Philosophy Conference at University of Canterbury, Kent, 1971)

4 A. L. Irion: *Psychology: a Study of a Science*, Vol. 2, 1959, pp. 546–59

5 R. B. Joynson: *Psychology and Common Sense*, p. 104 (Routledge & Kegan Paul, 1974)

6 *A Textbook of Human Psychology*, edited by H. J. Eysenck & G. D. Wilson, p. 3

7 Hans & Michael Eysenck: *Mindwatching*, p. 85 (Michael Joseph Ltd, 1981)

8 Alice Heim: *Intelligence & Personality*, p. 13 (Penguin Books Ltd, 1970)

9 David Krech, Richard S. Crutchfield & Egerton L. Ballachey: *Individual in Society*, p. 3 (McGraw-Hill Book Co., Inc., 1962)

10 P. E. Vernon: *Personality Assessment*, p. 2 (Methuen & Co., Ltd, 1966)

11 *Personality: Theory, Measurement & Research*, p. xi, edited by Fay Fransella (Methuen & Co., Ltd, 1981)

12 George Kaluger & Charles M. Unkovic: *Psychology & Sociology*, p. 10 (The C. V. Mosby Co., USA, 1969)

CHAPTER II

Planets: Functional Needs

As above, so below

The divine audacity of individual man that he should believe in his own unique identity among the abundance of awe-inspiring phenomena about him! The Earth environment teems with mind-boggling varieties of life-forms. His cosmic environment, embracing unimaginable distances, sparkles at night with mysterious patterns, expressions of powerful sources of energy . . .

Our human minds cannot comprehend the scale of the universe in terms of its stellar population and the immense distances involved. Galaxies are complex organizations of stars and interstellar matter, and an average galaxy may have a population of a thousand million stars.

On page 15 we read of the ancient Hermetic axiom 'as above, so below'. When we believe this, the distance between ourselves and a galaxy a billion light years away is of no real consequence. We no longer feel separated from our cosmic environment. We can believe that there must be a repetition of patterns descending from the greatest to the minutest scale, from the basic structure of the atom (less than a hundred-millionth of an inch in diameter) to the infinite universe as a whole. All is energy and subject to cycles of birth, growth and decay. Although modern cosmologists would vehemently disagree, there would appear to be an hierarchical structure to life, perfectly linking the atom with the largest known galaxy: the atom with its nucleus encircled by electrons, moons or satellites orbiting planets which revolve about the Sun, the Sun and other stars encircling the galactic centre. And what of our galaxy revolving about a distant cosmic centre? The scientist who would deny the as yet undiscovered but likely existence of subatomic and extragalactic hierarchical levels of the basic divine blueprint would indeed be a fool.

Our system of astrology does not contain any reference to distant galaxies and there is only one star involved – the Sun, with its encircling planets – and our Earth's satellite the Moon. Perhaps, thinking of the hierarchical levels of energy systems, each with its nucleus, the centuries-old concept of man's psychological make-up being linked with the planetary system is as natural and real as the warmth of the Sun's physical rays on our faces. Nobody who has seriously studied and tested astrology can think otherwise.

From carbon molecules to complex man

This chapter is about the planets and what each represents in psychological terms. For convenience we are referring to the Sun and Moon as 'planets' in addition to the eight actual planets which appear to revolve around the Earth.

We have seen in chapter 10 that the most primitive driving force in man is the need to survive or self-preservation. All other needs stem from this primary activity, which produces the inescapable interaction and involvement of the human organism with its environment. By tracing the evolution of man from this primitive driving force, I have developed the concept of the structure for survival, based on six classes of primary needs. These are the survival needs. Except, perhaps, for the sixth of these needs – to explore the environment for creative, inventive expediency – all could be basic manifestations of the desire for self-preservation in virtually all living organisms and not apply only to homo sapiens.

But man has evolved differently to any other organism. He is unique among the millions of living species on Earth. There are those of us who would attribute this to God creating man 'in His own image' and that it was therefore preordained he should evolve a brain and intelligence which progressively produce even greater potential for creativity and insight to the mysteries of life. I do believe it is man's destiny to have arrived at his present stage in evolution, wielding power through creativity and inspired intelligence, through mindless destruction of the Earth's resources, through love and gentleness, ruthless cruelty, genius and madness.

Despite his capacity to experience delight in being alive, man seems incapable of avoiding the infliction of suffering and at times unbearable stress upon himself and others in his quest for identity, his quenchless desire to know 'who he is', why he should be born a separate entity from all other human beings. Through this endless searching he inevitably realizes his own unique form of potentiality of self-expression and contribution to the evolution of mankind. He even realizes the creative power of happiness. But delight in being alive, the pleasure of stability, of successful achievement, love and sheer fun, never lasts. Always there is the experience of the 'law of opposites'. Without darkness we would not know light. Without unhappiness, happiness would become boring, a dead end. *Is* this true? At times we feel lost within a jungle of inconsistencies, bewildering contrasts, the trauma of conflicting experiences, the confusion and frustration of seemingly irreconcilable aspects of life, the stress of incompatibles.

Life would not exist without the forces of opposition. But opposition does not mean inevitable conflict between incompatible forces. Male and female can complement each other and become creative: 'the problem of opposites, as an inherent principle of human nature, forms a further stage in our process of realization.'[1]

And so man has survived against incredible odds and evolved to his present form. You and I each began as invisible-to-the-naked-eye seed as the result of our parents' sexual union. We did not suddenly appear on Earth in baby form at birth. We had first to grow stage by stage. Neither did the human species suddenly appear on Earth as full grown 'Adam and Eve' specimens of homo sapiens. As we noted in chapter 10 man's evolution took aeons for even the simplest thought or feeling reaction to manifest itself and have meaning.

Spanning billions of years from the early primitive and formless carbon molecules to the magnificently complex being that is today's man or woman, our species has not only survived but has evolved because it has *at critical stages discovered new ways of coping with and utilizing its environment.* We have inherited these instinctive adaptive responses to environmental challenges from, in some instances, millions of generations of our ancestors. Certain areas of human behaviour and activities of paramount importance developed in this way, I have named *functional needs*.

The psyche's functional needs

To avoid confusion we must distinguish between functional needs and survival needs. A survival need, as we have seen, is an activity vital for self-preservation, for staying alive, for maintaining an organism's identity. These needs are vital for any living organism though for our purposes in this book they have been presented in terms of human survival. The survival needs can illuminate one's understanding of deep-rooted compulsions in human behaviour and their aggravation of stress.

A functional need is an activity vital to the fulfilment of the psyche's unfolding of potentialities. More than this, each function is one of a group of related actions contributing to the larger action of the whole psyche and personality. Each function was developed as a result of the demands of necessity at various stages in man's evolution, as a vital adaptive response to the environment. In one sense a functional need can be seen as a survival need, but the distinctive difference is that functional needs fulfil the purpose of the psyche's identification with the human race. We are human creatures, not apes or kangaroos, because our ancestors developed these vital adaptive responses to the environment. You will understand this quite clearly when you think about each functional need in its correlation with a particular planet.

The fact that these needs are classed as *functional* implies that each is instrumental to the working of the human psyche in a useful, effective, specialized form and for the greater purpose of wholeness of experience and expression. We can also see the functional needs not just as expressions necessary for developing individual qualities, but indirectly as activity directed towards satisfying the need to survive.

Life means activity, and the human organism is a dynamic system of complex energy exchanges. Here, 'dynamic' implies a force producing motion. Each functional need generates a type of energy, expressed in activity and behaviour. The primary impulse that has produced each need for special activity and behaviour would seem to derive from a particular archetype originating in the Collective Unconscious in which all men and women have common roots.

Each planet represents a particular functional need, impossible for any human being not to express with varying degrees of satisfaction and efficiency. The choice of a single psychological expression to describe the functional need associated with a planet must inevitably be an over-simplification, but from each stem numerous variations of behaviour that share a common origin or impulse.

Functional needs associated with the planets

⊙ Sun: purposeful activity
☽ Moon: adaptation
☿ Mercury: communication
♀ Venus: evaluation
♂ Mars: exertion
♃ Jupiter: increase
♄ Saturn: structure
♅ Uranus: deviation
♆ Neptune: refinement
♇ Pluto: transcendence

You must learn these so that they can be easily remembered.

Description of categories

The Sun, the Moon and each individual planet will be interpreted as if it were an isolated factor within the psyche. But when viewed within the structure of a complete birth chart, the potential behaviour associated with a planet may be modified according to its interrelationship with the whole chart pattern. Here is an explanation of the several categories that describe each planet's function within the psyche.

Functional need: a primary activity necessary for the psyche's growth and survival. This is the mode or special kind of action by which a planet fulfils its purpose.

Focus on: the suggested most important or central expressions of the functional need. These can be seen as motives for satisfying the need. For instance, the Sun's functional need is action. To be doing something and also to be releasing energy are two major means of satisfying the need for action. Numerous other motives 'for action' may be seen to derive from these two that we are focusing on.

Definition: a further and more precise explanation of the functional need and how this relates to the environment.

Distinctive motives for experiencing [the functional need]: a motive is a means of satisfying a need. We can think of it as that which impels one to seek a goal of personal value and which gives meaningful direction to behaviour.

+ Stimulus reaction (comfortable): we may think of these as satisfying traits and characteristic and distinctive behaviour, where there is an absence of discomfort and uneasiness, where any stress registered is a stimulus that is enjoyed.

− Stress reaction (uncomfortable): we may think of these as unsatisfactory traits and characteristic and distinctive behaviour which reveal vulnerability to stress through the particular functional need. These reactions spring from probable disequilibrium creating discomfort, uneasiness, tenseness, strain.

SNs' influence: briefly, suggested ways by which particular survival needs will tend to influence the functional need.

Summary of [the planet's] psychological role: further helpful pointers concerning the planet's functional role in a chart and in the psyche.

The Sun ☉

Functional need: purposeful activity.

Focus on: doing; releasing energy; purposefulness.

Definition: to express activity purposefully, whether inwards and mentally or outwards and into the environment. The need to release energy, to be doing, as distinct from being inert.

Distinctive motives for experiencing action:

(a) Masculinity. To express the *masculine* principle in life, an assertion of strength, will-power, a seeking to engage masterfully with the environment. This applies to both male and female.

(b) Encountering the environment. Stemming from the primitive pre-conscious, instinctive reaction to anything outside the organism as being not just separate, but something to be engaged with, and energy used against or upon to ensure there is no threat to one's survival.

(c) Purposeful endeavour. Active intention or impulse to express oneself meaningfully with a definite end in view. That by which effort is directed to attain an objective.

(d) Achievement. The need to accomplish an action or feat expressive of one's identity as an individual. Derived from various primitive urges and manifesting itself, if successful, as the satisfaction in dealing with, managing, controlling and manipulating objects and the environment. To be better than others, superior.

(e) Mobility. The function necessary for the outflowing of energy and production of mobility, for animating psychic processes with active properties, facilitating movement.

(f) To be volitional. To have the power of willing or choosing a course of action, manifesting itself as self-conscious activity towards a determined end, primarily involving decision and intention.

+ Stimulus reaction (comfortable): expressive, purposeful, self-reliant, ability to effect results, independent, volitional, ambitious, determined.

– Stress reaction (uncomfortable): self-centred, authoritative, aggressive, dominant, power-seeking.

SNs' influence:

SNA: masculinity, assertion of strength and will-power, engaging with others, self-reliance, ambitious.

SNB: maintaining fitness and strength.

SNC: active engagement against any threat to security.

SND: the preservation of self-identity by utilizing another person for reproduction of self.

SNF: purposeful endeavour, effort directed to attain an objective, especially to accomplish an action or feat expressive of one's individual identity.

Summary of the Sun's psychological role: All forms of behaviour, outwardly or inwardly expressed, including the thinking and feeling processes, involve activity – the exertion of energy. This means that each planet represents some form of psychic activity or energy expenditure. The Sun, however, represents the very quintessence of the psyche's activity and self-expression, manifesting itself as *purposeful* activity.

Whether for male or female, the Sun represents the *masculine* principle of action. One can best realize the type of action by considering the human organism at its very primitive stage, when the male instinctively engaged with the environment to survive and matched his strength and guile against it for supremacy, so he could take from it what was necessary for survival. As man has evolved and become civilized, this basic need is still present but the motives for action are more complex and can be intelligently chosen.

We look to the Sun in a chart, by sign placing, angularity and aspects, for the potential ability to mobilize energies and resources in terms of purposeful activity and the possible motives that will be most naturally chosen to express the need for action.

The Moon ☽

Functional need: adaptation.

Focus on: equilibrium; vulnerability, receptiveness; rhythm.

Definition: to be as one with the environment, achieving a stable equilibrium between the inner demands of the psyche and the demands of the exterior world.

Distinctive motives for experiencing adaptation:

(a) Femininity. To express the *feminine* principle in life; receptiveness, impressionability, the need to nurture and protect others, sensitivity to environment, submissiveness, pliability and resilience. This applies to both male and female.

(b) To be as one with the environment. Stemming from a powerful original form of primitive mentality in which one may believe that there is a sense of 'universal oneness', that the concepts of time are not separated into past, present and future but all is in the present and myth, dream and reality are one experience. An awareness that is still a subtle feature of the feminine aspect of the psyche. It is one's need to never forget that oneself and the environment share and belong to a common reality and origin.

(c) To belong. Akin to (b), but experienced more as a desire to be with, to share and to belong to someone or something, as if to complete and fulfil oneself. It is an urge to participate in another's experience and reality, though it can also be a desire to be a part of and dependent on someone else. Both ☽ and ♀ represent functional needs of the psyche to be connected or joined with other people. The very important difference is that the ☽ represents a need to be emotionally and meaningfully connected, whilst ♀ represents a need to connect relatively, in terms of comparing and evaluating the relevant merits of the parties involved in a relationship. Both functions exercise the feelings.

(d) Empathy. Aligned with (b) and (c), but here the essence of concern is sympathy and a maternal-like instinct to understand in-depth the subject by putting oneself in the other person's place.

(e) Vulnerability. One's psyche is probably most vulnerable – capable of being wounded, open to attack, susceptible to emotional disturbance – through the Moon function. Hence one's continual (conscious or unconscious) striving to achieve a state of equilibrium with the environment, especially through this function, and despite the feminine characteristic of being prone to the potential imbalance of strong likes/dislikes. The Moon function also represents that part of the psyche where one would wish to be open and vulnerable to the environment's influence. This may be understood more clearly if one thinks of the Sun function desiring to touch other people and the environment as the masculine principle, whilst the Moon function desires to be touched as the receptive feminine principle.

(f) Rhythm. The psyche's rhythmic ebbing and flowing of energy as it interacts with the environment is seen as a process of learning to adapt for survival reasons and to stimulate creative potential. The ebbing and flowing is a continuous process for the purpose of achieving equilibrium between oneself and the environment. Through this process one's psyche:

  (i) assimilates the realities of experience for its own nourishment and growth;

  (ii) cultivates sensitivity through the feelings which can (1) improve its defences against environmental threats to safety and security and (2) generate creative potential; develop spontaneous reactions to environmental influence.

(g) Maintenance. The organism is dependent for its survival upon what it can receive in terms of nourishment – physical, emotional, spiritual – from the environment. Its health must be maintained through assimilation of nourishment and adaptation, which means being in harmony with the external environment.

(h) Protection. Defence of the organism and adaptation to the environment are interwoven. Psychologists tend to speak of an organism's instinctive 'defence mechanism'. I prefer to use the term 'protective mechanism', and the Moon's role within the psyche is a major factor for the organism's protection. The feminine principle's maternal features are an important aspect of this protective mechanism or system. The Moon function's normal form of alertness, to be receptive and impressionable to environmental activity, is to exercise a primitive survival technique, an early warning system of an imminent threat.

+ Stimulus reaction (comfortable): adaptable, alert, aware (vigilantly perceptive), assimilating, sensitive, impressionable, receptive, spontaneous, protective, tenacious, accommodating, participative, accessible, resilient, sociable, sympathetic, compassionate, imaginative, introspective, attentive, sentimental, romantic, pliable.

− Stress reaction (uncomfortable): vulnerable, possessive, clannish, restless, moody, unstable, neurotic (phobias, anxiety), touchy, indecisive, self-indulgent, morbidly sensitive, submissive, shy/timid, effeminate (male), easily embarrassed, prejudiced.

SNs' influence:

SNB: sensitive adaptability, impressionability, assimilation, desire for rhythmic interaction and empathy with environment.

SNC: defensive, protective, alertness, maternal.

SND: feminine receptiveness and sensitivity, desire to belong to someone and to involve oneself emotionally.

SNE: submissive, impressionable, accessible, vulnerability.

SNF: creativeness, sensitivity, imaginative, receptive, introspective.

Summary of the Moon's psychological role: The Moon represents the feminine principle in life – sensitivity, receptiveness, pliability, the need to nurture and protect. Whether male or female, the psyche of each of us is composed of this dual life-principle, the

Moon's feminine being complementary to the Sun's masculine features.

Through the masculine impulse we see ourselves and the environment as separate, whilst through the feminine impulse we feel as one with our environment and seek to receive the environment into ourselves. Our masculine side needs to be self-sufficient, the feminine side yearns to belong to someone or something, to participate in another's reality. This is the part of ourselves that would be sensitive to a rhythmic interaction of energy with our environment that subtly helps to regulate our measure of adaptation to our external world. It is here where we are most aware of vulnerability, weakness, helplessness; and yet we must be open and accessible if we are to fully receive others into ourselves.

We look to the Moon in a chart by sign placing, angularity and aspects for potential *sensitivity* to the environment (which also implies vulnerability) and the measure of the subject's potential for *adapting* to its external world. Effective adaptation means good health mentally, emotionally and physically; faulty adaptation implies inefficiency and ill-health. Thus, we also look to the Moon for the source of any psychological imbalance that may seriously undermine health.

Mercury ☿

Functional need: communication.

Focus on: information exchange; co-ordination; interpretation.

Definition: to establish communication and be connectively involved with the environment for information exchange and the interpretation and analysis of experience.

Distinctive motives for experiencing communication:

(a) Acquiring knowledge; inquisitiveness; perception. To have information and knowledge concerning the environment, by searching, investigating, inquiring into, examining systematically or in detail, questioning, and thus to fully comprehend one's external world relationship. To be perceptive: mental and sensory awareness and processing of information experienced through the environment for stimulation of immediate and appropriate responses.

(b) Analysis, interpretation. To separate, distinguish or ascertain the elements of anything and to subject it to critical inquiry. To attempt to explain its meaning, significance or purpose, and so strengthen one's role within the environment and satisfy the curiosity motive and quest for knowledge.

(c) Involvement, sociability. To be in contact with the environment for the exercise of mental, nervous and sensory faculties, the conscious projection of oneself, debative intercourse, exchange of ideas, transmission of sensory messages.

(d) Co-ordination. To not only co-ordinate the mental, nervous and sensory faculties for greatest efficiency, but to co-ordinate these with environmental features to produce beneficial results.

(e) Change, variety. To make changes, variations and readjustments to one's activities and focus of interest involving the environment, to avoid static and restrictive conditions and achieve wider and more diverse experience.

+ Stimulus reaction (comfortable): communicative, versatile, volatile, clever, inquisitive, analytical, sociable, studious, fluent, debative, shrewd, perceptive.

− Stress reaction (uncomfortable): excitable, nervous, restless, compulsive-talker, anxiety-prone, cunning, forgetful, meddlesome, inconstant, critical, careless.

SNs' influence:

SNB: acquiring knowledge of the environment's benefits through communication, critical inquiry and analysis.

SND: communication, connective involvement with environment, sociability.

SNF: acquiring knowledge; inquisitiveness; critical inquiry; co-ordination; urge for change and variety.

Summary of Mercury's psychological role: We look to Mercury in a chart by angularity and aspects for the potential ability to *communicate* with the environment for information exchange and the exercise of mental, nervous and sensory faculties. Each planet may be said to represent a particular feature of the psyche that communicates in its special way with the environment. But with Mercury, communication is the vital process to enable the psyche to co-ordinate its various faculties to achieve the greatest efficiency within itself and in its relationship with the external world, and for a clearer interpretation of experience. The activities of the nervous system aptly symbolize this function's constantly busy involvement with the environment.

Venus ♀

Functional need: evaluation.

Focus on: feeling-evaluation; interdependent relationships; attraction.

Definition: to experience and assess through the feelings (as distinct from rational judgement by the mental faculties) the value to oneself of environmental features for the purpose of developing interdependent relationships, reducing friction and disharmony to a minimum and attracting pleasing attention to oneself.

Distinctive motives for developing evaluation:

(a) Appreciation. To appreciate and be appreciated. To realize and to recognize the very quintessence of experiencing another person, situation, or environmental feature, and for one's true nature and worth to be equally recognized. To be sensitive to, or sensible of, any delicate impression or distinction. To be critically and emotionally aware of delicate subtle aesthetic or artistic values. This is the need to cherish a thing or person, and to be cherished. It is the feeling within the creative impulse: the essence of creativity. It is the process which imparts a distinct value in terms of acceptance or rejection; and this function can, as with the Moon function, be associated with strong likes/dislikes.

(b) Interdependent relationships; sociability. Stemming from a vital evolutionary stage of the primitive human organism's development: the achievement of efficient teamwork and greater strength and security through co-operation, clinging together in communities yet remaining interdependent for expressing individual qualities. To achieve co-operational patterns based on mutual sympathy, relating cohesively to others. This impulse teaches that one cannot survive without co-operation with and sympathetic attachment to fellow creatures. Its highest and most worthy objective is to be the means for love and compassion. Its most active manifestation is one's desire to behave sociably, to seek company, and to participate eagerly in group activities.

(c) Attraction. To stimulate emotion/feeling in others in order to draw attention to oneself, either for self-gratification or for recognition of one's self-estimation. A centripetal process, an essentially inner and subjective experience. Misused, it is the urge to tempt, to entice and allure for purely personal advantage. But in its essence it demands to be more than the physical aspect of a sexual relationship or the soliciting of attention: it is a means by which one can love and be loved, fulfil the need for affection and the need to share oneself intimately. Venus alone does not represent the ability to love, but the means and ability to relate to another through attraction and thence to evaluate the relationship or connection relatively. That is, to compare and evaluate the relevant merits of the other person with one's own. One could say that the Moon also represents a function which needs to attract. The fundamental difference is that Venus attracts in order to bring together two individuals to establish a relationship; whilst one's Moon function's attraction is only an affect of the need to receive another into oneself for sharing together in an experience of belonging to one another.

(d) Uniting or resolving opposites; harmony. To achieve harmony with one's environment and to reduce friction and disharmony to a minimum. To seek a complementary, mutually dependent relationship with another person, a consummating part to complete a whole. To balance, unify and smooth out the rough and the discordant and create cohesion and unity. The potential for diplomacy, compromise, reconciliation.

+ Stimulus reaction (comfortable): co-operative, attractive, harmonious, sympathetic, kindly, compassionate, compromising, considerate, gentle, sociable, friendly, amorous, placid, courteous, passive, creative, artistic, idealistic, aesthetic, cheerful, diplomatic.
− Stress reaction (uncomfortable): self-indulgent, acquisitive, indolent, vain, disagreeable, disorderly, selfish, flatterer, permissive, immoral, seductive, feeble, possessive.

SNs' influence:
SNB: co-operation with the environment.
SND: interdependent relationships, sociability; to appreciate and be appreciated; attracting others; sharing self with others; urge for harmony.
SNF: creativity; feeling-evaluation.

Summary of Venus's psychological role: We look to Venus in a chart by angularity and aspects for the potential ability to *evaluate* an experience or a feature of the environment through the *feelings*. One can see this as a further function of the psyche to learn about the environment, but in this case it is primarily for the purpose of forming interdependent relationships. In primitive times this arose as a need to be part of a community rather than fending for oneself alone. This evolved into a complex system of social interests and demands and, as feelings were refined, subtle expressions such as appreciation, aesthetic tastes and love for another person were developed. Therefore, we also look to Venus for the means of forming relationships through attraction, and where a contribution to emotional and sexual intimacy is sensitivity and the generation of sympathetic feeling.

Mars ♂

Functional need: exertion.

Focus on: impetus; stimulation; effort.

Definition: to facilitate action and exert oneself into and upon the environment.

Distinctive motives for experiencing exertion:

(a) Impulsion, stimulation. To try harder at a physical or mental task. The action of impelling or forcing onward; instigation, incitement; determination to action. To accelerate action. To rouse to action, impart additional energy to an activity. To quicken: animate, give or restore vigour to, excite, hasten.

(b) To be powerful, strong. To have the ability for effective action, the capacity for moral effort or endurance, vigour and intensity of feeling or conviction. To be forceful.

(c) Self-projection; competition. To be energetically objective, self-assertive. To strive against others for the same object, compete in a trial of ability. To struggle, make great efforts in spite of difficulties, especially to resist force or free oneself from constraint. The impetus for pioneering new ventures requiring stamina, enterprise, initiative.

(d) Effort. To activate a strenuous exertion of power, physical or mental. To influence the environment forcefully. To endeavour vigorously.

(e) Sex-drive; excitement. Sensual expression. Intense eagerness, zeal, the urge to move to strong emotion. Emotion inevitably accompanies all drives associated with the Mars function. The body experiences emotion when it is prepared or stimulated for particular action or reaction. Emotion is personal involvement in an experience, and sexual activity or any exciting situation will stimulate emotion. The more intimate the involvement, the more intense the emotion. Emotion serves to sustain and, in its less violent form, to facilitate action.

+ Stimulus reaction (comfortable): exertion, self-assertive,

    initiatory, enterprising, impulsive, competitive, pioneering, zealous, persuasive, direct, adventurous, incisive, ardent.
- Stress reaction (uncomfortable): combative, reckless, impatient, fanatical, agitative, irascible, over-excitable, pugnacious, quarrelsome, sensuous, militant, brusque, impetuous.

SNs' influence:

SNA: exertion, strenuous effort; active and objective self-projection; incitement to action; competitiveness.

SNB: endurance through strength and determination.

SNC: capacity to resist and compete against other forces.

SNF: competitiveness, enterprise.

Summary of Mars' psychological role: We look to Mars in a chart by angularity and aspects for the potential ability to facilitate (make easier) any form of activity by having the capacity for exertion and effort beyond just 'doing something' physically or mentally in the normal way. The Sun will show us the measure and mode of action; Mars will indicate the additional impetus, stimulation and effort the psyche is capable of and can impart to the activity. It can be seen why Mars has traditionally been associated with sexual stamina, with *emotional* excesses and difficulties, with successful warriors and their feats of bravery and with the exertions of international athletes.

Jupiter ♃

Functional need: increase.

Focus on: expansion; improvement; abundance.

Definition: to improve one's relationship with the environment, achieve increase in material benefits, deeper participation in experience and expansion of the consciousness.

Distinctive motives for experiencing increase:
- (a) Expansion, amplification. To increase – by adding to, enlarging, amplifying, magnifying, exaggerating. To widen the field of activity, spread one's influence, broaden one's experi-

ence. To open out, unfold one's potential. To extend one's interests, enlarge the area of application, range and scope. To prolong a satisfactory experience or advantageous situation. Ensure that there is ample of all that is wanted. Risk of indulging in excesses of behaviour, of exaggeration, extravagance.

(b) Improvement, advance. To improve oneself in every respect so that one's character matures and understanding of life widens, that the right action and decisions are taken. To achieve increase so as to spread one's gains among others for their benefit also, although sometimes for the acquiring and hoarding of the rewards of one's efforts. To make a profit, gain, benefit; to advance, go forward, progress, increase one's well-being. To excel at a task and surpass even the best that can be expected.

(c) Opportunism, optimism. To seek opportunities, to experience increase and improvement in one's relationship and standing with the environment. To 'look to the future' – for advancement, progress, improvement, expansion. To make the most of experiences. To be expedient and of optimistic disposition.

(d) Deep participation; exploration. To be self-explorative; ranging over the environment for the purpose of discovery, seeking new horizons. To understand, as distinct from just knowing. To enrich one's life by responsible, conscientious, just and lawful means and be morally accountable for one's actions, and thus achieve growth and maturity. To be liberal, generous, open-minded, philosophical, profound in thought and insight. To judge, in the sense of needing to form an opinion about someone or something as an act of understanding, distinct from seeking to criticize or condemn.

(e) Status; prominence. To improve one's status and to acquire the best things in life. To achieve position, standing, rank in relation to others and be conspicuous, eminent, remarkable. To make oneself greater and achieve special prominence. To develop the ability to gain an advantage over others – not necessarily in the sense of feeling superior or more powerful

– but so that one is responsible only to oneself and to one's conscience and thus gain the respect of others through making an impression. To put distinctive emphasis on one's significant features to accentuate these. Risk of extravagant or excessive behaviour, exhibitionism.

+ Stimulus reaction (comfortable): opportunist, expedient, explorative, generous, genial, jovial, buoyant, optimistic, exuberant, enthusiastic, tolerant, broadminded, profound, ambitious, progressive, idealistic.

– Stress reaction (uncomfortable): extremism, uncompromising, presumptuous, impertinent, dogmatic, voracious, aggrandizement, exaggeration, condescension, extravagance, exhibitionist, intemperate, fanatical, pompous, self-indulgent, reckless, self-righteous, dissipated.

SNs' influence:

SNA: seeking advantage over and improving one's rank in relation to others.

SNB: urge to achieve growth and maturity, opportunism, seeking improvement and profit from the environment.

SNF: urge to widen one's field of activity and experience, improving oneself, self-exploration, desire for growth and maturity.

Summary of Jupiter's psychological role: A basic feature in human life is the desire for improvement: success, advantages, growth and maturity, enrichment materially and spiritually. Society aptly thinks of a person who enjoys life to the fullest, delights in conviviality and good fellowship as being jovial – after the Roman god of good fortune, Jove or Jupiter. And so it is not just apt but quite correct that we look to Jupiter in a chart by angularity and aspects for the potential ability to achieve enjoyment and *increase* in every possible advantageous way. Increase and expansion implies reaching and developing beyond one's existing conditions and social status. Sometimes our efforts only result in exaggerative and extravagant forms of behaviour and unfortunate self-indulgence.

Saturn ♄

Functional need: structure.

Focus on: form; regulation; accuracy.

Definition: to develop self-control and realistic methods of regulating and organizing the environment for the establishment of stability and security.

Distinctive motives for developing formativeness:

(a) Form, structure. To construct an orderly framework within which to regulate energy expenditure and growth. To give shape or form to something, place in order, devise a structure, build an organized combination of mutually connected parts.

(b) Regulation, control, order. To regulate one's adjustment to circumstances to maintain control and order, be law-abiding. To be organized and have one's actions conform to established order; adhering to rules, principles, standards, habitual practice, codes of discipline and conduct.

(c) System, method. To adhere to a system: an orderly or regular method of procedure; a formal, definite, or established scheme; a set of principles.

(d) Accuracy, punctuality. To construct ideas coherently and logically and be accurate and distinct, precise, correct, exact, explicit, leaving nothing merely implied, but definite, certain. To be punctual, exactly observant of time.

(e) Stability; endurance; labour. To be stable, steadfast in resolution and purpose, powerful in resisting change and disturbance. To develop the ability for sustained, monotonous, laborious work requiring patience and self-discipline. To consolidate one's position and establish things on a secure basis, with a view to permanency. To endure difficult and painful experiences. To achieve regularity, marked by steadiness or uniformity of action and habitual behaviour, perseverance. To be staid, sober, temperate and avoid excesses. Risk of being too fixed and rigid.

(f) Limits, restriction, restraint. To develop boundaries or structural limits for regulating and controlling energy and growth; and to impose restrictions, restraint and prohibition on the actions of others. Risk of experiencing repression or a sense of isolation and loneliness; of becoming reserved, averse to showing familiarity and open expression; of inadequateness, incompetence, inability to fulfil requirements.

(g) Concentration, focus. To concentrate, direct or focus attention on a single matter or purpose to have it clearly defined and not weaken the action by scattering energy.

(h) Severity, strictness, seriousness. To be severe, unsparing in censure and criticism, austere, conforming to rigorous standards. To be strict, characterized by close and unrelaxing effort, enforcing authority, obedience and admitting no relaxation or indulgence. To be serious and reflective, of earnest purpose. To be punctilious, scrupulously exact and strictly observant of the nice points or details of action or behaviour. Likelihood of solemness, of rigidness, unyielding and rigorous.

(i) Conforming, obedience, discipline. To conform to accepted standards; be formal, behaving according to rule, lacking in ease or freedom. To have an attitude towards religious or social ethics that demands dedication to correct form, to a rigid code of conduct, rites and ceremonies – rather than a spirit of heartfelt devotion and humility. To be disciplined, observing a system of rules for conduct; obedient to a principle or an authority, dutiful. To be self-sacrificing.

(j) Conservation, economy. To conserve, keep in safety and intact. To be conservative, characterized by a tendency to preserve or keep unchanged and to maintain and take care of. To economize, to carefully and systematically manage resources.

(k) Practicality, rationality, realism. To formulate constructive and precise rules for the development of a realistic and practical code of behaviour. To be logical, conforming to the laws of correct reasoning in a proper and rational manner. To be rigidly observant of, exactly answerable to, fact and reality. To be interested in what constitutes an actual thing, as distinct from what is merely apparent or theoretical.

(l) Regularity, formula. To formulate, express in a formula, state systematically, express a form or structure which is reducible to some rule or principle.

(m) Preparation, readiness, planning. To plan, arrange or devise activities in advance. To prepare, put oneself or things in readiness.

(n) Protection, defence. To construct a self-protective system and be rigid, unyielding, inflexible.

+ Stimulus reaction (comfortable): realistic, practical, protective, stable, disciplined, organized, discriminating, perseverant, cautious, serious, reflective, strict, reserved, concentration, earnest, dedicated, patient, restrained, steadfast, regular, obedient, self-conscious, persistent, rigid, conforming, conservative, methodical, rational, punctilious, scrupulous, explicit, meticulous, accurate, punctual, thrifty, prudent, reliable.

− Stress reaction (uncomfortable): inhibited, pessimistic, repressive, fixed, unimaginative, matter-of-fact, materialistic, austere, fastidious, critical, obstructive, stubborn, suspicious, sceptical, narrow minded, shy, apathetic, apprehensive, melancholic, depressive, fatalistic, uncompromising, oppressive, merciless, dominating.

SNs' influence:

SNA: maintaining control of and organizing the environment.

SNB: ability to endure urge to conserve energy and resources, self-discipline, practicality.

SNC: urge to construct a self-protective system against the environment and establish stability and security, self-discipline.

SNE: conformable to established order and to authority, self-restraint.

SNF: urge to construct an orderly framework for ideas and creative energy, desire to have a clear and coherent understanding of anything.

Summary of Saturn's psychological role: For the human race to not only survive, but to continue to evolve for the benefit of all its members, individual man must learn to control and to regulate his behaviour and energy expenditure. He must adhere to codes of conduct and systems and structures devised by society for the benefit of all. Thus, we look to Saturn in a chart by angularity and aspects for the potential ability to develop self-control and a commonsense and responsible attitude to life. This stems from the basic primitive need for structure through which all successful societies have developed systems based on form, regulation and boundaries for control.

Uranus ♅

Functional need: deviation.

Focus on: originality; freedom; surprise.

Definition: to deviate from the normal in one's relationship with the environment; and thus stimulate the development of unfettered and original growth-patterns and the creatively exciting element of surprise.

Distinctive motives for experiencing deviation:

(a) Deviation; variation. To deviate from the normal anticipated course of behaviour for the creation of entirely new forms of expression. To seek novelty and the unusual and to make variations in self-expression and the structure of one's life-style and introduce variety.

(b) Originality: unconventionality. To be capable of original ideas or actions, derived independently of any other person or source. To be unconventional, unorthodox, disregarding or not according with social custom and established usage. Risk of eccentricity, peculiarity and abnormalities of behaviour, perverseness.

(c) Independence, freedom. To be independent, not influenced or biased by the opinions of others or subject to external control or authority. To be uninhibited, unrestrained, free, enjoying personal rights and liberty of action, acting of one's own will or choice and without restriction or limitation. Risk of broken relationships, separation, divorce.

(d) Invention, experiment. To be inventive, to discover or devise something never before known. To be experimental, inquisitive, questioning, researching, eager for knowledge, curious, explorative.

(e) Reform, change. To reform or remodel outmoded or retarding features of one's behaviour or of social structures. To seek changes, desire to convert one's behaviour or any thing into another and better form, free from previous faults or imperfections. Risk of rebelliousness, anarchy.

(f) Drama, excitement, surprise. To behave dramatically, with theatrical effect, strikingly and impressively. To shock others. Risk of impetuousness, excitability, explosiveness, disruptiveness.

+ Stimulus reaction (comfortable): deviating, original, experimental, frank, explorative, inquisitive, independent, unconventional, readiness, familiarity, informal, changeable, dramatic, adventurous, progressive.

− Stress reaction (uncomfortable): reckless, impatient, irresponsible, lawless, disruptive, eccentric, licentious, disorderly, inconstant, perverse, explosive, contrary, excitable, rebellious, fanatical, abrupt, impetuous, erratic, unreliable, wilful, freakish/abnormal, intolerant, autocratic, ruthless, capricious.

SNs' influence:

SNA: need for independence and freedom from external control or authority, expressive of one's self choosing to cope alone with exterior circumstances.

SNF: need to deviate from the normal and expected through originality, free and uninhibited expression, inventiveness, seeking reforms.

Summary of Uranus's psychological role: Through the Saturn function the psyche responds to the need for control, regulation and accuracy of energy release and expression. But to evolve and develop his potential man must seek beyond accepted boundaries and limits. Thus, we look to Uranus in a chart by angularity and aspects for the potential ability to *deviate* from the normal, for the desire to be free and uninhibited and to be original.

Neptune ♆

Functional need: refinement.

Focus on: sensitivity; subtlety; idealism.

Definition: to achieve refinement through a sensitive and subtle interpretation of the environment and through the ideal of perfection.

Distinctive motives for experiencing refinement:

(a) Refinement, sensitivity. To refine one's behaviour, thoughts and feelings and so clarify understanding of experience and free the psyche from imperfections or defects. To be sensitive, able to feel quickly and acutely, be mentally impressionable, keenly perceptive, intuitive. To be tender, expressing delicacy of feeling, gentleness, lovingness, kindness. Risk of being over-impressionable, easily influenced or affected by or moved to feeling.

(b) Idealism, perfection. To continuously elevate and revalue experience to achieve perfection in all that one does. To have ideals, seeking a standard of excellence, a conception of something as perfect in its kind, exercising the imagination. Risk of dissatisfaction with commonplace matters, hence vulnerability to glamour, sophistication, woolly-headedness, impracticality, day-dreaming and escapism through mysticism, drugs, sex, alcohol and sensational unconventional experiences.

(c) Subtlety, secrecy. To have subtlety, refinement or nicety of thought, delicate or keen perception. To have deep-felt mysterious experiences of hidden or secret things, inexplicable happenings. Risk of escapism, tendency to shirk unpleasant realities by withdrawing into a world of fantasy or seeking mental or emotional distractions.

(d) Inspiration, elevation, excitement. To seek inspiration and the elevation of oneself to a higher state of performance and accomplishment. To experience ecstasy as an overwhelming delight, rapture, uplifting state of feeling. To be romantic, readily influenced by the imagination, stimulating extravagant feelings and idealism which tend to 'go beyond what is rational and practical'. To be sentimental, characterized by refined and elevated feeling, expression of the tender emotions, love. Risk of trance condition, abnormal state of suspended consciousness, fantasy.

(e) Aestheticism. To have aesthetic taste, sensuous perception, appreciation or criticism of the beautiful and artistic.

(f) Spirituality, mysticism. To seek spirituality as an experience characterized by a high degree of refinement of thought and feeling; and devotional in the religious sense. To have mystical experiences, spiritually symbolic, esoteric or occult revelations. To be religious in the devout and solemnly dedicated sense of orthodox worship.

+ Stimulus reaction (comfortable): sensitive, subtle, refined, delicate, elegant, impressionable, tender, kindly, gentle, humane, secretive, idealistic, ecstatic, informal, day-dreamer, devotional, romantic, sentimental.

− Stress reaction (uncomfortable): escapist, impractical, unstable, sensuous, touchy, evasive, nebulous, absent-minded, hypersensitive, self-deceptive, deceitful, shy, vague, disorderly, gullible, vacillating, hallucinatory, worrier, alcoholic, anxiety-prone, phobia-prone, drug-addictive, brittle/fragile nature.

SNs' influence:
SNE: easily influenced, impressionable, idealistic, escapist.
SNF: idealistic, perfectionist, sensitive, keenly perceptive, acute imagination, spirituality, mysticism.

Summary of Neptune's psychological role: To fulfil the need for perfection of the initial divine impulse of creation, life must seek to realize perfection in its every manifestation. The archetype of perfection demands continuous improvement and refinement of human expression. Thus, we look to Neptune in a chart by angularity and aspects for the potential ability to achieve *refinement* of expression and a sensitivity that can be felt not only through the bodily senses but deep within the spiritual core of the psyche. Neptune may indicate an area of the psyche where the tilt towards genius or madness can be decided by the most delicate and subtle of mental or emotional pressures.

Pluto ♇

Functional need: transcendence.

Focus on: exceeding limits; compulsion; power.

Definition: to exceed known limits of human achievement and discovery through an irresistible compulsion to generate power.

Distinctive motives for experiencing transcendence:

(a) Achieving the impossible. To accept no limit to what can be achieved. To reach unimaginable heights of endeavour.

(b) Compulsion. To feel compelled to act and express oneself in a given determined and single-minded way without obligation to others or concern for personal safety. To feel as if forcibly driven from within, unable to relax one's attention from the activity or ambition which is the compulsion's objective, even if one wanted to.

(c) Surpassing or outdoing others. To be superior to other people in special qualities and attributes. To fiercely desire to be the best. To be somebody special, a rarity, 'superhuman', supreme. Hence, an intensely serious devotion to a pursuit, utter dedication, a powerful will to win or succeed.

(d) Fulfilling destiny. To believe that one is destined to make an extraordinary impact on the world or have an outstanding mission, calling or vocation in life. Hence, evidence perhaps of a 'missionary or crusading spirit' even in relatively parochial activities and always complete conviction that one is doing what is best and is performing the inevitable. Risk of taking life too seriously and intensely.

(e) Power. To exercise power and influence. Not just the kind employed upon the masses by propagandists, politicians, fanatical rulers and the acting profession, but also as the result of the discovery and development of a unique personal attribute. When misused, extreme cases of ruthless use of force, violation of the rights of others, coercion, or just sheer dominance, aggression, arrogance and militancy.

(f) Introspection. As equally powerful as the outgoing compulsion to act and to pursue objectives in specifically zealous and intensely energetic ways, is the compulsion for self-examination. To exhibit superior qualities or exert magical influence or power over others demands a severe examination and recognition of one's own weaknesses or faults so that these may be purged and the psyche strengthened and tuned to the utmost strength and efficiency. Thus, the need to expose, bring to the surface and into the open is developed, to make known what would otherwise be undesirably hidden; to eliminate, expel, eject if necessary by force, ruthlessly; to transform in composition or structure, renew, regenerate greater efficiency and vigour. This can also reflect in one's dealing with the environment.

(g) Sexual experience. One or more of a wide range of motives will stimulate a man or woman to seek 'sexual experience'. In the sense we are using 'sexual experience' here, we refer to an intimate relationship involving physical sex play and sexual intercourse. The Pluto function will be identified as seeking satisfaction particularly through the compulsive, intense desire and passion which almost always demands (forcefully from or, in mutual excitement, shared with the partner) consummation with orgasm. Within the excitement as the increasing and accelerating build-up of desire nears orgasm during the stimulation of the sexual organs, there is something akin to a mystical experience, as if the psyche can with a final ecstatic surge of energy plunge beyond even previous limits of explosive emotion and reveal a new exciting dimension of one's self and identity. Orgasm can be a moment of abandonment to the powerful inner compulsion, a moment of aloneness and vulnerability. Other functional needs will, of course, participate in sexual experience to provide the means for satisfaction, but the Pluto function is very much the compulsive expression of energy that seeks to transcend what is accepted as normality.

+ Stimulus reaction (comfortable): venturesome, enthusiastic, determination, great endurance, emphatic, dedicated, ambitious, concentration, outspoken, lack of pretence, hardworking, disciplined, serious worker, courageous, unorthodox, tough, independent, controversial, intense.

− Stress reaction (uncomfortable): restless, uncompromising, moody, ruthless, fanatical, at times an unbearable aloneness, iconoclastic (image breaker, assails accepted usages, breaker of rules), hurtfully frank, aggressive, blunt, critical, stubborn, aloof, arrogant, selfish, conceited, sexual excesses, discontented.

SNs' influence:

SNA: compulsive single-minded expression of power, need to be superior to others.

SNF: need to achieve 'the impossible' and reach beyond known boundaries for discovery and revelation of hidden truths; self-examination and self-discovery.

Summary of Pluto's psychological role: Through the Uranus function man seeks beyond accepted boundaries and limits by developing his potential to deviate from the normal and realize greater freedom and originality of expression. Through the Jupiter function man seeks to increase enjoyment, well-being and material benefits and advantages beyond his present conditions and social status. Both functions provide means for 'breaking out of' an existing framework which might limit progress towards developing personal potential in one's quest for identity. The Pluto function also provides the potential for breaking out of an existing framework, but with a profound difference.

Every man and woman will at some time, and perhaps frequently for certain individuals, have to accept that they 'know their limits' of successful expression in particular directions. Their accepted measure of abilities may be regarded as a bound beyond which further development or a more successful expression of their potential ceases to be possible. Even the Jupiter and Uranus functions cannot on their own take them further. In short, their potential improvement in a particular direction is finite. Yet human potential knows no bounds if one believes that man was made in the image of God. Pluto represents the compulsive need of an individual to seek his or her *infinite* potential.

We should realize, of course, that only a minority are able to successfully tap this reservoir of inner power and potential. These are the great statesmen and leaders, prominent men and women in public life, athletes who perform incredible feats of prowess and endurance, talented entertainers, composers and writers, all of whom will have Pluto prominently in their birth charts. We see Pluto's enthusiasm and restlessness in persons with great charisma, those ready to risk their reputation for their beliefs, those who will never dodge a fight whatever the odds against them. There are also the infamous characters who ruthlessly exploit, coerce or wreak suffering on other persons or the masses. But most of us merely react to the Pluto compulsion in quite inconspicuous ways, not realizing why we may suddenly have a compulsive desire to direct great energy and enthusiasm to extra work or to prove something of ourselves forcefully and with much determination.

We therefore look to Pluto in a chart by angularity and aspects for indications of how strongly and effectively the subject's need to *transcend* and exceed the limits of what might be expected of them can be developed. We must bear in mind also that inhibition and frustration of this source of power could erupt in deep-rooted psychological disorders. Subjects who react strongly to the compulsive desires of this functional need tend to see life far too much as a conflict with the environment and too little as an arena for playing games and relaxing. Pluto is also associated with eruptive periods when the door must be shut tight on particular features in life so that another door can be opened and new vistas be revealed for realizing entirely new potentialities.

Summary of chapter

1 The theme of this chapter is that each planet represents a vitally important functional need for every human being.

2 A functional need is an activity vital to the fulfilment of the psyche's unfolding of potentialities. Each function was developed as a result of the demands of necessity at various stages in man's evolution, as a vital adaptive response to the environment.

3 In one sense a functional need can be seen as a survival need, but the distinctive difference is that functional needs fulfil the purpose for the psyche's identification with the human race.

4 Each functional need – and therefore, for the purpose of astrological interpretation, each planet – is instrumental to the working of the human psyche in a useful, effective, specialized form and for the greater purpose of wholeness of experience and expression.

Notes

1 Dr Carl Jung: *Two Essays on Analytical Psychology*, p. 59 (Routledge & Kegan Paul, 1966)

CHAPTER 12

Signs: Diversity of Disposition (1)

In the next two chapters we will examine the twelve zodiacal signs and what their symbolism in the birth chart represents in terms of the psyche and human behaviour. In chapter 9 we read that the signs give diversity of purpose and direction to the specialized functional needs represented by the planets. Before we see exactly what this means, let us briefly make a few observations on the origin of the signs and constellations.

Origin of the signs

There are twelve signs of the zodiac or zodiacal signs:

♈	Aries	♎	Libra
♉	Taurus	♏	Scorpio
♊	Gemini	♐	Sagittarius
♋	Cancer	♑	Capricorn
♌	Leo	♒	Aquarius
♍	Virgo	♓	Pisces

There are also twelve zodiacal constellations bearing the same (or similar) names as the above signs. But as you read on page 49, the signs and constellations have only a mythological connection. In astrology we use the twelve signs, each 30° in length, and we do not speak at all of the constellations. And yet it is of more than historical interest to be aware of how the signs came to be vivid concepts of basic and significant variations in the nature of man.

All authorities are agreed that the zodiacal constellations

originated in that area of the Middle East now known as Iraq, but called Mesopotamia by the Greeks. It was here that the foundations of Western civilization were laid almost 10,000 years ago. It was the Mesopotamians who 'so richly developed the fundamental ideas about orientation and correspondences.'[1] They must be given full credit for founding astronomy and initiating the basic concepts of astrology. They laid the foundations for science.

Of the various tribes who settled in Mesopotamia, the Sumerians were among the greatest and earliest of inhabitants. Their significant period was between 3000 and 2000 BC. The origin of the zodiac constellations goes back to the Sumerians and in most cases the Babylonians continued to use the Sumerian symbols, but with Babylonian names. Egypt, Greece and later other countries followed the Babylonian system.

I would agree with many distinguished scholars who do not believe that the constellations were named firstly from fancied resemblances to certain figures and the subsequent stories composed around these figures. The stories or myths were already known from ancient times and the zodiacal constellations designed in order to illustrate them. I would go further than the speculations of these scholars and suggest that there was a deeper significance to the transference of the stories to the stars in the heavens: this linking of human life with the cosmos was an inevitable and profound new stage in man's seeking self-realization. Deification of the planets was one primitive reaction to an archetypal impulse; the composing of the zodiacal constellations was a further necessary unfolding of consciousness.

The first clear reference to zodiacal signs appears in an observation-text dated from year 6 of Dareios II (420–419 BC), one of the Persian kings during the Achaemenid conquest of Babylonia. The Greeks took over the zodiacal constellations from the Babylonians in the 6th century BC, or possibly even earlier, with scarce change in the names. But not until about 400 BC is there a clear use of these as signs (by Euktemon and Eudoxos) in calendars.

Biblical references

There are many references to astrology and the zodiacal signs in the Bible. I will mention but three occasions where there is interesting use of the symbolism of the signs.

In John's vision (Revelation 22:2) the zodiac is thought to be 'the tree of life with its twelve kinds of fruit, yielding its fruit each month.'

Again John, in the original version of the Bible (Revelation 4:2–7), has the vision of a throne set in heaven '. . . and round about the throne, were four beasts full of eyes before and behind. And the first was like a lion, and the second beast like a calf, and the third beast had a face as a man, and the fourth beast was like a flying eagle.' We recognize here the four Fixed signs: lion (Leo), calf (Taurus), man (Aquarius), and the eagle (Scorpio). The eighth sign was once depicted as an eagle, not a scorpion.

In the Old Testament book of Ezekiel 1:10 (revised version) we read an account of the Chaldean priest Ezekiel's vision of four living creatures: 'As for the likeness of their faces, each had the face of a man in front; the four had the face of a lion on the right side, the four had the face of an ox on the left side, and the four had the face of an eagle at the back.'

Each sign linked with a planet

Traditionally, a planet is said to 'rule' one or more signs. I do not accept the concept of 'rulership' in the sense that there could be some kind of mystical link between a planet and a sign. I prefer to think that there is an *affinity* between a planet and a sign such that traditionally the planet would be said to 'rule' due to both having certain significant similarities of traits. The ancients were aware of this affinity though, unfortunately, they coined the term 'rulership', implying that a particular planet has an influence over a particular sign.

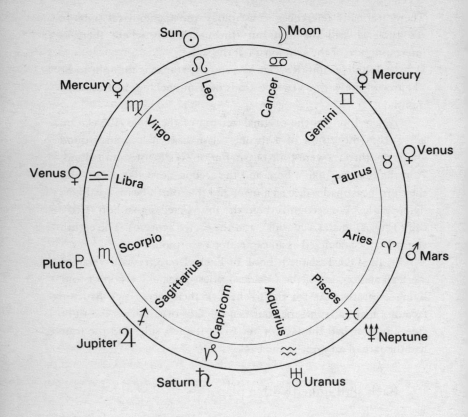

Figure 9

Planet–Sign affinity

Sun in the signs

The traits associated with each sign are most evident when the Sun is in that sign, although one must remember that the Sun's most natural function will be to express a sign's disposition in a purposefully active way. Each sign's traits are also emphasized when that sign is on the Ascendant, though here they are expressed specifically in terms of self-conscious adjustment to the environment. This is explained in more detail in chapter 16. A sign's traits and disposition are also given prominence in a subject's personality when the Moon 'occupies' that sign, with special relevance to sensitivity to the environment. The Moon by sign is dealt with in chapter 14. The system of astrological interpretation of personality traits taught in this book does not take into account the planets by their sign-placing. This is because we are presenting a system using only those chart features of absolute major importance, whereby the most significant personality features can be more clearly recognized. This is not to say that, for example, Mars in Taurus does not provide a glimpse of a potential subtle variation to the Mars functional need distinct from Mars in Pisces. Astrologers have tended to over-emphasize the planets in signs, resulting in misleading interpretations and a much less clear picture of a subject's real personality and potential.

The Sun enters each sign annually on approximately these dates:

♈ Aries around 21 March
♉ Taurus around 20 April
♊ Gemini around 21 May
♋ Cancer around 21 June
♌ Leo around 23 July
♍ Virgo around 23 August
♎ Libra around 23 September
♏ Scorpio around 23 October
♐ Sagittarius around 22 November
♑ Capricorn around 22 December

≈ Aquarius around 20 January
♓ Pisces around 19 February

Signs: diversity of disposition

We will recap what we said in chapter 9: the signs represent twelve different directions or courses of action, interest, behaviour. The signs are best described concisely as expressive of disposition – a tendency to act in a certain necessary and predictable manner, especially under given circumstances. But to understand the role of the signs more distinctly, an in-depth analysis is needed, and through this we will see each sign as a *quality of differentiation*. This alternative definition is rather 'a mouthful' and so normally you will think of the signs as expressive of disposition.

But what do we mean by a 'quality of differentiation'? Firstly, how do we define a quality as applied distinctively to the signs? A *quality* is an attribute or special feature designed for a particular purpose.

Secondly, what do we mean by differentiation? With this term we are thinking of 'progressive change, in evolution or in development'. The nature of the change we envisage is the need to discriminate and develop in a particular direction for the unfolding of human potential; and for devising new forms of adaptation.

The emphasis is on:
(a) human potential
(b) special feature
(c) progressive change, evolution, development
(d) discrimination
(e) particular direction
(f) adaptation

or, concisely: the particular purpose and direction for human potential and for improved adaptation. Each of the twelve signs is therefore a quality or special feature, vital for a particular purpose or direction for human potential and improved adaptation.

The evolution of the human species to its present incredibly complex and wonderfully expressive and self-conscious being would not have been possible without a series of periodic 'decisions' by the organism for increased differentiation in its means of coping with and adapting to the environment. Since the earliest of primordial stages in the destined-to-be-human organism's development the vital breakthroughs from periodic threats of stagnation in growth would have been increased complexity, variation, originality, plasticity and adaptation. The instinctive goal, apart from survival, is greater efficiency in coping with and adapting to the environment. The very essence of such a progressive process of development would have produced increasing self-awareness and intelligence.

This, surely, is what is meant by the 'survival of the fittest'. Not the survival of the physically strongest, but of the fittest in terms of being most fitted to deal successfully with the challenges and threats of the environment.

All evolutionary growth, whether of living organisms or of the growth and development of the expressions of human potential through activities and interests such as art, music, language construction, literature, science and technology, the formation of communities and social aggregations has progressed from the homogeneous (simplicity, uniformity) to the heterogeneous (complexity, multiformity, diversity).

The signs represent twelve different directions or courses of action, interest and behaviour necessary for the development of the whole potential unique to being human. In this way we see them as twelve necessary qualities of differentiation.

The planets represent functional needs in man. Without the signs and their qualities of differentiation or disposition, man would tend to remain in a world of relatively simple uniformity and unrealized diversity of creative and individual potential.

In understanding the role played in the birth chart (and in the psyche) by the signs, it is very important that we never forget that each human being has within him or her the psychological potential represented by all twelve signs. Because you have in your own chart the Sun in Gemini, Scorpio rising and the Moon in Pisces, this does not mean that you have the potential to develop only the traits of these three signs. You would be capable of behaving at times according to the directions given by any of the other nine signs and dependent for the strength of manifestation upon how these signs interrelate with the whole chart pattern. But . . . the signs most prominent in your chart (in our example case, particularly Gemini, Scorpio and Pisces) would indicate traits likely to be most evident in your behaviour and direction of interests.

Numerical classification of signs

Traditionally, the twelve signs have been classified into three groupings:

Polarities (positive and negative): two sub-groups of six signs each.
Quadruplicities or Qualities (Cardinal, Fixed, Mutable): three sub-groups of four signs each.
Triplicities or Elements (Fire, Earth, Air, Water): four sub-groups of three signs each.

These classifications have been known for centuries. Considerable discussion has been stimulated by the necessity of arranging the signs in this way, into these particular distinctive groups, especially from those holding the esoteric (mystical, spiritual) viewpoint. Those of us who seek a likely and realistic reason for their existence see them as an orderly manifestation of psychic or psychological functions. They provide each sign with three fundamental properties or attributes, arising from particular relationships with other signs in the circle of twelve. These relationships enable us to see more clearly the pattern of potential wholeness inherent in the nature of man and the universe.

Dr Carl Jung has written of numbers:

There is something peculiar, one might even say mysterious, about numbers . . . The most elementary quality about an object is whether it is one or many. Number helps more than anything else to bring order into the chaos of appearances. It is the predestined instrument for creating order or for apprehending an already existing, but still unknown, regular arrangement or 'orderedness'. It may well be the most primitive element of order in the human mind, seeing that the numbers one to four occur with the greatest frequency and have the widest incidence. In other words, primitive patterns of order are mostly triads or tetrads.[2]

He goes on to define number psychologically as 'an *archetype of order* which has become conscious'.

The three classifications or groupings of the signs will now be described in more detail. My view of these, though basically aligned with traditional definitions, presents a much revised concept of the function represented by the signs. Briefly, with their new designations:

Attitude (polarities): attitude stemming from objective/subjective orientations.

Mental type (quadruplicities): characteristic manifestation of the mental processes.

Temperament (triplicities): affective (emotional/feeling) nature; potential nervous expression.

Polarities: attitude

The twelve signs are seen as two distinct sets or groups, in alternate order:

Odd-numbered signs: 1, 3, 5, 7, 9, 11 = ♈ ♊ ♌ ♎ ♐ ♒
Even-numbered signs: 2, 4, 6, 8, 10, 12 = ♉ ♋ ♍ ♏ ♑ ♓

Traditionally these have been named *positive* (odd-numbered) and *negative* (even-numbered) signs. The ancients, many centuries ago, recognized these two opposing groups of signs in terms of human behaviour and activities. They referred to them as *masculine* and *feminine* respectively.

These must be thought of as two groups representing two opposing *attitudes* inherent in each of us. The dominant attitude for the odd-numbered signs tends to be directed to objects and events outside oneself. The resultant behaviour is more frequently extraverted (sociable, outgoing, taking chances, impulsive) than introverted. The dominant attitude for the even-numbered signs tends to be directed within oneself, subjectively. The resultant behaviour is more frequently introverted (introspective, reserved, taking no chances, serious) than extraverted.

We are distinguishing between an attitude and its resultant behaviour. An attitude has primeval roots in the elementary need to be successful. Its function is orientation, the organism's instinctive orientation to a position in which it feels most comfortable and pleasurable. It is a basic attitude of adaptation to the environment, by which a desired end or purpose can most effectively be attained. Thus it is a process of orientating oneself to a position that feels right and best for oneself in relation to other features of the environment and other people at any given moment. The resultant behaviour is one's emotional and mental activity arising from the orientation and necessary to achieve successful expression through the desired attitude.

The attitudes represented by the polarities are not learned attitudes in the conventionally defined framework: learned from parental influence, association with groups one is attracted to, the society one belongs to and so on. The potential to process the dominant orientation and attitude is present at birth. As one develops from childhood to adulthood, the other learned attitudes will give opportunities for developing and satisfying the dominant (objective or subjective) attitude. Where the latter is virtually inhibited, stress will be evident. It follows therefore that a dominant attitude may form into a consistent, habitual, evaluative and organized psychic structure powerfully determining one's behaviour and distinctly recognizable as the familiar extraverted or introverted disposition. But with most of us there will be a more or less equal balance between objective and subjective orientations; or, any 'dominance' in one direction will only be occasionally evident, and not consistently.

Objective attitude (odd-numbered signs)
Directing interest outside oneself, with probable development of
    extraverted behaviour.

Stemming from instinctive orientation in this direction as the most conducive to comfortable and pleasurable experience and the satisfaction of the need to be successful.

Priorities: external activities; status; influential relationships; a busy social environment.

Subjective attitude (even-numbered signs)

Directing interest within oneself, with probable development of introverted behaviour.

Stemming from instinctive orientation in this direction as the most conducive to comfortable and pleasurable experience and the satisfaction of the need to be successful.

Priorities: inner psychic activity; quiet and well-ordered environment; studying, reading, ideas, creativeness.

Quadruplicities

The traditional classification of the signs into three sub-groups of four signs each is known as the *quadruplicities* or *qualities*. These are:

Cardinal: ♈ ♋ ♎ ♑
Fixed: ♉ ♌ ♏ ♒
Mutable: ♊ ♍ ♐ ♓

Referring to figure 10, we can see that each quadruplicity forms a 'square'. In other words, the four signs in each quadruplicity or sub-group are in square aspect (90°) to the adjoining signs in their group and, of course, in opposition aspect (180°) to their opposite sign. One could say that this implies that the four signs within a quadruplicity are incompatible. But incompatibility only applies in relation to attitude (polarities), in which signs are objective versus subjective, and temperament (triplicities); since it will be noted that in each quadruplicity the Fire, Earth, Air and Water elements are represented. In terms of their respective quadruplicity or mental type the four signs have a common function vital for human expression.

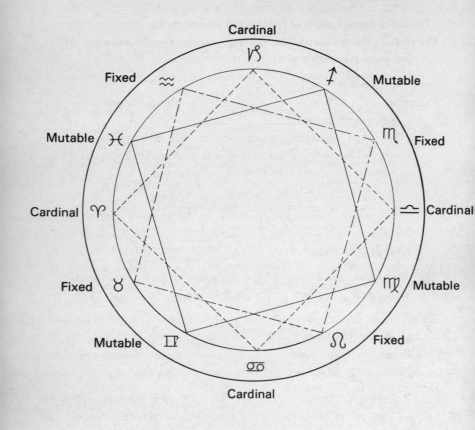

Figure 10

The Quadruplicities (mental type)

Quadruplicities: mental type

The three quadruplicities, Cardinal, Fixed and Mutable, represent three characteristic forms of mental type, appropriate expressions of the mental processes.

We would classify mental processes or cognitive processes as the thinking and knowing aspects of experience; awareness, perception, comprehension; the receiving and processing of information about the environment; communication by symbols; creation of objective structures of knowledge; judgement, problem-solving, decision making; and reasoning, especially intellectually – as opposed to emotional and volitional processes; anticipation, remembering, observing, conscious and organized learning.

Strictly speaking we cannot isolate a purely mental process, that which conjures up our thoughts and by which we have conscious awareness, from the rest of our being. Any mental activity is at the same time a bodily activity. Our thinking about what we can see, hear and feel may be influenced by a complexity of factors involving memories, wishes, imaginings and various other subtle emotions. Hence, our thinking and cognitive processes cannot be separated from emotion. Cognition is only one of many interrelated processes instrumental for our individual modes of reaction to the environment and for our striving to express ourselves and satisfy our needs.

However, within the complex structure of the psyche's emotional and mental activities, we can distinguish a mental type in terms of emphasis on a characteristic mode of development of the mental processes. The Cardinal, Fixed and Mutable signs provide the three types of emphases. These are:

Cardinal: actuation; directness
Mental processes manifest themselves as frank and uncomplicated,
with a tendency to generate activity.

Fixed: concentration; perseverance, fixity
Habitually and tenaciously held viewpoints. The tendency is to be
uncompromising and rigid in opinions.

Mutable: dispersion; changeable, flexible

A tendency for the mental processes to adapt to changing conditions and stimulate the psyche's interests in varied and widespread directions.

Triplicities

The traditional classification of the signs into four sub-groups of three signs each is known as the triplicities or elements. These are:

Fire: ♈ ♌ ♐
Earth: ♉ ♍ ♑
Air: ♊ ♎ ♒
Water: ♋ ♏ ♓

Referring to figure 11, you will see that each triplicity forms a 'triangle'. In other words, the three signs in each triplicity or sub-group are in trine aspect (120°). One could say that this implies that signs within a triplicity are compatible, which is true in terms of each triplicity representing a characteristic temperament. But the three signs within each triplicity are incompatible where mental type (quadruplicities) are concerned. For example, of the three fire signs, Aries is Cardinal, Leo is Fixed and Sagittarius is Mutable.

Triplicities: temperament

The four triplicities, Fire, Earth, Air and Water, represent four characteristic modes of temperament, appropriate expressions of the affective (emotional/feeling) nature and of potential nervous activity.

We would distinguish 'temperament' as one's general nervous and affective nature, as opposed to one's mental and intellectual nature. 'Affective' embraces the feelings and emotions. 'Feeling' is a subjective process that evaluates a given content on the basis of 'like or dislike', 'pleasant or unpleasant'. When one's mind

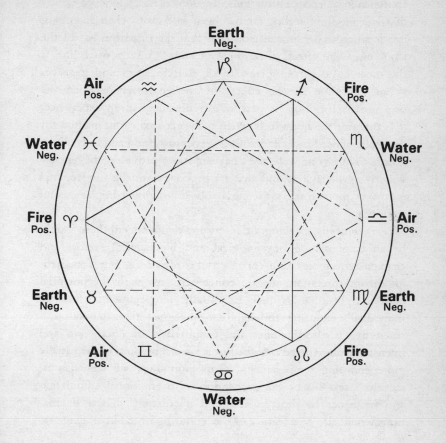

Figure 11

The Triplicities (temperaments)

apprehends objects or situations, an immediate experience occurs that is a mode of feeling. It has been said that 'when an organism is stimulated, the consciousness that the organism has of the stimulus is the affect, affection or feeling. A state of feeling is the most basic perceptible state of consciousness and it serves as an indication of the effects of the environment upon the organism.'[3] 'Emotion' is personal involvement in an experience; it is the way the body feels when it is prepared or stimulated for particular action. Indeed, emotion serves to sustain and to facilitate action. Thus, one can see that emotion provides the energy underlying behaviour and that its processes are the fundamental means of motivation, also, inevitably, involving complex neural activities.

Technically speaking, in describing temperament there should be an emphasis on physiological and biochemical factors and characteristic motor (muscular activity) responses. But, for astrological interpretation, we are concerned only with the potential behaviour of an individual. Essentially, temperament defines an individual's enduring and habitual emotional characteristics and reactivity. It also includes the peculiarities of fluctuation and intensity in short-lived moods. But if we can predict the potentially more enduring temperament of an individual, we will also be able to assess his or her susceptibility to emotional stimulation and frequency of short-lived mood fluctuations. These fluctuations would also be a feature of the 'enduring or habitual' temperament.

The characteristic modes of temperament represented by each of the four triplicities are:

Fire: propulsion; eagerness

The temperament is imbued with a keen desire, eagerness, even impatience, to drive forward or onward in response to inner motives or reactions to environmental stimuli. This can manifest not only in obvious self-projective or extraverted behaviour, but also as emotionally-charged stimulus and 'colouring' to mental activity and self-expression.

Earth: deliberation; criticalness

The temperament is imbued with intensity and caution, emotionally restrained for the exercise of careful judgement, judicious evaluation, observation. It is as if the organism's primitive and inherent fear of insecurity permeates even now every form of action and response. This manifests itself as an underlying discrimination, a seeking for errors and imperfections and an instinctive need for careful consideration before committing oneself.

Air: interaction; looseness

The temperament is imbued with elasticity and the quality of unrestrained action or feeling. The innate desire is for reciprocal activity and participation with the environment, acting upon each other and through each other. Hence, accessibility is the keynote of this temperament.

Water: assimilation; fluidity

The temperament is imbued with the attributes for stimulating a ready flow of emotion and for absorbing and incorporating experiences through the feelings and nervous system into the psyche. Thus, environmental influences are keenly and sensitively registered.

This completes the first part of our description of the zodiacal signs. In the next chapter we will interpret each sign individually through the unification of the three classifications (attitude, mental type, temperament) according to the particular combinations relating to each sign.

Summary of chapter

1 The theme of this chapter is that each sign represents a particular form of disposition, or a quality of differentiation. Each is a special feature within the psyche, vital for giving diversity of purpose and direction to the functional needs represented by the planets.

2 The twelve signs are classified into three groupings. Traditionally these are polarities, quadruplicities and triplicities. We now know these as attitude, mental type and temperament.

3 The traits associated with a sign are most evident when that sign is occupied by the Sun, the Ascendant or the Moon.

Notes

1 Jack Lindsay: *Origins of Astrology*, p. 28 (Frederick Muller, 1971)

2 Dr Carl Jung: *The Structure and Dynamics of the Psyche*, p. 456 (Pantheon Books Inc., New York, 1960)

3 John H. Ewen: *Handbook of Psychology*, p. 24 (Sylviro Publications Ltd, 1950)

CHAPTER 13

Signs: Diversity of Disposition (2)

Twelve unique diversities of disposition

In the previous chapter you saw how each sign is associated with three fundamental properties or attributes, three distinct processes by which the psyche functions: attitude, mental type and temperament.

Each of these processes has different modes of expression, arising from numerical relationships between each of the signs in the circle of twelve. This orderly arrangement or manifestation of psychological functions, based on units of two, three and four, shows all twelve signs to be necessarily integrated and yet representing twelve unique and basic diversities of dispo sition. Each represents a particular purpose or direction for human potential and for the psyche's improved adaptation to its environment.

We all share basic behaviour

Unless an individual has a severe abnormality and is deprived of a basic form of behaviour or instinctively-generated reaction to particular environmental stimuli, all human beings are capable of similar behaviour, emotions, feelings, outwardly recognizable responses to basic drives and survival needs. We are all capable of laughing, hating, loving, of feeling anxiety, desire, pleasure, fear, excitement.

But naturally, because each of us is unique, not everyone expresses any particular trait in exactly the same measure or frequency. It is understandable that psychologists, who do not have an individual's birth chart to refer to, have no reliable basis on which to be able to predict that individual's potential behaviour patterns and probable frequency of certain traits.

The particular traits or characteristic reactions to stimuli or stress that are given in this chapter for each of the twelve signs are those which, for a stated sign, are potentially more prominent than the average expected frequency among the population.

It is very important to realize this. For instance, Pisceans tend to be imaginative whilst Capricornians tend to be unimaginative; Capricornians tend to be practical but Pisceans tend to be impractical. Taureans tend to be stubborn, Leos tend to be generous, Virgoans tend to be critical, and so on. Even if we do not 'belong to' any of the Sun-signs given above, most of us, if not all, will possess to some degree its related trait. Thus, if our Sun-sign is not Taurus, we will probably admit to being 'stubborn' on occasions. However, with Taureans, stubbornness is a potentially characteristic trait, associated with the purpose and evolutional direction of the Taurean quality within all humans – but very pronounced and evident in persons born when the Sun was in Taurus.

I frequently use the word 'potential' or 'potentially' with reference to traits and behaviour. This is because no predicted trait will necessarily happen with certainty. It is predicted as a latent capacity or possibility, of sufficient possibility to justify being classified as a potentially characteristic trait. Other factors in the complex chart pattern might tend to inhibit and modify the predicted trait, and circumstances of birth environment, parental influence and the course of events will produce or restrict opportunities for the trait to be developed and realized. Despite the profusion of environmental variables likely to encourage or discourage a trait's development, the individual astrological chart is a unique and incredibly reliable blueprint of personality.

A couple of examples should suffice to illustrate what has just been said about most of us sharing any given trait or response.

A highly successful research study I devised[1] testing the relation between the signs and neuroticism and extroverted/introverted personality traits provided a vast amount of interesting material from the fifty-seven questions answered. 2,324 samples were used – men and women from all walks of life and from seventy countries of birth. All answered Professor Hans Eysenck's Personality Inventory and gave their birth data.

To the question, 'Are you rather lively?', 73.6 per cent of the 2,324 subjects replied 'yes'. But more Sun–Aries than other signs considered themselves lively (80.2 per cent), whilst Sun–Capricorns were fewest (68.4 per cent). Only 11.8 per cent separates 'most from least' but the figures are pertinent. We know how lively, active and excitable Aries can be, and how reserved and cautious so many of the Capricornians we know are. Of course, we are only considering one chart factor – the Sun by sign – and not the whole chart pattern. However, as 73.6 per cent of the total sample consider themselves to be 'lively' personalities, it would be reasonable to suggest that seven out of every ten persons in, say, the British Isles, would more or less fit that category. It is, therefore, brilliant observation on the part of astrologers over the centuries to have distinguished between those signs connected with a 'more lively than average' personality and other signs connected with a 'less than average liveliness'.

Another question asked was, 'Are you moody?' Traditionally the sign most associated with a moody temperament has been Cancer. More Cancer subjects than any other sign considered themselves 'moody' (68.8 per cent). But a large percentage of all other signs can also be moody, 58.3 per cent of the 2,324 samples. Fewest Librans consider themselves prone to moodiness (51.7 per cent).

Diversities of disposition associated with the signs

♈	Aries	to initiate, be active
♉	Taurus	to sustain, be acquisitive
♊	Gemini	to transmit, be volatile
♋	Cancer	to contain, be defensive
♌	Leo	to display, be managerial

♍ Virgo	to analyse, be discriminating
♎ Libra	to relate, be appreciative
♏ Scorpio	to scrutinize, be intensely penetrating
♐ Sagittarius	to extend, be explorative
♑ Capricorn	to construct, be calculative
♒ Aquarius	to innovate, be observant
♓ Pisces	to merge, be impressionable

You should learn these so that they can be easily remembered.

Description of categories

Each sign will be interpreted as if it were an isolated factor within the psyche. But when viewed within the structure of a complete birth chart, the potential behaviour associated with a sign may be modified according to its interrelationship with the whole chart pattern. The special human potential represented by each sign will be most evident when the sign is occupied by the Sun, and also, according to their particular functions within the psyche, when occupied by either the Ascendant or the Moon. Here is an explanation of the several categories that describe each sign's disposition.

Numerical position within the zodiacal circle: the traditional designation within the one–twelve sequence.

Period of the year when occupied by the Sun: the approximate dates annually; these may vary by one day some years, due to the Leap Year.

Planet affinity: traditionally known as 'ruling planet', but that claim is now unacceptable (see page 127). Until future research enlightens us with a new concept of planet–sign links through certain similarities of expression, I prefer to view each sign's form of disposition as being compatible with a particular planet's function within the psyche. 'Compatible', in the sense that the psyche's responses to a particular functional need (e.g. Mars: exertion) can be of a similar nature to the psyche's responses associated with a particular disposition –

in this example, Aries' special purpose or direction to initiate and to be active.

Disposition: a special feature which gives a particular purpose or direction of action and behaviour to the functional needs (planets), vital for human potential and growth and for improved adaptation to the environment.

Attitude (polarity): basic attitude of adaptation to the environment.

Mental type (quadruplicity): characteristic manifestation of the mental processes.

Temperament (triplicity): affective (emotional/feeling) nature; potential nervous expression.

+ = stimulus reaction (comfortable): characteristic and distinctive behaviour that is satisfying and without discomfort and uneasiness; where any stress registered is a stimulus that is enjoyed.

− = stress reaction (uncomfortable): characteristic and distinctive behaviour that is unsatisfying and reveals vulnerability to stress; springing from probable disequilibrium creating discomfort, uneasiness, tenseness, strain.

Further characteristics: additional features.

Aries ♈

First zodiacal sign.

Sun is in Aries around 21 March to 19 April.

Planet affinity: Mars ♂

Disposition: to initiate, be active.

Greater efficiency through taking the initiative, facilitating the first actions, steps and procedures; characterized by activity.

Attitude (polarity): objective; directing interest outside oneself; tending to extraversion.

Mental type (Cardinal): actuation; directness. Frank and uncomplicated; generates activity.

Temperament (Fire): propulsion; eagerness. Forward and onward seeking; impatience; self-projection.

+ : action, directness, initiative.

Self-reliant, independent, quick, adventurous, enthusiastic to reach a goal, pioneering, singleness of purpose, audacious (bold, daring, impudent), frank, competitive, determined, spontaneous.

− : impatient, restless, impulsive.

Too self-centred, must have own way, 'me first', inconsiderate, quick temper, takes risks, accident-prone, over-excitable and emotional, pugnacious, fanatical, aggressive, narrow of vision, dislike of routine, inertia and restraint, headstrong, frequently 'competing' within a relationship, tactless, desire for conquests, over-active with insufficient relaxation.

Further characteristics: meet opposition head-on; can conceive the start and end of an activity but overlook details in between; want quick results; enjoy excitement and bustle; uncooperative.

Taurus ♉

Second zodiacal sign.

Sun is in Taurus around 20 April to 20 May.

Planet affinity: Venus ♀

Disposition: to sustain, be acquisitive.

Greater efficiency through gaining and maintaining strength by endurance, sustainment, provision; characterized by acquisitiveness.

Attitude (polarity): subjective; directing interest within oneself; tending to introversion.

Mental type (Fixed): concentration; perseverance; fixity. Habit-forming, tenacious, uncompromising, rigid.

Temperament (Earth): deliberation; criticalness. Intensity, caution; fear of insecurity; discrimination.

+ : tenacity, deliberation, endurance, restraint.

Industrious, patient, circumspect (prudent, discreet, vigilant, consider consequences), steadfast, acquisitive, consistent, security-conscious, steady plodder.

− : uncompromising, possessive, stubborn.

Inflexibly prejudiced, intolerant, stodgy, materialistic, routine-obsessed, brood, hesitant, procrastinate, resent contradiction.

Further characteristics: love food and comfort; desire to build; avoid abstractions; conform; avoid risk-taking; enjoy being productive; reliable because predictable; powerful fear of insecurity; ideally suited to the Civil Service, banking, accountancy, or where there is a secure and routine job with the reward of a pension at the end.

Gemini ♊

Third zodiacal sign.

Sun is in Gemini around 21 May to 20 June.

Planet affinity: Mercury ☿

Disposition: to transmit, be volatile.

Greater efficiency through transmitting, passing on or spreading about, conveying; characterized by lightness, rapid movement, volatility.

Attitude (polarity): objective; directing interest outside oneself; tending to extraversion.

Mental type (Mutable): dispersion; changeable; flexible. Adaptable; varied and widespread interests.

Temperament (Air): interaction; looseness. Elasticity; unrestrained action/feeling; desire for reciprocal activity, participation; accessibility.

+ : flexible, communicative, inquisitive.

Interactive, volatile, adaptable, versatile, gregarious.

− : restless, diffusive, inconsistent.

Superficial, fickle, vacillating, impatient, lack of concentration, changeable.

Further characteristics: exploratory; talkative; middle-man or agent roles; likely to have a 'second string to his or her bow'; needs to have varied and widespread interests and to be ready to make changes and new contacts; readily accessible for exchange of ideas and conversation.

Cancer ♋

Fourth zodiacal sign.

Sun is in Cancer around 21 June to 22 July.

Planet affinity: Moon ☽

Disposition: to contain, be defensive.

Greater efficiency through holding together, holding on to, containing energy; characterized by defensiveness.

Attitude (polarity): subjective; directing interest within oneself; tending to introversion.

Mental type (Cardinal): actuation; directness. Frank and uncomplicated; generates activity.

Temperament (Water): assimilation; fluidity. Readily emotional; keenly and sensitively influenced.

+ : tenacious, retentive, protective.

Resourceful, shrewd, acquisitive, receptive, conservative, cautious, assimilative, imaginative, defensive.

− : moody, over-possessive, deeply emotional.

Easily hurt and touchy, acutely sensitive beneath a hard-to-penetrate exterior, restless, self-conscious, jealous, irrationally prejudiced, impatient.

Further characteristics: loves to collect things; females very maternal; tears and laughter come easily; protective of own kith and kin; strong likes and dislikes; sensuous; sentimental; cling to the past and to tradition; intuitive; try to ignore inner shyness; outwardly strong-minded but inwardly sensitive and emotional; prefer company of known and trusted friends; romantic.

Leo ♌

Fifth zodiacal sign.

Sun is in Leo around 23 July to 22 August.

Planet affinity: Sun ☉

Disposition: to display, be managerial.

Greater efficiency through achieving prominence, exhibiting for effect; characterized by management and organization.

Attitude (polarity): objective; directing interest outside oneself; tending to extraversion.

Mental type (Fixed): concentration; perseverance, fixity. Habit-forming, tenacious, uncompromising, rigid.

Temperament (Fire): propulsion; eagerness. Forward and onward seeking; impatience; self-projection.

+ : self-assured, opportunist, enthusiastic.

Persevering, self-projective, organizer, optimistic, ambitious, generous, frank, gregarious, demonstrative.

– : exhibitionism, self-esteem, self-indulgent.

Affectation, uncompromising, impatient, manipulation of others, power-seeking, self-dramatization, conceit, exaggerative, condescending, snobbish, prejudiced, dominating, autocratic, lack of consideration of details, intolerant, arrogant, presumptuous (impudent, over-confident), extravagant, ostentatious.

Further characteristics: self-display; desire to entertain and to impress and influence others; must upstage others; extravagant moods; showmanship; social climber; potential for leadership; can be a bore.

Virgo ♍

Sixth zodiacal sign.

Sun is in Virgo around 23 August to 22 September.

Planet affinity: Mercury ☿

Disposition: to analyse; be discriminating.

Greater efficiency through determining critically the fundamental elements of anything for close scrutiny, or to find its essence, trace underlying principles, or for an accurate resolution of an overall structure or nature; characterized by discrimination.

Attitude (polarity): subjective; directing interest within oneself; tending to introversion.

Mental type (Mutable): dispersion; changeable, flexible. Adaptable; varied and widespread interests.

Temperament (Earth): deliberation; criticalness. Intensity; caution; fear of insecurity; discrimination.

+ : discriminating, inquisitive, observant.

Analytical, flexible, precise, methodical, conscientious, industrious, shrewd, discerning, assimilate details of experience, thoroughness, undemonstrative.

− : hypercritical, perfectionist.

Fastidious, diffident (lacking self-confidence), sceptical, cynical, irritable, slow to forgive, intolerant, pedantic, interfering.

Further characteristics: attention to detail; rationalizing; interest in abstracts, systems, techniques, methods; charming modesty; outwardly coolly affectionate; sexual experimentation; choose friends carefully; interpret and improve upon original ideas of others; capacity for ingenious improvisation; fear of insecurity; evaluates life by facts and logic; introspective; over-specialization.

Libra ♎

Seventh zodiacal sign.

Sun is in Libra around 23 September to 22 October.

Planet affinity: Venus ♀

Disposition: to relate, be appreciative.

Greater efficiency through establishing a relation between oneself and the environment, between other people, that can be understood and evaluated; characterized by appreciation.

Attitude (polarity): objective; directing interest outside oneself; tending to extraversion.

Mental type (Cardinal): actuation; directness. Frank and uncomplicated; generates activity.

Temperament (Air): interaction; looseness. Elasticity; unrestrained action/feeling; desire for reciprocal activity, participation; accessibility.

+ : co-operative, communicative, compromise.

Optimistic, diplomatic, adaptable, tactful, debative, desiring to please, sociability, idealistic.

− : indecisive, too easy-going, lack of discipline.

Easily influenced, lack of confidence, procrastination, avoid taking 'sides', vacillation, unable to say 'no'.

Further characteristics: capacity to relate to and accommodate other people; ability to bring people together; powerful need to appreciate others and to be appreciated; accessible; romantic; dislike of disharmony and coarseness; instinctive seeking for harmony and balance; artistic perception; desire to reconcile opposites; correct evaluation of situations and people is important; need for social and emotional security; capacity for seeing both sides of an argument; passionately aroused by an injustice; good at flattering and vulnerable to flattery; freely make concessions for sake of peace and harmony; allow others to make decisions for them.

Scorpio ♏

Eighth zodiacal sign.

Sun is in Scorpio around 23 October to 21 November.

Planet affinity: Pluto ♇

Disposition: to scrutinize, be intensely penetrative.

Greater efficiency through critical enquiry and search, close observation and examination; characterized by intense penetration.

Attitude (polarity): subjective; directing interest within oneself; tending to introversion.

Mental type (Fixed): concentration; perseverance, fixity. Habit-forming; tenacious, uncompromising, rigid.

Temperament (Water): assimilation; fluidity. Readily emotional; keenly and sensitively influenced.

+ : penetrative reasoning and depth of feeling; subtlety, tenacity.

Concentration, perseverance, intense, shrewd, industrious, discerning, inquisitive.

− : obstinate, dogmatic, critical.

Uncompromising, brooding resentment, jealousy, suspicious, dominant, sarcastic, possessive, revengeful, easily hurt, forceful.

Further characteristics: need to scrutinize, search, examine in depth anything that interests or challenges; strong likes and dislikes; strong convictions; intuitive; introspective; capacity for powerfully and often subtly influencing others; magnetic charm; dislikes trivialities and superficialities; seek to gain access to the inner content or meaning of anything which interests and attracts; pervasive manner; capacity for endurance; subtle and secretive.

Sagittarius ♐

Ninth zodiacal sign.

Sun is in Sagittarius around 22 November to 21 December.

Planet affinity: Jupiter ♃

Disposition: to extend, be explorative.

Greater efficiency through reaching forth beyond normal limits, expanding and extending range or scope; characterized by exploration.

Attitude (polarity): objective; directing interest outside oneself; tending to extraversion.

Mental type (Mutable): dispersion; changeable, flexible. Adaptable; varied and widespread interests.

Temperament (Fire): propulsion; eagerness. Forward and onward seeking; impatience; self-projection.

+ : exploration, opportunism, competitiveness.

Enthusiasm, adaptable, optimism, inquisitive, self-projection, sociable, frank, versatile, spontaneity.

− : impulsive, extremist, erratic.

Impatient, extravagant, exaggerative, restless, unsubtle, moody, careless, unmethodical.

Further characteristics: idealist; an interpreter and translator rather than inventor; wide-ranging interests; prefers independence; philosophical; over-talkative; likes gambling and taking risks; great capacity for fun, enjoyment, sport; likes changes; high-spirited; accident-prone; capacity for counselling, promoting, educating.

Capricorn ♑

Tenth zodiacal sign.

Sun is in Capricorn around 22 December to 19 January.

Planet affinity: Saturn ♄

Disposition: to construct, be calculative.

Greater efficiency through applying logic and planning to the fitting together of relevant parts for the forming of structures; characterized by calculation.

Attitude (polarity): subjective; directing interest within oneself; tending to introversion.

Mental type (Cardinal): actuation; directness. Frank and uncomplicated; generates activity.

Temperament (Earth): deliberation; criticalness. Intensity, caution; fear of insecurity; discrimination.

+ : discrimination, deliberation, self-reliance.

Caution, patience, perseverance, prudence, determination, self-control, practicality, shrewdness.

− : critical, over-cautious, severe.

Authoritarian, too rigidly conforming to conventional and disciplined behaviour, too matter-of-fact and materialistic, pessimism, procrastination, scheming, selfish.

Further characteristics: cool and calculating; capacity to bear hardship and frustration; dutiful and disciplined; a 'wet blanket'; economizing and resourceful; capacity for constructive and productive type of employment; conservative; slow and plodding; good sense of humour − as if compensating the basic severe nature; meticulous attention to detail; undemonstrative; capacity for routine work with an ultimate useful purpose; unimaginative.

Aquarius ♒

Eleventh zodiacal sign.

Sun is in Aquarius around 20 January to 18 February.

Planet affinity: Uranus ♅

Disposition: to innovate, be observant.

Attitude (polarity): objective; directing interest outside oneself; tending to extroversion.

Mental type (Fixed): concentration; perseverance, fixity. Habit-forming, tenacious, uncompromising, rigid.

Temperament (Air): interaction; looseness. Elasticity; unrestrained action/feeling; desire for reciprocal activity, participation; accessibility.

+ : innovative, observant, detached.

Idealistic, imaginative, independent, perceptive, inquisitive, attentive.

− : tactless, contrary, wilful.

Dogmatic, unpredictable, eccentric, touchy, rebellious, erratic, antisocial, cold and unemotional detachment, brusque, untidy.

Further characteristics: originality; progressive thinker; attracted to the unusual and unorthodox; intuitive; inventive; fanatically unconventional, cranky; complex and contradictory; an observer rather than a participator; capacity for taking others by surprise; social idealist and theoretical reformer; more attracted to groups than to individuals; like to keep their private thoughts secret.

Pisces ♓

Twelfth zodiacal sign.

Sun is in Pisces around 19 February to 20 March.

Planet affinity: Neptune ♆

Disposition: to merge, be impressionable.

Greater efficiency through experiencing absorption into something else, blending, intermingling, immersing; characterized by impressionability, sensitivity.

Attitude (polarity): subjective; directing interest within oneself; tending to introversion.

Mental type (Mutable): dispersion; changeable, flexible. Adaptable; varied and widespread interests.

Temperament (Water): assimilation; fluidity. Readily emotional; keenly and sensitively influenced.

+ : impressionability, intimacy, sociability.

Sympathetic, receptive, assimilative, creative and vivid imagination, compassionate.

− : indecisive, hypersensitive, too subjective, escapist.

Nebulous, submissive, impractical, careless, touchy, gullible, extravagant, restless, dramatization, difficulty in cultivating complete detachment from disturbing influences, vacillation, petulant irritability, temperamental and moody.

Further characteristics: easy-going; intuitive; secretive; need for creative and artistic expression; enter into the feelings of others; very sensitive to environmental influences; shy; reflect and absorb moods of others; idealistic; romantic; over-dependence on others; timidity; lack of discrimination; drift easily into habits, good or bad; dissolve easily into tears; unpunctual; untidy; unmethodical; undisciplined.

Summary of chapter

1 The theme of this chapter is to show that each sign representing a particular purpose or direction for human potential expresses traits or reactions to stimuli or stress characteristic to that sign, because these are potentially more prominent than the average frequency among the total signs.

2 All human beings are capable of similar behaviour, emotions, feelings, outwardly recognizable responses to basic drives and survival needs. But because each of us is unique, not everyone expresses any particular trait in exactly the same measure or frequency. A prominent sign or signs in an individual's birth chart are a reliable indication of potentially prominent traits or responses characteristic to that individual.

Note

1 *Mayo–Eysenck Research*: see Appendix I.

CHAPTER 14

The Moon in the Signs

The traits of the sign occupied by the Moon will tend to be prominent features affecting general behaviour and responses to environmental influences. We know that the signs occupied by both the Sun and the Ascendant will also be highly important chart features. In each case, whether it be the Sun, Moon or Ascendant, the traits of the sign each occupies will be basically similar – for instance, when each occupies Aries, we will find the characteristic disposition of Aries to initiate and be active is clearly evident, even though these traits will be integrated with other varied and contrasting features of the subject's unique personality.

The subtle difference, however, will be how these three important features of the psyche affect the Aries traits. That part of the psyche represented by the Sun will express these initiating, restless and activity-seeking traits through the more masculine principle of purposeful endeavour. As we will see in chapter 16, the Ascendant represents a need to be sensitively self-conscious, particularly where personal relationships are concerned; where it is important, if mostly subconsciously, to impress others with one's own unique value and abilities; and where self-interests might easily become selfish self-centred objectives. Hence, when Aries is on the Ascendant, that sign's tendency to restless activity and enthusiastic self-projection will find an apt outlet.

With the Moon however, a sign's traits will be highlighted by an emphasis on emotional colouring and an underlying feminine type of sensitivity – not the Ascendant's self-conscious sensitivity where the focus is on self and self interests, but a sensitivity to the environment and other people. This is due to this function's need to be emotionally and meaningfully connected to others. This is an area where the subject is likely to be particularly vulnerable to stress, not just because it is an acutely sensitive area of the psyche, but also because this is where there is a significant desire to be accessible to other people.

The function of the Moon, in terms of 'a psychological need for an individual, will be given a particular purpose or direction of action and behaviour according to the sign it occupies. This means that someone with the Moon in Aries will be disposed to (will tend to) seek adaptation to others and the environment through the Moon's feminine form of sensitivity by taking the initiative and being energetically active, quick and forthright. The sensitivity and emotionality of the Moon's function will tend to be very evident because of the restlessness, impulsiveness, excitableness and, at times, aggressiveness of the Aries disposition.

Characteristic disposition of each sign occupied by the Moon

The signs give diversity of purpose and direction to the Moon's functional need of adaptation to the environment through sensitivity, coupled with the need to be susceptible and accessible to others. Hence, emphasis will be on the emotions, feelings and acute vulnerability to emotional stress. (However, do bear in mind that the traits listed for each sign in chapter 13 will all be potential features, as these have been focused on when linked with the Moon; this is why the interpretation formula for the Moon in chapter 22 reminds you to refer to a sign's major classifications of 'attitude, mental type and temperament'.) But, as we have just indicated, emphasis in the Moon's case will be on the emotions, feelings and resultant vulnerability in this area.

Successful and sensitive adaptation to others and the environment is best achieved through:

Aries ♈: taking the initiative, being energetically active, quick, forthright, enthusiastic. Emotional vulnerability through being over-excitable, impatient, restless, impulsive.

Taurus ♉: persistence and endurance, being acquisitive, patient, deliberate. Emotional vulnerability through being possessive, uncompromising, stubborn.

Gemini ♊: flexibility, being communicative, inquisitive, versatile. Emotional vulnerability through being restless, inconsistent, superficial, impatient.

Cancer ♋: shrewdness and tenacity, being resourceful, cautious, defensive. Emotional vulnerability through being easily hurt and touchy, moody, too self-conscious.

Leo ♌: self-projection and organization, being opportunist, demonstrative. Emotional vulnerability through being self-indulgent, exhibitionist, dominating.

Virgo ♍: discrimination and discernment, being inquisitive, observant, methodical. Emotional vulnerability through being too perfectionist, hypercritical, interfering.

Libra ♎: co-operation and compromise, being appreciative, optimistic, tactful. Emotional vulnerability through being too easy-going, indecisive, procrastinating.

Scorpio ♏: subtlety and depth of feeling, being intensely inquisitive and discerning. Emotional vulnerability through being too critical, possessive and brooding.

Sagittarius ♐: versatility and opportunism, being variously active, optimistic, enthusiastic. Emotional vulnerability through being too impulsive, restless, erratic.

Capricorn ♑: deliberation and determination, being calculating, persevering, prudent. Emotional vulnerability through being too severe, over-cautious, pessimistic.

Aquarius ♒: innovation and perceptiveness, being idealistic, imaginative, keenly observant. Emotional vulnerability through being contrary, rebellious, too independent.

Pisces ♓: impressionability and receptiveness, being easy-going, idealistic, sympathetic. Emotional vulnerability through being hypersensitive, indecisive, moody, gullible.

Summary of chapter

The aim of this chapter is to show the importance of the sign in which the Moon is placed. Not only are the general traits associated with the sign made potentially more prominent in the subject's behaviour and responses, but of most significance will be the more emotionally-charged traits and spontaneous feeling-reactions. This is because the functional need represented by the Moon within the psyche seeks to express the powerful feminine principle in both men and women.

CHAPTER 15

The Houses: Traditional Mundane Matters

We will not be interpreting houses in the traditional, or any other way, but we will be showing these equal 30° areas on our illustrated chart form with very brief lines, along with the number of each house, as shown in figure 14 (page 181). This is for three reasons. Firstly, these lines, separated by 30° all round the chart commencing from the Ascendant, are helpful when entering the sign divisions; secondly, any reader who wishes for research or personal choice to interpret the planets in the houses can do so (it is appreciated that for many who have been taught that the houses are an essential feature of charting it will not at first be easy to disregard these); and thirdly, virtually all printed chart forms that can be bought for entering data will include the house cusps.

Why use houses?

The traditional name, originating in antiquity, for the twelve sections of a chart that almost always begin at the Ascendant with the first house and are numbered in an anti-clockwise direction is 'houses'. These houses refer mostly to mundane or 'worldly' matters (rather than psychological features), such as the fourth house, 'home and family' and the tenth house, 'career and business affairs'. I always recommended my students to the Equal House System (each house is of equal 30°), but in all other house systems the houses vary in length, according to which system is used.

Why need there be houses? I won't speak for the traditionalists in answering this question. Nor would I dispute the sincerity of those astrologers who still believe the houses to be valid chart factors not to be ignored. I used the houses and taught students to interpret them for years, though with progressively decreasing confidence in their generally accepted interpretations. I now ignore them and would answer the above question by saying that no existing interpretation of the houses that I am aware of warrants their inclusion in a chart analysis. The main reason I say this is that emphasis on house positioning of planets can often produce misleading statements about the individual concerned. This situation is amplified because there are such a variety of 'schools of thought', each with widely differing interpretations for each house. I did not finally reject the houses from my personal chart analyses lightly. My decision was based on the study of thousands of charts where case histories were known.

Present state of house interpretations does not entail a loss to astrology

With the study of these thousands of charts it became clear that traditional houses were an unnecessary complication, but that the angles (Asc., IC, Desc., MC) that are the axes for house systems were a vitally important feature for predicting a subject's personality. My intensive research over many years resulted in the identification of four sectors of environmental relationships, which are dealt with in chapter 16. The vital role of these sectors in a chart analysis fully justifies and compensates for the rejection of traditional houses, and we need have no fear that the absence of houses deprives us of important and unique areas of the psyche's potentialities.

Summary of chapter

The theme of this chapter is that the astrological houses can be ignored without depriving a chart analysis of vital features. Indeed, it is possible that erroneous interpretations involving houses may be given greater emphasis than other dependable chart factors.

CHAPTER 16

The Angles: Environmental Relationships

Angles produced by Earth's axial rotation

Let us remind ourselves what the angles are. The angles of the birth chart are produced by the Earth's axial rotation. They are the Asc.–Desc. horizon axis and the MC–IC axis, as illustrated in figures 1 and 4. For those readers who have never erected a birth chart, we will explain how to enter the angles in the next chapter.

We can see how important the Earth's rotation through the complete circle of 360° in roughly twenty-four hours makes the *exact* time of birth for an accurate interpretation of the angles. The sign changes on the MC/IC every two hours, though for the Asc./Desc., the length of time a sign occupies these angles varies.

The angles provide a dimension of uniqueness

The angles can tell us a great deal about the subject whose birth chart is being interpreted. For an accurate interpretation of the angles and their relationship to the planets and signs, the time of birth should be known exactly, or within an error-margin of ten–fifteen minutes. Many are unsure of their time of birth to 'within an hour or more'. In these cases it is still possible to rectify the angles according to a probable near-exact time of birth, although here it should be remembered that interpretation would be based on a 'speculative' time.

The angles give a vitally important dimension of uniqueness to the individual concerned, showing how he or she differs psychologically from the thousands of other babies born on the same date.

There are three ways in which the angles can provide vital information and guidelines concerning significant facets of an individual's behaviour and responses to environmental stimulation and challenges:

1 by relating the functional needs (planets) to the sectors of environmental relationships through planetary aspects to angles;

2 by planets in Distinctive Zones;

3 by the sign on the Ascendant and to a much lesser degree the signs on the other three angles (IC, Desc., MC).

Figure 12 illustrates these three ways, with reference to Janet's chart. For simplicity only three planets and the sign on the Ascendant are shown. (1) Saturn is related to the Ascendant by trine aspect and to the Descendant by sextile aspect; (2) Moon is in Distinctive Zone 1 and Jupiter in Zone 2, both in conjunction with the Ascendant; (3) Sagittarius is the sign on the Ascendant.

Sectors of Environmental Relationship (SERs)

My intensive research over many years of 'house interpretations' and the angles of the birth chart, as mentioned in the previous chapter, has resulted in my identifying four vitally important sectors associated with our various inevitable relationships with the environment. These I have called *sectors of environmental relationships*, and each of the four angles of a chart focuses on a particular sector. To whatever extent we like to mix with other people, or are forced to relate to them through business or personal circumstances, whether we prefer animals, nature or our own company to socializing, other people are the most important features of our environment. We need others, whether we like the fact or not. And there are four basic ways of relating to others, through which we can develop our interests and potentialities and learn to identify our true selves.

My research involving the angles and my identification of the four sectors in no way followed the superb astrological research of Michel and Françoise Gauquelin, the French husband–wife

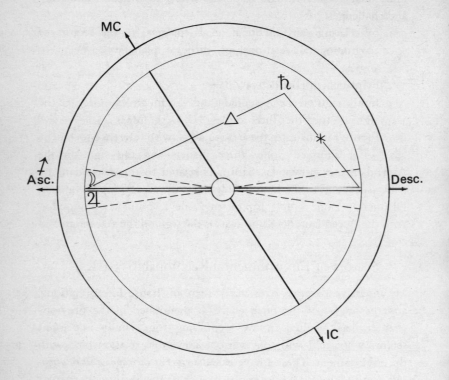

Figure 12

The angles provide vital information.
Example: 1 ♄ △ Asc., ✳ Desc.
          2 ☽ in Distinctive Zone 1;
            ♃ in Distinctive Zone 2
          3 ⚹ Asc.

psychologists. The basis of their research was the division of the diurnal rotation of the Earth (beginning clockwise from the Ascendant) into 36 sectors. They gave prominence to planets rising near the Ascendant, culminating near the MC, and setting near the Descendant. It was, nevertheless, extremely interesting and encouraging to find their research giving such significance to the angles of the chart.

We will call the four basic ways of relating to our environment or other people simply: Me, Us, You and Them. Each is represented by an area or sector of the chart extending 8° either side of an angle (see figure 13). A sector is of importance to the person concerned according to which planet or planets are either placed in that sector or form an aspect to its angle from another part of the chart.

Me, Us, You, Them: focal areas of relating

Me sector: 16° area centring on the Ascendant.
Here my relationship with the environment will be dominated by
 self-centred interests and the desire to be valued for my own
 efforts. Emphasis on a self-centred relationship with the
 environment. Self-interests must come first – but not necessar
 ily in a totally selfish way. The need to make others recognize
 my unique value and to prove to myself what I am capable of
 achieving on my own. Stress risk largely as a result of my
 own choice of interest, activity, behaviour.
Us sector: 16° area centring on the IC.
Here my relationship with the environment will be dominated by
 the joint and interdependent interests of you and me and my
 need to share with you. Emphasis on a you-and-me-together
 relationship. The need to share myself with someone else on
 a one-to-one basis for mutual interest and benefit. Stress risk
 to me largely as a result of sharing choice of action with you.
You sector: 16° area centring on the Descendant.
Here my relationship with the environment will be dominated by
 your interests, behaviour and impact upon me and my own
 need to receive from you. One is not always aware of this

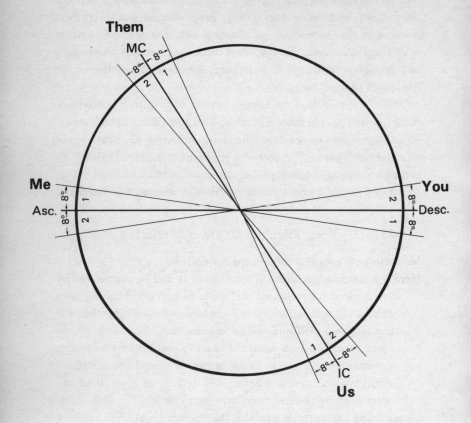

Figure 13

Sectors of environmental relationships and
Distinctive Zones

need to receive from a particular person and it is often a puzzle why, without having much or anything in common, or where there is generally discord, one must maintain this relationship. Sometimes circumstances make the continued contact unavoidable. Those of us who have a strongly-aspected You sector have significant lessons to learn and opportunities to grow in this way. Emphasis on a you-centred relationship. Your interests and behaviour are a major environmental influence and stimulation to my own behaviour. Stress risk to me largely as a result of your actions and behaviour.

Them: sector 16° area centring on the MC.

Here my relationship with the environment will be dominated by the interests and demands of society generally and my own need to contribute to society. Emphasis on a society-orientated relationship. The need to conform, sociologically, with an aggregate of persons living or working together in a more or less ordered structure. The need to relate to others through business interests and the achievement of status. Stress risk to me largely as a result of contact and involvement with society generally and its demands.

Distinctive zones: potential for achieving distinction

This is a name I have given to the sectors of environmental relationships (SERs) when each is divided into two zones as shown in figure 13. Zone 1 extends 8° before an angle; Zone 2 extends 8° following an angle, moving in an anti-clockwise direction, the direct motion of the planets and the sequence of the signs. We are, in effect, calling the SERs distinctive zones, which they are. But the reason for each sector's division into two zones and the naming of these 'distinctive' is that this gives a further dimension for the interpretation of an individual's potential. The function of a planet placed in either of these zones can be enhanced and through this there can be the potential for achieving some act or expression of *distinction*. Conversely, there may be unfavourable notoriety. This especially applies to those with a planet or planets in Zone 1 above the Ascendant or at the MC.

Apart from their functions as amplifiers and enhancers of the functional needs and as pointers to specific relationships with the environment and potential distinctive activity, the angles also indicate through these same planets and aspects linked with them, where the psyche will tend to be very vulnerable to the environment. This vulnerability will be essential for successful adaptation to the environment.

Zone 1: Tendency to restlessness, risk-taking. Often a compulsive exposing of oneself to risk of danger, loss, hurt by taking chances. May go to extremes of exertion. Can sometimes prove advantageous through seizing opportunities for personal betterment and distinction.

Zone 2: Tendency for a more controlled type of exertion. As with Zone 1, there is an urge to be active and self-expressive in terms of the planet's function, but with less risk-taking and more likelihood of any restlessness being controlled and the energies held in reserve.

Sign on the Ascendant, or ascending sign

Usually when we speak of the Ascendant we mean the sign on this angle of the chart. This ascending sign indicates a psychological feature of immense importance to the successful realization of the psyche's potential. In terms of a self-centred or what-I-want choice of action and expression, the focal point is the Ascendant. An apt designation, which we will use, for the special psychological function represented by the Ascendant is 'self-conscious adjustment'. Some other chart features are inevitably associated with 'self-consciousness', and the Ascendant can be seen as a focal point for all self-conscious activities of the psyche – and thus, is probably one's most sensitive expression of self-consciousness. This can be better understood when we bear in mind that the Ascendant is the focal point for the Me sector of environmental relationships.

By 'self-conscious adjustment' we mean that awareness of

oneself as a separate and unique being to all other people is the primary motive in the mode of expression or attitude, mental type and temperament of the ascending sign. Also, this self-consciousness is a vital feature for adapting oneself successfully to the environment. Its role is 'adjustment'. One does not want to lose sight of oneself as a unique person. To this end, through the Ascendant's traits, one needs to make an impression on others. 'Adjustment' implies making changes, and this is why the attitude and traits associated with the Ascendant are a source of particular vulnerability to stress. Relief from or avoidance of stress is achieved through coming to terms with necessary adjustments involving changes in one's relation to others and the environment, and by coping with sensitivity.

Strength and satisfaction through confidence in oneself depends considerably on the type of Ascendant and its measure of integration with the rest of the chart pattern. The potential for this is indicated by the ascending sign and planetary aspects to the rising degree of the Ascendant, especially through a planet being in conjunction with the Ascendant.

Sign on the lower meridian or IC

The sign on the IC is rarely given importance. The results of my own research suggest that the sign's traits are only subtly evident and even then only in relation to joint and interdependent interests on a one-to-one basis of the subject with another person. In other words, only in relation to the Us sector of the angles. Planets' aspects to the IC can modify the sign's traits slightly; mostly this applies to the conjunction.

Sign on the Descendant (Desc.)

The sign on the Descendant is rarely given importance. The results of my own research suggest that the sign's traits are only subtly evident and even then only in relation to the subject's need of a you-centred relationship. In other words, only in relation to the You sector of the angles. Planets' aspects to the Descendant can modify the sign's traits slightly; mostly this applies to the conjunction.

Sign on the Midheaven or MC

The sign on the MC is rarely given importance. The results of my own research suggest that the sign's traits are only subtly evident and even then only in relation to the interests and demands of society generally and the need to relate to others through business interests and the achievement of status. In other words, only in relation to the Them sector of the angles. Planets' aspects to the MC can modify the sign's traits slightly; mostly this applies to the conjunction.

Planets aspecting the four angles

The following are guidelines for interpreting each planet's aspects to the angles. Because each angle is at the centre of the SER it relates to, interpretation is in terms of the respective SER. For example, if the Moon is in conjunction with or square to the Ascendant, the interpretation will refer to the Me sector. Always remember that the Sun, Moon and each planet represent functional needs, each need being a different expression of the psyche in relation to its environment, personal growth and survival. Therefore, as an example, Mars aspecting the Descendant in the You sector will represent a different expression of the psyche to the Sun or the Moon aspecting the Descendant in the same You sector. When we interpret Janet's chart you will see how we can use these guidelines.

The interpretational value of an aspect is determined by three grades of strength or significance. The *conjunction* (♂) represents the top grade or that of most significance; *major* aspects (□ △ ♂°) and the *sextile* (✶) are of considerable significance, though not quite that of the conjunction; and the *minor* aspects (∟ ⬓) also represent expressions of significance, but are classified as the lower grade. With experience one learns how to interpret these three groups of aspects differently.

Sun aspecting the angles

Purposeful activity, particularly through:

Ascendant: + one's own efforts and choice of objectives.
(Me Sector)   − with resultant stress, especially through self-centredness and excessive demands on self.

IC: + mutual interests and shared choice of objectives
(Us Sector)   with another person.
   − with resultant stress, especially through difficulty in compromising.

Descendant: + the impact upon and challenge to oneself of
(You Sector)   another person.
   − with resultant stress, especially through difficulty in tolerating another's influence.

MC: + one's own determined contribution to the
(Them Sector)   needs and demands of society.
   − with resultant stress, especially through power-seeking, or dissatisfaction with the demands of society.

Moon aspecting the angles

Sensitive and meaningful adaptation to the environment, particularly through:

Ascendant: + the need to choose one's own environment.
(Me Sector)   − with resultant stress, especially through vulnerability, self-preoccupation, insecurity.

IC: + sharing oneself with another person,
(Us Sector)   participating in a mutual choice of environment.
   − with resultant stress, especially through possessiveness.

Descendant: + the influence and stimulation of another
(You Sector)   person.
                   − with resultant stress, especially through over-
                     defensive or submissive reactions.
MC: + conforming to the influence and demands of
(Them Sector)   society.
                   − with resultant stress, especially through
                     discontentment and anxiety.

Mercury aspecting the angles

Communication and an inquisitive involvement with the environment, particularly through:

Ascendant: + conscious and excitative projection of self.
(Me Sector)   − with resultant stress, especially through
                     restlessness and nervous exhaustion.
IC: + connective contact and co-ordination with
(Us Sector)   another person.
                   − with resultant stress, especially through
                     meddlesomeness and over-conscientiousness.
Descendant: + acquisition and analysis of knowledge of
(You Sector)   another person.
                   − with resultant stress, especially through over-
                     criticalness and nervous tension.
MC: + information exchange and acute mental and
(Them Sector)   sensory awareness to the needs and demands
                     of society.
                   − with resultant stress, especially through anxiety
                     and instability.

Venus aspecting the angles

To seek relationships and feelingly evaluate the environment, particularly through:

Ascendant: + being appreciated and being liked.

(Me Sector)	− with resultant stress, especially through self-indulgence and vanity.
IC: (US Sector)	+ co-operation with another person based on mutual sympathy and attraction.
	− with resultant stress, especially through permissiveness or emotional disappointment.
Descendant: (You Sector)	+ appreciating another person by recognizing their value to oneself.
	− with resultant stress, especially through inferiority feelings or being too perfectionist.
MC: (Them Sector)	+ behaving sociably, participating in group activities and being of value within the community.
	− with resultant stress, especially through feeling socially inadequate.

Mars aspecting the angles

Exertion and active stimulation of the environment, particularly through:

Ascendant: (Me Sector)	+ personal initiative and energetic self-assertion.
	− with resultant stress, especially through restlessness and over-impulsiveness.
IC: (Us Sector)	+ active emotional involvement with another person.
	− with resultant stress, especially through emotional conflict.
Descendant: (You Sector)	+ energetic encouragement of another person's self-expression.
	− with resultant stress, especially through impatience and quarrelsomeness.
MC: (Them Sector)	+ a competitive and adventurous involvement with society.
	− with resultant stress, especially through recklessness and aggression.

Jupiter aspecting the angles

To achieve increase and improvement, particularly through:

Ascendant: (Me Sector)	+ personal growth, maturity and making an impression.
	− with resultant stress, especially through extravagance and self-aggrandizement.
IC: (Us Sector)	+ a generous and genial relationship with another person.
	− with resultant stress, especially through exaggerated enthusiasms of oneself conflicting with another's less enthusiastic responses.
Descendant: (You Sector)	+ benefiting by another person's advantages and influence.
	− with resultant stress, especially through over-optimism or inability to accept inferiority.
MC: (Them Sector)	+ an opportunist and optimistic involvement with society.
	− with resultant stress, especially through presumptuous status-seeking or exhibitionism.

Saturn aspecting the angles

Self-control and regulation and organization of the environment, particularly through:

Ascendant: (Me Sector)	+ self-discipline and responsibility.
	− with resultant stress, especially through egotism or inhibition.
IC: (Us Sector)	+ a stable and reliable relationship with another person.
	− with resultant stress, especially through apathy and criticalness.
Descendant: (You Sector)	+ a commonsense desire to learn from the example of another person.

	−	with resultant stress, especially through inferiority feelings or being suspicious of others' motives.
MC:	+	a realistic and enduring desire to conform to the needs and demands of society.
(Them Sector)	−	with resultant stress, especially through lack of imagination and stubbornness.

Uranus aspecting the angles

Deviation from the normal and an uninhibited experience of the environment, particularly through:

Ascendant:.	+	independence and originality.
(Me Sector)	−	with resultant stress, especially through wilfulness and eccentricity.
IC:	+	an unconventional and frank relationship with another person.
(Us Sector)	−	with resultant stress, especially through contrariness and impetuosity.
Descendant:	+	seeking exciting and unusual influences and stimulation from another person.
(You Sector)	−	with resultant stress, especially through over-excitability and instability.
MC:	+	an unorthodox and original contribution to and involvement with society.
(Them Sector)	−	with resultant stress, especially through rebelliousness and irrational behaviour.

Neptune aspecting the angles

To achieve refinement, sensitivity and subtlety, particularly through:

Ascendant:	+	idealism and perfectionism.
(Me Sector)	−	with resultant stress, especially through nebulousness and self-deception.

IC: (Us Sector)	+ an idealistic and elevating relationship with another person. − with resultant stress, especially through touchiness and irrational expectations of another.
Descendant: (You Sector)	+ an inspired and impressionable reaction to another person's influence. − with resultant stress, especially through gullibility and self-denigration.
MC: (Them Sector)	+ a keenly perceptive and imaginative attitude to the needs and demands of society. − with resultant stress, especially through impracticality and escapism.

Pluto aspecting the angles

To exceed known limits and make an extraordinary impact on the environment, particularly through:

Ascendant: (Me Sector)	+ self-confidence and enthusiasm. − with resultant stress, especially through arrogance and selfishness.
IC: (Us Sector)	+ an intense and persuasive sharing of enthusiasm with another person. − with resultant stress, especially through emotional excesses.
Descendant: (Us Sector)	+ a compelling and determined effort to learn through another person. − with resultant stress, especially through obsessiveness and discontentment.
MC: (Them Sector)	+ dedication and endurance in meeting the needs and demands of society. − with resultant stress, especially through excessive obstinacy and fanaticism.

Summary of chapter

1 The theme of this chapter is that the angles of a chart represent four basic types of relationship we can form with our environment, and that the form of relationship or relationships which are likely to prove most significant in our life can be indicated in our birth chart.

2 The angles provide a vitally important dimension of uniqueness to the individual concerned and reveal features of the psyche that will tend to be very vulnerable to environmental pressures and influence. At the same time these features are particularly important for one's adaptation to the environment.

3 Each of the sectors of environmental relationships is divided into two zones, known as Distinctive Zones. A planet placed in one of these zones indicates the potential for achieving some act or expression of distinction.

4 The angles intensify and amplify the function associated with a planet aspecting them.

5 The sign on the angle at the eastern horizon (Ascendant) reveals psychological features of immense importance to the individual concerned.

CHAPTER 17

Constructing the Birth Chart

In chapter 1 I explained why this book does not deal with the calculation of a birth chart. However, I feel it may be helpful to make various comments on constructing a birth chart. My students have always been taught to enter signs, planets, figures and aspect lines in a chart methodically, and so that they are clear to read. We are, of course, working with Janet's chart, illustrated in figure 1 (page xvi).

At this point it would be helpful if you have a 'blank' chart form by you so that you can follow the instructions given in this chapter for entering Janet's chart details onto the form. At present there are no printed charts available drawn to the design as illustrated in figure 14, that is, with the very brief house cusps a uniform 30° in size and commencing from the Ascendant, according to the Equal House System. You can obtain blocks or loose quantities of chart forms from: Fowler's, 1201–3 High Road, Chadwell Heath, Romford, Essex RM6 4DH, England. They can supply two designs: either showing house cusps that extend fully to the chart centre, or showing no house cusps but instead the small 360° divisions of the complete chart circle. You can, of course, draw your own charts, similar to the design illustrated in figure 14. For this you will need a pair of compasses with a steel point at one end and a pencil at the other end, plus a ruler and pen and paper!

The birth chart's basic structure

To avoid any confusion, as we have just mentioned chart forms containing house cusps, we would repeat that we are not employ-

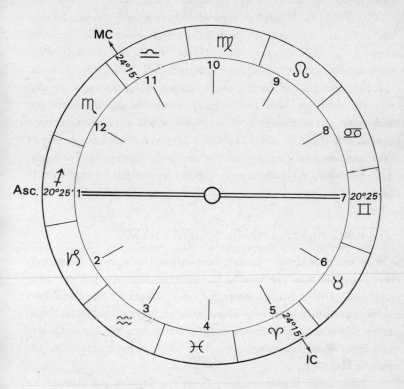

Figure 14

Basic chart framework: angles, signs and houses

ing houses in our system of personality interpretation. At the beginning of chapter 15 it was explained why house cusps happen to be shown as very brief lines in figures 1 and 14.

It would be helpful to remind ourselves of the symbolism of the chart by referring to page 52 and to figure 4 in the same chapter. In this diagram the MC–IC axis cuts through what traditionally would be houses eight and two. When you draw in the MC and IC for Janet's chart, shown in figure 14, their axis will cut through what traditionally would be the eleventh and fifth houses. The tilt of the MC–IC angle will vary with different charts. But the Asc.–Desc. axis or angle will always be shown as exactly horizontal in the chart, symbolizing the horizon at birth. The Ascendant (Asc.) is always entered on the left or eastern side of the chart.

Entering the Ascendant, signs and MC

Let us examine closely Janet's chart (shown in figure 1, page xvi) and visualize how we would have entered the Ascendant, signs and MC onto a blank chart that only contained the basic two circles, the horizontal Asc.–Desc. axis, and the abbreviated house cusps. Assuming that from Janet's birth data we have already calculated the Ascendant and MC angles, these are: Asc ♐ 20°25′; MC ♎ 24°15′.

First, enter the Ascendant. Write the degrees and minutes to the left of the horizontal line (east point of horizon) that, of course, marks the first house cusp. Write the figures boldly so that they are clear to read.

Before we enter the Sagittarian symbol (♐) we must enter the dividing lines between the signs. Remember that each sign is 30° in length and that the signs rotate in an *anti-clockwise* direction. Janet's Ascendant is 20°, which is two-thirds of the distance through the sign. Thus, two-thirds or 20° will be above the horizon and one-third below the horizon. See how this is done in figure 14. Enter the rest of the sign divisions similarly. To make a really tidy job of charting, draw these lines with a ruler (lining the ruler up with the centre of the chart). It may be useful to obtain a protractor if you are drawing your own chart-wheel. This is a draughtsman's instrument that is marked with the full circle of 360°. It would then be a simple job to mark off exactly the thirty degrees for each sign.

Now you can enter ♐ just above the 20°25′ as shown in figure 14. Enter each sign's symbol neatly midway between the sign divisions. Put an arrow, as shown in figure 14, to indicate where the MC-degree is. Estimate proportionately where this should be in a sign of 30°. Make the arrow project beyond the outer circle of the chart and write 'MC' alongside it, and the degrees and minutes as shown in figures 1 and 14.

Do the rotating signs move in the opposite direction to the planets?

You may have wondered why the numbering of the signs is in an anti-clockwise direction, whilst the planets are said to rise at the Ascendant in a clockwise direction? And not only the planets – the signs also rise in a clockwise direction, contrary to their numbered direction! This can be proven by assuming, for example, that Janet was born two hours later, at 11.25 p.m. GMT. Approximately ♑ 20° would then be on the Ascendant and ♐, Janet's Ascendant for birth at 9.25 p.m. GMT, would be fully above the horizon. 'Why then,' you might ask, 'isn't the sign sequence in a clockwise direction?'

The explanation is that in reality the planets do move through the signs in an anti-clockwise direction when plotted in a chart – this is their direct motion. This means the signs also move in the same direction, as we have shown. But because the Earth, rotating on its axis, moves at a much greater speed than the planets moving in their orbits, the planets and signs *appear* to be moving in the opposite (clockwise) direction and rising in the eastern horizon at the Ascendant. If the Earth was motionless, fixed in space, neither rotating on its axis nor orbiting the Sun, we would be able to trace the paths of the Sun, Moon and planets following an anti-clockwise arc over our heads.

Entering the planets and Moon's nodes in the chart

It is preferable, after calculating the positions of the planets' and Moon's nodes, to first list these according to the sign each occupies in the correct sign sequence, beginning with Aries (if a planet is in that sign). We will extract these from figure 1, as follows:

☊	North node:	♉	13°12'
☉	Sun:	♊	2°38'
☿	Mercury:	♊	24°46'
♅	Uranus:	♊	24°52'
♀	Venus:	♋	9°16'
♇	Pluto:	♌	12°44'
♄	Saturn:	♌	16°56'
♂	Mars:	♍	2°06'
♆	Neptune:	♎	10°26'R*
☋	South node:	♏	13°12'
☽	Moon:	♐	13°06'
♃	Jupiter:	♐	26°45'R*

* See 'retrograde motion', chapter 8, p. 72.

It would seem a simple job to enter the planets and nodes and their degrees and minutes just as they appear in figure 1, because these are already entered in this illustration. But to do this neatly and efficiently, for these to appear as in figure 1, one has to work to a method. There are a few important rules to bear in mind, as follows:

1 Each chart you erect is going to reflect the measure of your efficiency as an astrologer.

2 The planets' symbols must be drawn boldly and clearly, and must be easy to read at a glance.

3 Keep the planets' symbols upright. Don't twist the chart around as each planet is entered, otherwise some symbols

will be on their side and others upside down. This is annoyingly confusing to read. Avoid doing this by keeping the chart form upright in front of you as you enter each planet.

4 Don't enter a planet into the chart until you have listed all (as we have done for Janet). When several planets are grouped together, enter these in a methodical way so that it is clear which sign each is in. A typical instance occurs with Janet's chart (see figure 1). ☿ and ♅ are in that small 10° area at the end of ♊, whilst ♀ is in ♋ at 9°16′. If you were to enter ♀ first, it may happen that you do not allow enough space between ♀ and the Descendant for both ☿ and ♅. So . . . the latter two must be entered before ♀.

5 Always place the planets close to the rim of the chart, as shown in figure 1. The planets' degrees and minutes should be in line with the centre of the chart, rather as if they were forming an invisible spoke of a wheel. This will look efficiently done and neat, and when you come to enter aspect lines it will clearly be seen which planet a particular line is intended for.

6 Allow a reasonable space in the middle of the chart for entering aspect lines (described in chapter 18). Confusion will arise if aspect lines pass through figures or planets' symbols.

7 It is important to see clearly which sign a planet is in, especially when several planets are bunched together near the end and beginning of adjoining signs. Therefore, as you enter each planet, make a small line or dot linking it with the sign it is in, as has been done in figure 1.

You can now enter the planets in Janet's chart.

Summary of chapter

1 The aim of this chapter is to not only instruct how to enter the angles, signs and planets in a chart, but to indicate how important it is to always make a tidy and methodical job of charting. A well-presented chart reflects an efficient and conscientious mind.

2 For the moment of a given birth, the exact relationship of the ecliptic (planets' path) to the birthplace is represented by the signs relative to the angles in the birth chart.

CHAPTER 18

Aspects: Connection between Planets

We have dealt with the signs, planets and angles as chart features for interpreting psychological potential. We will now examine the derivation of the fourth interpretational feature: aspects between planets, and between planets and angles.

What is an aspect?

As we have seen in chapter 6, astronomy provides the framework for astrological interpretation. Without the calculated positions of the Sun, Moon and planets provided by astronomers, the astrologer would have no tools or equipment. 'Astronomy is a science concerned with observing, recording, accounting for and predicting the motions of the celestial bodies, and determining their physical elements.'[1] Astrology is the interpretation of this phenomena in terms of human psychology.

Because the Sun, Moon and planets are ceaselessly hurtling around the sky in their respective orbits as seen from the Earth, these bodies are continually changing position relative to one another. These changing positions provide valuable information for the astrologer, and certain of these positions are known as *aspects*.

The definition, therefore, of an aspect is the angular distance between two bodies measured along the ecliptic in celestial longitude, as viewed from the earth.

The aspects we will use

Traditionally, aspects have been classified into two types, major or minor. For interpretational purposes major aspects are considered of more significance than minor aspects and, therefore, are allotted a wider *orb*. An orb is an allowance of a certain number of degrees either side of an exact aspect. Thus, even when two planets are not forming an exact aspect, they are still said to form that aspect if the number of degrees separating them is within the limits of the orb the aspect is allowed. For example, an exact trine aspect (△) is 120°; if the distance between the two planets were 126°, the trine aspect would still apply, because the orb allowed is 8° (a trine applies between 112°–128°).

A considerable number of aspects have been devised over the centuries, each representing a number which can divide the circle of 360° into equal parts, or is itself a meaningful proportion of the circle. For instance, the 90° square aspect (□) is one-quarter of a circle, whilst the 135° sesquiquadrate (⊡) is three-eighths of a circle: the square measures one part of four equal parts, whereas the sesquiquadrate measures an unequal yet meaningful proportion of a circle.

The following are those aspects we will use in our studies:

			Orb	Aspect limits	Circle ratio
☌	0°	conjunction	8°	0°–8°	$\frac{1}{360}$
∟	45°	semi-square	4°	41°–49°	$\frac{1}{8}$
✳	60°	sextile	6°	54°–66°	$\frac{1}{6}$
□	90°	square	8°	82°–98°	$\frac{1}{4}$
△	120°	trine	8°	112°–128°	$\frac{1}{3}$
⊡	135°	sesquiquadrate	4°	131°–139°	$\frac{3}{8}$
☍	180°	opposition	8°	172°–180°	$\frac{1}{2}$

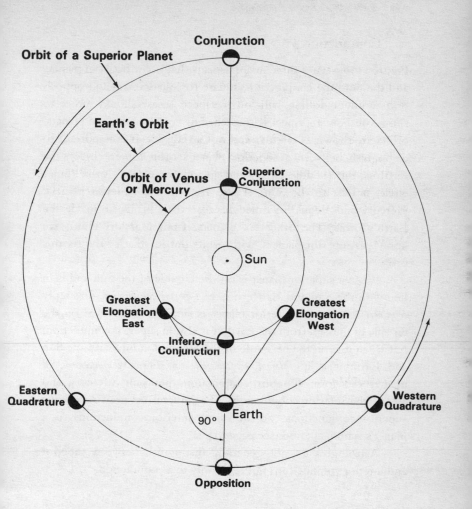

Figure 15

Planetary aspects and elongations

Conjunction

Figure 15 illustrates three major aspects that occur between planets and the Sun: the conjunction, square (or quadrature) and opposition. Without dealing with other aspects, these should suffice to show you how an aspect is formed. For convenience, the planets' orbits are shown as circular and not as ellipses. It is important to distinguish between a superior planet's orbit (outer circle), the Earth's orbit (middle circle) and an inferior planet's orbit (inner circle, nearest to the Sun). There are only two inferior planets, Mercury and Venus, so-called because their orbits lie inside the Earth's orbit. The other six planets, from Mars to Pluto, are known as superior planets, with orbits outside that of the Earth's orbit.

When a superior planet is on the far side of the Sun and is in line with the Sun and Earth, it is in *superior conjunction*, or simply *conjunction*. When an inferior planet is similarly positioned on the far side of the Sun from the Earth it is also in superior conjunction; but when it is on the near side of the Sun and in line with the Sun and Earth it is in *inferior conjunction*, or simply *conjunction*. All planets can form superior conjunction, but only Mercury and Venus the inferior conjunction. The interval between successive superior conjunctions, or successive inferior conjunctions, is a planet's synodic period (see page 61).

Astrologers do not generally distinguish between superior and inferior conjunctions but refer only to a conjunction.

Square or quadrature

The square aspect or quadrature *to the Sun* can only be formed by the superior planets and is due to their having orbits larger than the Earth's. The Moon, of course, because it orbits the Earth, also forms this aspect. When a planet's angular distance along the ecliptic from the Sun is 90° the astrologer calls this a *square* (□) aspect; whereas the astronomer speaks of the planet being at quadrature (figure 15).

Viewed from the Earth, a planet is at eastern quadrature when it is 90° eastwards of the Sun, midway between conjunction and opposition. In the Moon's case, this would be in its first quarter. When a planet is at western quadrature it is 90° westwards of the Sun at apparent midpoint between opposition and conjunction. For the Moon this would be last quarter.

Opposition

Mercury and Venus cannot be in opposition to the Sun as seen from the Earth as their orbits are inside the Earth's orbit. A superior planet (or the Moon) is in opposition to the Sun when the Sun, Earth and planet/Moon are approximately or directly in line with the Earth in the middle. A planet is also at its closest point in its orbit to the Earth (perigee) at opposition, and at its furthest point (apogee) at conjunction the Sun. This is clearly depicted in figure 15.

Elongation

Astrologers do not use the term 'elongation', nor do they observe (or attempt to interpret the possible significance of) the critical periods when Mercury or Venus reach their *greatest elongation* east or west. Maybe we are denying ourselves something richly important in terms of corresponding behaviour by the omission of research into these orbital limits.

The apparent angular distance of a planet east or west at any time from its centre of motion (the Sun) is called its elongation. Thus, when a planet is in conjunction with the Sun, elongation is nil; when it is square to the Sun, elongation is 90°; when it is in opposition to the Sun, elongation is 180°. However, the expression 'at elongation' usually means the planet's *maximum* angular distance during a particular orbit of the Sun. Where the inferior planets are concerned, Mercury can only be just over 28° from the Sun (viewed from the Earth) at *greatest elongation east or west*; Venus can only attain a distance of about 48° at these angular limits.

Finding the aspects

Happy are the astrological students and astrologers in the 1990s who now have their own personal computers and programmes for calculating birth charts. We of my generation had to struggle the hard and laborious, time-consuming way – and to think that we considered logarithms heaven-sent! Those readers who do not yet have a personal computer can receive computer-calculated charts (see chapter 1. page 3). We are not, therefore, teaching you a step-by-step method of calculating the aspects for Janet's chart, but are listing them similarly to how they would appear on a chart form, as in figure 16. If for practice you wish to calculate these aspects yourself, it would not be a wasted effort, but a useful exercise.

Aspects to the angles

As you have read in chapter 16, aspects to the angles are of immense importance for interpretation, indicating very personal psychological features. On average, the Ascendant and MC change by 1° every four minutes. This implies that the more accurate the known birth time, the more confident one can be of planetary aspects to the angles being within the required orb (the same as for planet to planet), and therefore being of value. Janet's time of birth is correct to within five minutes, and so the margin of error for the angles is roughly 1° either side of the figures shown in her chart. It is important to know, if possible, the probable margin of error for any special birth data you wish to chart and interpret.

Aspects to Moon's nodes

To my knowledge, no research has been undertaken to ascertain the probable true value of the Moon's nodes in terms of psychological traits. Yet I still think these points should be entered in a chart and studied for possible clues, especially where aspects with planets are concerned.

	☽	☿	♀	♂	♃	♄	♅	♆	♇	Asc.	IC	Desc.	MC
☉	·	·	·	□	·	·	·	△	·	·	·	·	·
☽		·	·	·	·	△	·	*	△	☌	⚼	☍	∠
☿			·	·	☍	·	☌	·	∠	☍	*	☌	△
♀				·	·	·	·	□	·	·	·	·	·
♂					△	·	·	·	·	·	·	·	·
♃						·	☍	·	⚼	☌	△	☍	*
♄							·	·	☌	△	·	*	·
♅								·	∠	☍	*	☌	△
♆									*	·	·	·	·
♇										△	·	·	·

Figure 16

Janet's aspects

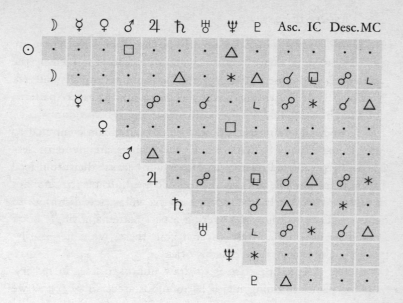

Aspect lines

In figure 1 many planets are seen to be linked by lines. These are *aspect lines*. At a glance one can see all the aspects formed by the planets, except those to the angles, which are not normally entered. The experienced astrologer will recognize various aspect patterns that can be associated with particular patterns of behaviour.

Aspect lines are usually only entered in charts computed to the Equal House System, where the planets are more or less correctly positioned relative to each other because they are placed as near as possible to the degree occupied. If planets are not positioned accurately, the aspect patterns will appear distorted. In this book we will not be covering aspect patterns; a single book could be devoted entirely to analyzing these, with, necessarily, many example charts and case histories.

The accepted practice is to draw unbroken lines in red ink linking planets forming major harmonious aspects (✳ △); as we cannot use colours in figure 1 these are shown as thin unbroken lines. Major disharmonious aspects (□ ☍) are normally drawn as black unbroken lines; in figure 1 these are shown as thick unbroken lines. Minor aspects (∟ ⊡) are shown as broken lines in black. It is not felt necessary to link planets in ☌ as this contact is obvious.

Be methodical entering aspect lines, as otherwise the result could be a confused mess, with lines perhaps running through planets' symbols and figures! The best method is to use a pair of compasses with a pencil in one end or a pair of dividers. Stick a point in the chart centre and carefully set the other point so that, at the same distance from the chart centre, a tiny 'dot' is marked against each planet. It is a simple matter to join, using a ruler, any two dots with the correct type of line where two planets are in aspect.

Summary of chapter

1 The aim of this chapter is to show what is meant by an aspect between any two celestial bodies – the Sun, Moon or a planet

– as a result of their interrelating orbits as seen from the Earth, and how these can be clearly identified in a birth chart.

2 Aspects represent or symbolize a specific connection between two bodies in terms of psychological traits and drives.

Notes

1 Jeff Mayo: *The Astrologer's Astronomical Handbook*, p. 7 (L. N. Fowler & Co., Ltd, 1982)

CHAPTER 19

Aspects: Focus on the Satisfaction of Special Needs

The search for satisfaction

The search for satisfaction goes on continuously, both consciously and unconsciously. Ceaselessly the psyche is engaged in the process of realizing or producing a satisfying stimulus, situation or experience that meets a need, or represents a goal. The attainment of a goal, the gratification of an appetite or desire, the release from suspense or removal of a doubt or difficulty produce the simple yet profound feeling-state of satisfaction. Every act of self-expression, mental or physical, throughout every day, is energized by a desire for satisfaction in some measure or form.

The experience of pleasure — a dominating force activating and controlling behaviour — is the natural reaction to the satisfaction derived from the attainment of a drive or goal.

The search for satisfaction is not confined to the human race. Animals, indeed all organisms and tissues, though not feeling pleasure as we know it, strive to do only that which is satisfying and pleasant: doing what is best for their normal existence and survival.

If man, or any organism, were incapable of experiencing the satisfaction of achievement and fulfilment, in whatever form this may be experienced, all would become extinct. Survival would be meaningless, without an incentive.

The essence of the need and desire to experience satisfaction is *self-fulfilment*: realization of potential, accomplishment, to compensate for and supply what is lacking, to make complete. In a thousand different ways each day, each one of us seeks to experience satisfaction. However small or seemingly insignificant each effort made, the single goal (which embraces the need to survive) is self-fulfilment.

How an aspect focuses on satisfying a special need

When we speak of an aspect focusing on the satisfaction of a special need, we mean that the combined functional needs of two aspecting planets reveal where that person has a special need to achieve satisfaction through self-fulfilment. We might describe the 'special need' as the unfolding of a special quality of self-expression, vital for the realization of unique potential.

Basically, an aspect tells us that because two planets happen to be x number of degrees apart, they indicate the potential for the psyche to behave in certain significant ways. An aspect stimulates or activates the functional need associated with a planet. This means that two planets' functional needs are activated. But in no way can a particular functional need lose its identity, its purpose. Planets in aspect can only interact one with the other. By 'interaction' we mean reciprocal or complementary action.

We have said that the 'special need' can be seen as the unfolding of a special quality of self-expression. But we must not forget, of course, that there is always the risk of the reverse materializing: *dissatisfaction*. As an example, an aspect between ☉ ♄ equals purposeful activity plus regulation and control. Here we are shown that purposeful activity becomes a special need and will achieve most satisfaction when such active energies are regulated and controlled. We would probably find the development of determination, discipline, practicality and caution, the execution and results of which the person should find provide satisfactory rewards. But, negatively, this could also make for criticalness, obstruction, severity and a cool and calculating attitude, resulting in a basically dissatisfying feedback from such behaviour that others will disapprove of.

We have seen that an aspect accentuates two particular functional needs and therefore indicates a significant feature of the psyche of potential stress and of the particular activity and behaviour associated with the search for satisfaction (with risk of acute dissatisfaction).

Satisfaction versus dissatisfaction

Let us briefly define these two concepts.

Satisfaction is fulfilment, pleasure, contentment. Any stimulus, situation or experience that meets a need or represents a goal. Making content by the fulfilment of a desire or the supply of a want. Gratification or pleasure at the attainment of a goal. To supply what is lacking in, make complete. To fulfil by compensating for.

A desire to achieve satisfaction can in many instances produce a self-centred person indulging in selfish activities and behaviour. One then gives free course to one's inclination, and to gratify a desire or appetite. There is an absence of restraint and discipline. It becomes a habitual indulgence of desire. This can so easily produce only dissatisfaction.

Dissatisfaction is disapproval, discontent. A feeling of being deprived of the gratification or fulfilment of a desire. Displeasure, often mixed with resentment, anger, frustration.

The concepts I have chosen after years of research, of satisfaction and dissatisfaction, fit so realistically the role of an aspect and its two-pronged potential. Two-pronged because it depends entirely upon the individual's reaction to given circumstances and his/her overall make-up whether the energies and feelings involved in the aspect stimulation achieve satisfaction, dissatisfaction or simply a null effect. The traditional concepts of favourable and unfavourable, or good and bad, can be forgotten.

Three basic groups of aspects

There are actually seven different aspects we shall use, and these are classified into three basic groups. There are other minor aspects used by some astrologers, but I have found these seven to be the most significant and quite adequate. The interpretation of the aspects that are given presently for the respective pairings of planets apply to any of the seven aspects that a particular pair of planets can form. But when interpreting for a given chart, one should consider a slight modification according to which of the three following groups an aspect belongs to.

Group 1 ♂ *Intenseness*. Strictly speaking, the ♂ is not an aspect but a similar position of two planets. For convenience we always refer to it as an aspect. The essence of this planetary relationship is that it is a convergence towards the same point. Hence we might think of it as a direct focusing of the two functions represented by the planets. This tends to create an intenseness in the search for satisfaction, which is likely to be evident in the behaviour associated with the two planets.

Group 2 ✳ △ *Confidence/over-confidence*. The 'confidence' we refer to is a feeling or thought that one expects to make very little effort for things to work out as one desires. It does not mean self-assurance. It means reliance on other people, fate, good luck and, by taking the line of least resistance, to easily achieve satisfaction. It can lead to over-confidence, passiveness, indolence, apathy. It is not at all uncommon for several trine aspects to occur in a criminal's chart.

Group 3 ∟ □ ⊡ ♂ *Uneasiness*. These aspects (especially the major □ and ♂) can be sources of powerful energy drawn on by the person concerned. One usually must make great efforts to achieve satisfaction. Inevitably there is a tendency to restlessness, uneasiness, agitation. There is risk of conflict, friction, discord. These aspects can have a separative 'influence', resulting in a breaking down of conditions and relationships to provide fresh material through one's traumatic experiences for building new and stronger structures and qualities of character.

Classification of aspect features

Functional needs: each planet's functional need or specialized activity and adaptive response to the environment. We remind ourselves of these because when two planets form an aspect, these important functions of the psyche are stimulated and provide through their interaction the potential for the satisfaction of a special need or, conversely, indicate the type of resultant dissatisfaction.

Focus on special need: significant expressions of each functional need, seen as vital motives for satisfying the need.

Outer planets: this only refers to aspects between ♃ ♄ ♅ ♆ and ♇, known as the five 'outer planets', due to their being outside the asteroid belt lying between ♂ and ♃. Because their orbital motion appears to be quite slow due to their great distance from the Earth, aspects between these planets extend (within orb) over considerable periods. Thus, potential behaviour associated with their aspects are only considered to be significant in a personal or individual sense when both planets concerned also aspect an angle of the birth chart.

Pertinent features: characteristic motives or behaviour stimulated by the two planets' interaction that greatly influence the search for satisfaction or the resultant dissatisfaction.

+ : activity and behaviour associated with the search for satisfaction. The traits in italics are particularly appropriate.

− : activity and behaviour through which dissatisfaction is likely to result. The traits in italics are particularly appropriate.

The complete aspects
☉ ☽

Functional needs: ☉ purposeful activity; ☽ adaptation.

Focus on special need: great sense of self; self-consciousness.

Pertinent features: purposeful activity and mobility contribute to a satisfying adaptation to the environment; effective adaptation contributes to a satisfying expression of purposeful activity. To be able to *choose* and *determine* one's actions; highly perceptive and sensitive to one's uniqueness and therefore given to making comparisons and looking for common ground in others; strong self-preservation instincts.

☉ ☽ + : *dedication, intensely influential, insight.* Serious, responsible, shrewd, ambitious, purposeful, hardworking, single-

minded, self-determined, self-reliant, strong-willed, strong
likes and dislikes, intense, resourceful, fiercely defends own
beliefs, tenacious, impressive, alert, individualistic, active,
forthright, enthusiastic, persuasive, powerfully protective,
intensely sensitive.

⊙ ☽ −: *possessive, self-opinionated, self-involved.* Partisan (prejudiced, unreasoning or fanatical adherence), arrogant, brusque,
hurtfully outspoken, presumptuous, supercilious (loftily superior), self-centred, over-accentuated confidence, prejudiced,
tense, habit-prone, extremely vulnerable, self-conscious,
anxiety-prone, acutely emotional.

⊙ ☿

Functional needs: ⊙ purposeful activity; ☿ communication.

Focus on special need: releasing energy purposefully; information
exchange, co-ordination and interpretation.

Pertinent features: purposeful activity involving mobility, decision-
making and intention contribute to a satisfying communication with others and translation of experience; connective
involvement with and perceptive interpretation of the environment contribute to satisfying purposeful activity. Much
nervous/mental activity; prone to make changes, to readjust.

⊙ ☿ +: *volatile, skilfully influential, versatile.* Sociable, perceptive,
articulate, inquisitive, spontaneous, flexible, witty, adroit,
manipulative, skilled debater, alert, restlessly energetic, outspoken, fluent, studious, can talk at length, mercurial.

⊙ ☿ −: *unsettled, interfering, excitable.* Highly-strung, diffusive,
unemotional, impatient, powerful in argument, indecisive,
nervous, critical, dissipate nervous energy, compulsive talker,
irritable, lacking concentration, restless.

⊙ ♀

Functional needs: ⊙ purposeful activity; ♀ evaluation.

Focus on special need: releasing energy purposefully; evaluating
and establishing relationships.

Pertinent features: purposeful activity contributes to a satisfying development of interdependent relationships; sensitively and feelingly evaluated relationships contribute to satisfaction through purposeful activity and encounters with the environment. Strong likes and dislikes; readily display need of affection; sexual attraction, desire for intimacy; must 'put a value on everything'.

☉ ♀ + : *strength of feeling, feelingly influential, appreciative.* Sociable, warm, diplomatic, charm, strong sense of values, engaging openness, pleasure-seeking, power to attract, good-humoured, gregarious, demanding appreciation, courteous, sympathetic, compromising, artistic and aesthetic expression, romantic.

☉ ♀ − : *self-indulgent, self-centred.* Perfectionist, seductive, vain, sensuous, affected, fault-finding, promiscuous, flatterer, narcissism, effeminate (male), pursuit of glamour (female).

☉ ♂

Functional needs: ☉ purposeful activity; ♂ exertion.

Focus on special need: releasing energy purposefully; stimulation and acceleration of effort.

Pertinent features: purposeful activity contributes to a satisfying mobilization and exertion of energy; stimulation and acceleration of effort contribute to satisfying purposeful activity. Active emotional release; readily aroused sex drive; primitive need for action and exertion; a restlessness − though not necessarily implying the possession of 'abundant energy'.

☉ ♂ + : *irrepressibly active, vigorously influential, impulsive.* Determination, vigour, strength, enthusiasm, drive, competitive, eager, courageous, hardworker, high pressure, seeks challenges, fighter, spontaneity, intense, initiative (pioneering, crusading, adventuresome), tireless effort, stamina, objectivity, directness, strong-willed, persuasive, self-assertive, outspoken, quickness, constantly hurrying, demonstrative.

☉ ♂ − : *restlessly/uneasily energetic, power-seeking, combative.* Excit-

able, impatient, sensual, aggressive, forceful, hasty, venturesome, risk-taking, quarrelsome, tough-minded, authoritative,
dominant, selfish, arrogant, brusque, militant, pugnacious,
fanatical, forcefully argumentative, violent, accident-prone,
foolhardy, quick-tempered, irritable, brashly assertive, truculent (ferociously aggressive, defiant, fierce), impetuous, activist, hyperactive.

⊙ ♃

Functional needs: ⊙ purposeful activity; ♃ increase.

Focus on special need: releasing energy purposefully; opportunism
and expediency.

Pertinent features: purposeful activity contributes to a satisfying
increase in benefits and improvement within oneself; opportunism and expediency contribute to satisfaction through
purposeful activity, to accomplish impressive feats or goals;
urge for recognition; desire for 'space'; enjoyment of life;
voracious appetite for self-expansive interests and activities;
to gain advantage over the environment.

⊙ ♃ + : *enthusiastic, enthusiastically influential, generous.* Opportunist,
optimistic, responsible, ambitious, purposeful, open, outspoken, conscientious, proud, resourceful, social climbing, dedicated, gregarious, showmanship, conspicuousness, confident,
self-expansive, to make an impression, unselfconscious, self-
reliant, hardworking, bighearted, competitive, explorative,
jovial, sense of humour, broadminded, idealistic, philosophical, flamboyant, exuberant.

⊙ ♃ − : *extremist, domineering, exaggerative.* Uncompromising,
dogmatic, pompous, conceited, self-indulgent, reckless, self-
opinionated, boastful, arrogant, bombastic, excessive pursuit
of pleasure, over-confident, status-symbol interests, self-
aggrandizement, power-seeking, authoritative, egotistical, presumptuous, supercilious (loftily superior), extravagant, impertinent, intemperate, dissipated, wasteful, excessive moralizing,
ostentatious, gambler, fanaticism, exhibitionism.

⊙ ♄

Functional needs: ⊙ purposeful activity; ♄ structure.

Focus on special need: releasing energy purposefully; regulation and control.

Pertinent features: purposeful activity, involving decision-making and intention, contribute to satisfaction through realistic methods of regulating and organizing the environment; self-control, planning and endurance contribute to satisfaction through purposeful activity; devotion to duty; often success achieved only through personal sacrifice and dedication; slow developer; cautiousness; inhibitions; scant regard for others' feelings.

⊙ ♄ + : *determination, severely influential, diligent*. Disciplined, realistic, serious, dedicated, endurance, persistent, perseverance, resolute, responsible, strong-willed, adamant, dutiful, cool-headed, planner, organizer, manipulation, hardworking, shrewd, careful, conscientious, precise, fortitude, firmness, single-minded, concentration, resourceful, efficient, tough-minded, consistent, ambitious, self-reliant, masculinity, self-conscious, intense, courageous, earnest, solemn, practical, reserved, conforming, scrupulous, thoughtful, security-conscious, pragmatic, materialistic.

⊙ ♄ − : *critical, oppressively influential, austere*. Stubborn, obstructive, uncompromising, dominating, authoritative, merciless, self-centred, pessimistic, arrogant, unemotional, primitive, demanding, selfish, autocratic, manipulation of others, shy, power-seeking, supercilious (loftily superior, contemptuously indifferent), unimaginative, apprehensive, cool/calculating, inhibited, blunt, lonely, aloof, self-deprecation, cold, dour, strict.

⊙ ♅

Functional needs: ⊙ purposeful activity; ♅ deviation.

Focus on special need: releasing energy purposefully; deviation from the normal.

Pertinent features: purposeful activity contributes to satisfaction through deviations from the normal; originality, independence and surprise contribute to satisfaction through purposeful activity. Sudden variations of mood; sense of the dramatic; to be different from others; relationship problems – sudden unexpected separations, break-ups; controversial; life-patterns eventful, unusual, insecure, erratic; desire for 'space'.

☉ ♅ + : *autonomous, strikingly influential, originality.* Independent, quick, unpredictable, unorthodox, freedom-loving, experimental, inquisitive, curiosity, questioning, explorative, venturesome, outspoken, spontaneity, improvisation, brisk, energetic, innovative, enthusiastic, self-reliant, strong-willed, inventive, impulsive, impromptu, novelty-stimulated activities, irrepressible, unrestrained.

☉ ♅ − : *wilful, wayward, autocratic, disruptive.* Excitable, restless, rebellious, highly-strung, impatient, changeable, intolerant, ruthless, antagonistic, divisive, accident-prone, indiscreet, insecure, irritable, unreliable, brusque, tactless, eccentric, unstable, impetuous, reckless, explosive temper, contrary, nervous tension, erratic, anarchy, perversion, fanaticism.

☉ ♆

Functional needs: ☉ purposeful activity; ♆ refinement.

Focus on special need: releasing energy purposefully; sensitivity, subtlety, and inspiration.

Pertinent features: purposeful activity contributes to satisfaction through a sensitive and subtle interpretation of the environment; inspiration and idealism contribute to satisfaction through purposeful activity. Idealistic; can live in disorder, muddle; reluctance to face problems or hard tasks 'squarely'; easily betrayed, let down; scandals; mystery; disappointments; seldom recognize own motives; relish privacy.

☉ ♆ + : *idealistic, subtly influential, subtle.* Sensitive, perfectionist, creative, ecstatic, inspiration, charm, unorthodox, easy-going, warm, devout, generous, soft-hearted, aestheticism, impressionable, intuitive, modest, deftness, affable, imaginative.

⊙ ♆ − : *dramatization, extravagant, escapist.* Sensuous, evasive, disorderly, self-deceptive, fastidious, sensationalist, irresponsible, unreliable, shy, emotionally unsettled/confused, self-deprecation, insecurity, self-centred, permissiveness, vain, misplaced self-confidence, unstable, vague, vacillating, secretive, cunning, moody, gullible, untidy, effeminacy (male), impractical.

⊙ ♇

Functional needs: ⊙ purposeful activity; ♇ transcendence.

Focus on special need: releasing energy purposefully; compulsive and extraordinary striving.

Pertinent features: purposeful activity and mobility contribute to satisfaction through outdoing others and seeking to achieve the impossible; compulsion to generate power and to be superior to others contribute to satisfaction through purposeful activity. To transform lifestyle and thinking patterns; to transcend barriers rather than fight them; crusader; finds an opponent's weakness and exploits it; driven on by a deep inner compulsion; has a feeling of being outside or above society; extraordinary reserves of vitality; powerful influence over others; breaker of rules; fascinated with power.

⊙ ♇ + : *aggressive enterprise, conspicuously influential, enigmatic.* Hard and serious worker, hard-driving, dedicated, leadership, ambitious, intense, high ideals, enthusiastic, open directness, outspoken, conspicuous, forthright, courage, drive, forceful, determined, energetic, passion, cool precision, controversial, ability to change, tenacious, vigorous, likes a challenge, self-assured, flair for publicity, pronounced opinions, self-reliance, desire to make a powerful impression, single-minded, persistent effort, dramatization, outspoken critic, unorthodox, tough, stirs things up.

⊙ ♇ − : *uncompromising, self-righteous, rebellious.* Arrogant, showmanship, blunt, exacting (severe demands on self and others), hard-hitting, combative, low estimation of performance, militant, stormy partnerships, impatient, loud, provocative, iconoclastic (a breaker or destroyer of images), tyrannical, workaholic, bombastic, autocratic, aggressive, authoritative, impatient to have control, dominating, restless, reckless, ruthless, loneliness, feels an outcast, reserved, eccentric, irreverent, relentless, obsessions, compulsions, suicidal, hyperactive.

☽ ☿

Functional needs: ☽ adaptation; ☿ communication.

Focus on special need: effective adaptation and receptiveness; information exchange, co-ordination and interpretation.

Pertinent features: effective adaptation and receptiveness contribute to a satisfying communication with others and translation of experience; connective involvement with and perceptive interpretation of the environment contribute to satisfaction through adaptation. To explain and describe things; constantly, restlessly gathering facts and information; need for periodical rest and relaxation; risk of nervous/emotional overstrain, stress or nervous breakdown.

☽ ☿ + : *adaptable, accessible, inquisitive*. Perceptive, alert, sociable, lucid, shrewd, changeable, flexible, quickly responsive, involvement, pliability, resilience, assimilative, receptive, spontaneous, lively imagination, reflective, adroit, keenly observant, talkative, attention to detail, fluent, awareness.

☽ ☿ − : *vacillating, indecisive, prying*. Restless, inconsistent, excitable, moody, highly-strung, frivolous, inco-ordination, error-prone, fluctuating, nervous, gossipy, worrisome, much nervous energy, forgetful, anxiety-prone, instability, hysterics.

☽ ♀

Functional needs: ☽ adaptation; ♀ evaluation.

Focus on special need: effective adaptation and receptiveness; evaluating and establishing relationships.

Pertinent features: effective adaptation and receptiveness contributes to a satisfying development of interdependent relationships; sensitively and feelingly evaluated relationships contribute to satisfaction through adaptation. To achieve equilibrium; critical sense of balance, rhythm, harmony; to belong to someone; to share with others; femininity; receptive, impressionable; to attach self to others; vulnerable through feelings/emotions; capacity for entering into or sharing the feelings of others; to have an accurate perception of relative values and perspective.

☽ ♀ + : *co-operative, involvement, attraction.* Deep instinctive awareness of reality, receptive, sociable feeling/emotional participation, accessible, charm, easy-going, obliging, insight, compassionate, need for security, easy to live with, strong likes/dislikes, passive, compromising, sympathetic, empathy, considerate, assimilative, accommodating, romantic, sentimental, affectionate, aesthetic taste, graceful, tender, tranquil, placid, appreciative.

☽ ♀ − : *self-conscious, submissive, fickle.* Self-indulgent, sensuous, shy, permissive, possessive, fastidious, emotional dissipation, touchy, gourmet, vanity, effeminacy (male), self-centred, enticement, passive, promiscuous, hypersensitive.

☽ ♂

Functional needs: ☽ adaptation; ♂ exertion.

Focus on special need: effective adaptation and receptiveness; stimulation and acceleration of effort.

Pertinent features: effective adaptation and receptiveness contributes to a satisfying mobilizing and exertion of effort; stimulation and acceleration of effort contribute to satisfaction through adaptation. Strong and easily aroused likes and dislikes.

☽ ♂ + : *spontaneous, open directness, persuasive.* Alert, impulsive, lively, industrious, volatile emotions, resilient, tenacious, warm, forthright, ardent, intense, enthusiastic.

☽ ♂ − : *sensuous, touchy, impetuous.* Restless, wasteful, extreme and turbulent moods, excitable, over-reaction, instability, self-indulgent, acquisitive, selfish, irritable, quick-tempered, irascible, quarrelsome, promiscuous, hyperactive, depravity.

☽ ♃

Functional needs: ☽ adaptation; ♃ increase.

Focus on special need: effective adaptation and receptiveness; opportunism and expediency.

Pertinent features: effective adaptation and receptiveness contribute to a satisfying increase in benefits and improvement within oneself; opportunism and expediency contribute to satisfaction through adaptation. To nurture and protect; to flourish − develop vigorously and luxuriantly; love of basic comforts; to make others contented; risk of emotional instability.

☽ ♃ + : *generous, caring, exuberant.* Sociable, ready sense of humour, genial, open, tolerant, excessively protective, gregarious, philosophical, devotion, charm, empathy, sympathetic, contentment, kindliness, resilient, warm, optimism, jovial, compassion, flamboyance, philanthropic, charitable, candour, strong opinions, buoyant.

☽ ♃ − : *over-reaction, instability, intemperate.* Restless, self-indulgence, exaggerated emotions, prejudiced, moody, sensuous, gourmet, exhibitionist, greedy, patronizing, careless, wanton, extravagantly generous, promiscuous.

☽ ♄

Functional needs: ☽ adaptation; ♄ structure.

Focus on special need: effective adaptation and receptiveness; regulation and control.

Pertinent features: effective adaptation and receptiveness contribute to satisfaction through realistic methods of regulating and organizing the environment; self-control, planning and endurance contribute to satisfaction through adaptation. Deep instinctive awareness to reality and to vulnerability; risk of emotional disappointments; strong or dutiful family links; rigid deep-rooted habits; dependence on rituals and tradition.

☽ ♄ + : *cautious, vigilant, security-conscious.* Defensive, protective, dutiful, tenacious, hardworking, conscientious, responsible, steadfast, patient, shrewd, concentration, realistic, reserved, acquisitive, discriminating, endurance, devoted, introspective, reflective, devout, pride, plasticity, passive, cool precision, thrifty, self-denial, disciplined, methodical, scrupulous, conforming, fortitude, restrained.

☽ ♄ − : *apprehensive, self-pitying, distrustful.* Suspicious, sense of inadequacy, emotionally vulnerable, misunderstood, obstinate, critical, hesitant, standoffish, diffident (lacking self-confidence, modest, shy), morbid sensitivity, fastidious, easily discouraged, habit-prone, 'wet blanket', indecisive, dependence on others, submissive, possessive, timid, prejudiced, self-deprecation, easily embarrassed, discontentment, self-conscious, easily offended, pessimistic, emotionally inhibited, selfish, avaricious, callous, emotionally cool, melancholy, depressive, inflexible, restrained, brooding, clannish, masochist, claustrophobia, depressive-type phobias.

☽ ♅

Functional needs: ☽ adaptation; ♅ deviation.

Focus on special need: effective adaptation and receptiveness; deviation from the normal.

Pertinent features: effective adaptation and receptiveness contribute to satisfaction through deviations from the normal; originality, independence and surprise contribute to satisfaction through adaptation. Personal magnetism; uncannily perceptive and sensitive to the environment; sudden emotional outbursts; feminist activist.

☽ ♅ + : *ingenuity, imaginative, resilience.* Inventive, versatile, impulsive, improvization, lively, controversial, unorthodox, inquisitive, alert, informal, humour, uninhibited, whimsical.

)) ♅ − : *erratic, agitated, contrary*. Restless, swift mood changes, capricious, unstable, excitable, unusual and peculiar habits, fitful, touchy, vacillation, inconstant, disruptive, eccentric, perverse, irregular, highly-strung, homosexual, impetuous.

)) ♆

Functional needs:)) adaptation; ♆ refinement.

Focus on special need: effective adaptation and receptiveness; sensitivity, subtlety and inspiration.

Pertinent features: effective adaptation and receptiveness contribute to satisfaction through a sensitive and subtle interpretation of the environment; inspiration and idealism contribute to satisfaction through adaptation. Vulnerability; disarmingly quiet and gentle; seeks 'line of least resistance'; mysticism and devotional religion; to seek enlightenment (in terms of awareness to something as yet only acutely sensed or experienced intuitively); sensibility (capacity for refined emotion; delicate sensitiveness of taste).

)) ♆ + : *acute sensitivity, empathy, easy-going*. Perceptive, impressionable, imaginative, subtle, impartiality, controversial, creative, unorthodox, psychic, romantic, enlightenment, tenderness, accessible, considerate, intuitive, anticipation (intuitive preconception), appreciative, sympathetic, idealist.

)) ♆ − : *unreliable, moody, escapist*. Inconstant, vacillating, self-deception, submissive, susceptible to feeling/emotional disturbance, morbidly sensitive, sensuous, easily embarrassed, prejudiced, vain, fastidious, restless, touchy, shy, effeminate (male), deceitful, self-deprecation, confused, superstitious, anxious, diffuse, unstable, dreamy, hypersensitive, alcohol/drug addiction.

☽ ♇

Functional needs: ☽ adaptation; ♇ transcendence.

Focus on special need: effective adaptation and receptiveness; compulsive and extraordinary striving.

Pertinent features: effective adaptation and receptiveness contribute to satisfaction through outdoing others and seeking to achieve the impossible; compulsive and extraordinary striving contribute to satisfaction through adaptation. Powerfully ruled by emotions; could be 'torn apart' by intense moods; concerned with social issues; deep-rooted, powerfully influencing habits.

☽ ♇ +: *intense, introspection, compulsion.* Determination, perseverance, flair (instinctive discernment), enigmatic, enthusiasm, spontaneity, diligence, ability to change, dedication, quiet strength, buoyant, imaginative, simplistic, vigilant, reserved, sensitive, controversial, unorthodox, strong opinions, missionary spirit, informality.

☽ ♇ −: *obstinacy, self-absorbed, brooding.* Restless, self-centred, undisciplined, overly suspicious, uncomfortable in limelight, moody, gourmet, ill-tempered, feminist activist, explosively-emotional, secretive, obsessional.

☿ ♀

Functional needs: ☿ communication; ♀ evaluation.

Focus on special need: information exchange, co-ordination and interpretation; evaluating and establishing relationships.

Pertinent features: connective involvement with and perceptive interpretation of the environment contribute to a satisfying development of interdependent relationships; sensitively and feelingly evaluated relationships contribute to satisfaction through communication with others and translation of experience. Ability to estimate persons at their exact value; ability to co-ordinate and harmonize differing features.

☿ ♀ +: *discernment, fluency, affable.* Adaptable, sociable, tactful, diplomatic, discerning appreciation, mediation, emotional involvement, sympathetic perception (apprehension), skilled debater, ease of conversation, charm, courtesy, articulate, easy-going.

☿ ♀ − : *inconsistent, meddlesome, frivolous*. Tactless, incompetent, indiscreet, indecisive, flighty, flirtatious, a 'charming liar', awkward.

☿ ♂

Functional needs: ☿ communication; ♂ exertion.

Focus on special need: information exchange, co-ordination and interpretation; stimulation and acceleration of effort.

Pertinent features: connective involvement with and perceptive interpretation of the environment contribute to a satisfying mobilizing and exertion of effort; stimulation and acceleration of effort contribute to satisfaction through communication with others and translation of experience. High pressure mental activity: ability to get straight to the point; nervously restless; insomnia.

☿ ♂ + : *agility, acumen (quick perception), incisive*. Impulsive, outspoken, alert, volatile, direct, lively, dexterity, persuasive, quick thinker, mental vigour, brisk, mercurial, quick-witted, sharp wit, readiness, communicative.

☿ ♂ − : *restless, agitation, tactless*. Nervous impatience, careless, petulant, awkwardness, impertinent, nervous excitability, forceful opinions, flighty, spiteful, compulsive talker, much nervous energy, argumentative, fault-finding, sarcastic, provocative, gossiper, quick-tempered, brusque, irritable, blunt, metal strain, nervous breakdown, hysterics.

☿ ♃

Functional needs: ☿ communication; ♃ increase.

Focus on special need: information exchange, co-ordination and interpretation; opportunism and expediency.

Pertinent features: connective involvement with and perceptive interpretation of the environment contribute to a satisfying increase in benefits and improvement within oneself; opportunism and expediency contribute to satisfaction through communication with others and translation of experience. Abundant mental energy; desire to learn and study; exaggerated mental expression.

☿ ♃ + : *broad-minded, diversification, emphatic.* Optimistic, witty, cheerful, depth of thinking, sagacious, open-minded, skilful debater, much nervous energy, versatile, discerning.

☿ ♃ − : *misjudgement, dispersive, indiscriminate.* Awkwardness, indiscreet, highly-strung, compulsive talker, gossiper, censorious, blatant (loudly obtrusive), verbose (long-winded, excessive wordiness).

☿ ♄

Functional needs: ☿ communication; ♄ structure.

Focus on special need: information exchange, co-ordination and interpretation; regulation and control.

Pertinent features: connective involvement with and perceptive interpretation of the environment contribute to satisfaction through realistic methods of regulating and organizing the environment; self-control, planning and endurance contribute to satisfaction through communication with others and translation of experience. Slow but sure learner; risk of mental inhibition, claustrophobia or depression.

☿ ♄ + : *concentration, analytical, calculative.* Tact, exactness, accuracy, deliberation, discerning, attentive, discrimination, profound, conciseness, shrewd, manipulation, rational, dispassionate, studious, articulate, pensive, contemplative, quiet, moderation, thoughtful, sagacious (mentally acute), impartiality, logical, serious, cautious, stern, cool precision, matter-of-fact, meticulous, observant.

☿ ♄ − : *tedious, fastidious, pessimistic.* Exacting, absent-minded, apprehensive, critical, narrow-minded, hesitant, over-cautious, shy, nervous, diffidence, lacking confidence, meddle-some, unemotional, restrained, cunning, stammering, melancholy, embarrassment, boring, prying, carping, obstinate, hypercritical, prejudiced, cynical, suspicious, anxiety.

☿ ⛢

Functional needs: ☿ communication; ⛢ deviation.

Focus on special need: information exchange, co-ordination and interpretation; deviation from the normal.

Pertinent features: connective involvement with and perceptive interpretation of the environment contribute to satisfaction through deviation from the normal; originality, independence and surprise contribute to satisfaction through communication with others and translation of experience. Provocative or controversial ideas; risk of mental aberrations, nervous 'spasms'.

☿ ⛢ + : *inquisitive, lucid, inventive*. Impromptu/improvisation, unorthodox, witty, independent, ingenious, quick, spontaneous, eloquent, curiosity, dramatic impact, changeable, diversity, flexible, versatile, articulate, perceptive, dexterity, skilled debater, originality, open-minded.

☿ ⛢ − : *unsettled, edgy, eccentric*. Irregular (abnormal, unsystematic), highly-strung, impulsive, excitable, impatient, restless, inconsistent, critical, irritable, nervous tension, tactless, cranky, contradictory, brusque, insolent, rebellious, perverse, activist, homosexual.

☿ ♆

Functional needs: ☿ communication; ♆ refinement.

Focus on special need: information exchange, co-ordination and interpretation; sensitivity, subtlety and inspiration.

Pertinent features: connective involvement with and perceptive interpretation of the environment contribute to satisfaction through a sensitive and subtle interpretation of the environ-

environment; inspiration and idealism contribute to satisfaction through communication with others and translation of experience. Sensitive to music and the finer points of thought-communication; easily disturbed nervous system; risk of phobias, anxieties, delusions, hallucinations.

☿ ♆ + : *discerning, imaginative, deftness.* Insight, idealism, inspiration, quiet, unorthodox, intuitive, controversial, abstruse (difficult to understand), meticulous, finely discriminative, dexterous, astute.

☿ ♆ − : *confused, absent-minded, elusive.* Capricious, unreliable, daydreamer, muddled-thinking, unco-ordinated, gullible, vague, impractical, schemer, restless, agitated, embarrassment, inconstant, uneasiness, indecisive, crafty, dishonest, deceitful, subtle cunning, escapist, panic, thin-skinned, diffusive, deceptive, hysteria.

☿ ♇

Functional needs: ☿ communication; ♇ transcendence.

Focus on special need: information exchange, co-ordination and interpretation; compulsive and extraordinary striving.

Pertinent features: connective involvement with and perceptive interpretation of the environment contribute to satisfaction through outdoing others and seeking to achieve the impossible; compulsive and extraordinary striving contribute to satisfaction through communication with others and translation of experience. Much nervous energy; risk of deep-rooted neuroses, obsessive-compulsive expression.

☿ ♇ + : *forthright, incisive, concentration.* Discerning (discriminating, insight, penetration), curiosity, enigmatic, persuasive, spontaneous, outspoken, enthusiasm, unorthodox, intense.

☿ ♇ − : *obsessive, cunning, brooding.* Mischievous, highly-strung, malicious, spiteful, intellectual arrogance, forcefully argumentative, compulsive talker, rude, prying, piercingly critical, explosive outbursts, abrupt, sarcastic, hyperactive, acute nervous tension.

♀♂

Functional needs: ♀ evaluation; ♂ exertion.

Focus on special need: evaluating and establishing relationships; stimulation and acceleration of effort.

Pertinent features: sensitively and feelingly evaluated relationships contribute to a satisfying mobilizing and exertion of effort; stimulation and acceleration of effort contribute to a satisfying development of interdependent relationships. Love of fun, amusement, good living, excitement; sexually active; emotional conflicts and stress.

♀♂ + : *demonstrative, enticement, ardour.* Warm, amorous, passionate, persuasive, devoted.

♀♂ − : *sensuous, seductive, erotic.* Permissive, fickle, self-centred, gambler, acquisitive, fractious (irritable, peevish), lustful, voluptuous (addicted to sensual pleasure), activist, feminine militancy.

♀♃

Functional needs: ♀ evaluation; ♃ increase.

Focus on special need: evaluating and establishing relationships; opportunism and expediency.

Pertinent features: sensitively and feelingly evaluated relationships contribute to a satisfying increase in benefits and improvement within oneself; opportunism and expediency contribute to a satisfying development of interdependent relationships. Pleasures and enjoyments.

♀♃ + : *depth of feeling, genial, optimistic.* Sociable, gregarious, creative, delightful humour, affable, diplomatic, conciliatory, quietly confident, ardent affections, flamboyant, generous feeling nature, exuberant.

♀♃ − : *self-opinionated, vain, self-aggrandizement.* Excessive emotion, exaggerated feelings, self-indulgent, acquisitive, capricious, licentious, affective, permissive, gourmet.

♀ ♄

Functional needs: ♀ evaluation; ♄ structure.

Focus on special need: evaluating and establishing relationships; regulation and control.

Pertinent features: sensitively and feelingly evaluated relationships contribute to satisfaction through realistic methods of regulating and organizing the environment; self-control, planning and endurance contribute to a satisfying development of interdependent relationships. Content to limit feeling/emotional expression; to cling tightly to familiar and acceptable relationships; consistent adherence to familiar habits, values and principles; affection and loving taken very seriously; conflict between duty and pleasure; social rituals.

♀ ♄ + : *discriminating, moderate, dispassionate.* Quiet, calm, compromising, loyal, consistent, supportive, serious, flair, stern values, passive, sedate, devoted, conscientious, scrupulous, trustworthy.

♀ ♄ − : *critical, possessive, austere.* Diffident, shy, rigid values, inhibited, apathetic, fastidious, emotional deprivation, unappreciated, acquisitive, unsociable, undemonstrative, reluctant, ritualistic, covetous, masochism.

♀ ♅

Functional needs: ♀ evaluation; ♅ deviation.

Focus on special need: evaluating and establishing relationships; deviation from the normal.

Pertinent features: sensitively and feelingly evaluated relationships contribute to satisfaction through deviations from the normal; originality, independence and surprise contribute to a satisfying development of interdependent relationships. Difficult to live with; seek new, novel and unorthodox relationships; short-lived but dramatic relationships; abnormal and excitable feelings; adventures in love; feminine militancy; extreme emotional tension.

♀ ♅ + : *magnetism, unusual tastes, spontaneous feeling-reactions.* Allure-ment, enchanting, unorthodox values, sexually versatile, enticement, romantic, independent, unpredictable, freedom-loving, experimental.

♀ ♅ − : *emotionally restless, eccentric tastes, perverse feelings.* Excitable, melodramatic, emotionally dissatisfied, capricious (incon-stant), promiscuity, extremely touchy, sensual, permissive, waywardness, sexual deviations, inconsistent, disruptive, activ-ist, sadism.

♀ ♆

Functional needs: ♀ evaluation; ♆ refinement.

Focus on special need: evaluating and establishing relationships; sensitivity, subtlety and inspiration.

Pertinent features: sensitively and feelingly evaluated relation-ships contribute to satisfaction through a sensitive and subtle interpretation of the environment; inspiration and idealism contribute to a satisfying development of interdependent relationships. Given to sensuous delights; childlike enjoy-ment; especially sensitive to music, harmony, rhythm, art; seek mystical-orientated stimulants; dreamy and visionary; disillusionments in love; emotional disappointments due to unrealistic expectations.

♀ ♆ + : *sympathetic, idealistic, placid.* Equanimity (composure, calmness), gentle, romantic, sentimental, courteous, aesthetic tastes, elusive charm, conscientious, easy-going, compassion-ate, tenderness, enticement, amiable, delicately sensitive, naive, refined tastes, affectionate.

♀ ♆ − : *confused feelings, vain, fastidious.* Indolent, restless idealist, weak, vulnerable through feelings, unreliable associations, self-indulgent sensuality, fickle, beguiling (win the attention of by sly means), permissive, abandonment, drug addiction, homosexuality.

♀ ♇

Functional needs: ♀ evaluation; ♇ transcendence.

Focus on special need: evaluating and establishing relationships; compulsive and extraordinary striving.

Pertinent features: sensitively and feelingly evaluated relationships contribute to satisfaction through outdoing others and seeking to achieve the impossible; compulsive and extraordinary striving contribute to a satisfying development of interdependent relationships. Deep-rooted compulsive feelings; seek deep emotional relationships, with full exposure of feelings involved; need to eliminate disturbing feelings, lest these become obsessional and neurotic; obsessional likes and dislikes, preferences and opinions; seek feeling gratification at all cost; compulsive sexual desires.

♀ ♇ +: *magnetic charm, strong likes/dislikes, impartiality.* Approachable, warmth, amorous, shrewd.

♀ ♇ −: *self-centred, explosive feelings, self-aggrandizement.* Seems aloof to strangers, self-opinionated, permissive, self-conscious, infatuated.

♂ ♃

Functional needs: ♂ exertion; ♃ increase.

Focus on special need: stimulation and acceleration of effort; opportunism and expediency.

Pertinent features: stimulation and acceleration of effort contribute to a satisfying increase in benefits and improvement within oneself; opportunism and expediency contribute to a satisfying mobilizing and exertion of effort. Voracious sexual appetite; militant crusades or causes; ability to actively enjoy life; abundant emotional energy; excessive excitability; emotional excesses.

♂ ♃ +: *boundless energy, enthusiasm, venturesome.* Emphatic, ambitious, open directness, courageous, determination, ebullient, intense, competitive, intensely persuasive, enterprising, outgoing, adventurous, audacious, philanthropist, great sense of humour, initiative, evangelistic, vigorous.

♂ ♃ – : *over-reaction, extremist, extravagant.* Forceful, boisterous, impatient, aggressively exaggerative, wasteful, intemperate, exasperating, lustful, agitator, reckless, blustering, bullying, dissipated energies, impudent, aggressive, defiant, provocative, quick-tempered, unruly, uncompromising, over-bearing, boastful, gourmet, blatant, avaricious, compulsive gambling, fanatical.

♂ ♄

Functional needs: ♂ exertion; ♄ structure.

Focus on special need: stimulation and acceleration of effort; regulation and control.

Pertinent features: stimulation and acceleration of effort contribute to satisfaction through realistic methods of regulating and organizing the environment; self-control, planning and endurance contribute to a satisfying mobilizing and exertion of effort. Controlled enthusiasm; powerful and calculating; must have own way; excessive emphasis on discipline; alternating excitement and dread of committing oneself; stop–start, hot–cold moods; accident-prone.

♂ ♄ + : *industrious, endurance, determination.* Tenacious, perseverance, fearless, ambitious, great impact, leadership, hard-worker, frank, impulsively persuasive, fighter, explicit, compelling, authoritative, strong-willed, resolute, indomitable.

♂ ♄ – : *obstinate, ruthless, arrogant.* Materialistic, power-complex, aggressive, tough-minded, rigorous (stern, severe, strict), violent, rough, blunt, harsh, cynical, selfish, callous, exacting, acrimonious (irritating bitterness), sadistic, cruel, high stress.

♂ ♅

Functional needs: ♂ exertion; ♅ deviation.

Focus on special need: stimulation and acceleration of effort; deviation from the normal.

Pertinent features: stimulation and acceleration of effort contribute to satisfaction through deviations from the normal; originality, independence and surprise contribute to a satisfying mobilizing and exertion of effort. Volcanic (capable of sudden and violently explosive activity); short-lived enthusiasms; violent aberrations of mood; sexual abnormalities.

♂ ♅ + : *enterprising, spontaneity, uninhibited*. Unorthodox, self-willed, daring, irrepressible, controversial, frank, independent, pioneering, explorative, venturesome, adventurous, quick-acting, impulsive, demonstrative, readiness, initiative, alert.

♂ ♅ − : *rebellious, reckless, disruptive*. Melodramatic (sensational), restless, unrestrained, abrupt, destructive, excitable, erratic, eccentric, provocative, impatient, tactless, abusive, irritable, edgy, militant, explosive, defiant, audacious, inconsiderate, sadistic, hysteria, instability, suicidal, activist, anarchistic, fanatical, highly-strung.

♂ ♆

Functional needs: ♂ exertion; ♆ refinement.

Focus on special need: stimulation and acceleration of effort; sensitivity, subtlety and inspiration.

Pertinent features: stimulation and acceleration of effort contribute to satisfaction through a sensitive and subtle interpretation of the environment; inspiration and idealism contribute to a satisfying mobilizing and exertion of effort. Active inspiration (rather than enthusiasm); pursuit of glamour and adventure; energetic creativity; emotionally-coloured imagination.

♂ ♆ + : *dramatization, active idealism, inspired fervour*. Flamboyance, sensitive animation, vivid imagination, excitement, crusader, evangelical passions.

♂ ♆ − : *affectation, misapplied enthusiasms, fanaticism*. Self-indulgence, exhibitionist, excitable, sensationalism, abandonment, dissipation of energy, impudence, subtle cruelty, extremist, activist, cunning, panic-prone, sensuous, drug/alcohol addiction, hypo-chondriac, hyper-emotional, homosexual, irrational fears, pho-bias, sexual fantasies, sadistic.

♂ ♇

Functional needs: ♂ exertion; ♇ transcendence.

Focus on special need: stimulation and acceleration of effort; compulsive and extraordinary striving.

Pertinent features: stimulation and acceleration of effort contribute to satisfaction through outdoing others and seeking to achieve the impossible; compulsive and extraordinary striving contribute to a satisfying mobilizing and exertion of effort. Tend to take the law into own hands; powerful and sustained efforts; volcanic (capable of sudden and violently explosive activity); power-loving; risk of emotional crises or nervous breakdown.

♂ ♇ + : *intense, hard worker, utter conviction.* Tough-minded, quick acting, hard-hitting, boundless energy, high pressure activity, outspoken, crusader, likes a challenge, ambitious, dedication, enthusiasm, fighter, determination, pioneering, trenchant (incisive), assertive, adventurous, volatile, unorthodox, venturesome.

♂ ♇ − : *arrogant, uncompromising, obsessive.* Reckless, militant, rest-less, aggressive, activist, abrasive, hurtfully outspoken, un-subtle, provocative, pugnacious, unmanageable, abusive, impatient, malicious, truculent, rebellious, ruthless, moody, explosive temper, fanatical, hyperactive, obsessive, hysteria.

♃ ♄

Functional needs: ♃ increase; ♄ structure.

Focus on special need: opportunism and expediency; regulation and control.

Outer planets: a ♃ ♄ aspect is only considered of personal significance if both planets aspect an angle of the chart.

Pertinent features: opportunism and expediency contribute to satisfaction through realistic methods of regulating and organizing the environment; self-control, planning and endurance contribute to a satisfying increase in benefits and improvement within oneself. Benefit through steady growth and hard work; broadminded planning and organization; self-expression through conformist patterns of disciplined behaviour.

♃ ♄ + : *profound, resourceful, conscientious*. Emphatic, conventional, conservative, diplomatic, responsible, shrewd, outspoken critic, hard worker, intense, impressive, protective, earnest, ambitious, self-assurance, realistic, philosophical, contemplative, manipulative, organization.

♃ ♄ − : *exacting, dogmatic, pompous*. Arrogant, autocratic, unsettled, cynical, sceptical, uncompromising, pessimistic.

♃ ♅

Functional needs: ♃ increase; ♅ deviation.

Focus on special need: opportunism and expediency; deviation from the normal.

Outer planets: a ♃ ♅ aspect is only considered of personal significance if both planets aspect an angle of the chart.

Pertinent features: Opportunism and expediency contribute to satisfaction through deviations from the normal; originality, independence and surprise contribute to a satisfying increase in benefits and improvement within oneself. Need for 'space'; progressive; strong sense of the dramatic.

♃ ♅ + : *freedom-loving, independent, open-minded*. Spontaneous, alert, outspoken, controversial, flamboyant, explorative, inquisitive, demonstrative, generous, good-humoured, enthusiastic, progressive, unorthodox, innovative, dramatization.

♃ ♅ − : *injudicious, disobedient, rebellious*. Careless, extremist, gambler, selfish, ill-disciplined, restless, fanatical, extravagant, exaggerative, impertinent, destructive, disruptive, militant, impatient, excitable, activist, religious mania.

♃ ♆

Functional needs: ♃ increase; ♆ refinement.

Focus on special need: opportunism and expediency; sensitivity, subtlety and inspiration.

Outer planets: a ♃ ♆ aspect is only considered of personal significance if both planets aspect an angle of the chart.

Pertinent features: opportunism and expediency contribute to satisfaction through a sensitive and subtle interpretation of the environment; inspiration and idealism contribute to a satisfying increase in benefits and improvement within oneself. Capable of an ecstatic form of enthusiasm; quixotic moods (striving with lofty enthusiasm for visionary ideals).

♃ ♆ + : *idealism, dramatization, spontaneous generosity*. Enthusiasm, delightful humour, charm, sympathetic, compassionate, philanthropic, altruistic, flattery, quietly confident, meditative.

♃ ♆ − : *over-confident, excessive emotion, extravagant generosity*. Careless, extravagant tastes, over-magnified imagination, dissipated, vague, indecisive, gourmet, wasteful, unreliable, self-deprecation, aimlessness, escapist, instability, hysteria, hypersensitive, drug/alcohol addiction, delusions, hallucinations, highly-strung, religious mania.

♃ ♇

Functional needs: ♃ increase; ♇ transcendence.

Focus on special need: opportunism and expediency; compulsive and extraordinary striving.

Outer planets: a ♃ ♇ aspect is only considered of personal significance if both planets aspect an angle of the chart.

Pertinent features: opportunism and expediency contribute to satisfaction through outdoing others and seeking to achieve the impossible; compulsive and extraordinary striving contribute to a satisfying increase in benefits and improvement within oneself. Determined to prove one's superiority in some way.

♃ ♇ + : *optimistic, impressive, productive.* Unflappable confidence, hard worker, dedication, fortitude, shrewd, leadership, flamboyant, abundant energy, outspoken, determined, enthusiastic, intense, ambitious in a big way, responsible, insight, self-assured, idealist, influential, generous, conspicuous.

♃ ♇ − : *egotistical, exhibitionism, ruthless.* Plutocratic (power through wealth, worship of wealth), supercilious (loftily superior), showmanship, uncompromising, self-aggrandizement, power-seeking, self-righteous, bombastic, over-ambitious, arrogant, gourmet, exaggeration, refuse to admit to personal faults.

♄ ♅

Functional needs: ♄ structure; ♅ deviation.

Focus on special need: regulation and control; deviation from the normal.

Outer planets: a ♄ ♅ aspect is only considered of personal significance if both planets aspect an angle of the chart.

Pertinent features: self-control, planning and endurance contribute to satisfaction through deviations from the normal; originality, independence and surprise contribute to satisfaction through realistic methods of regulating and organizing the environment. Practical innovation; controlled originality; research; scientific leaning; nervous tension.

♄ ♅ + : *self-willed, shrewd, impartiality.* Determination, hard-working, precise, articulate, resourceful, inventive, productive, aggressive.

♄ ♅ − : *critical, brusque, wilfully obstinate.* Selfish, uncompromising, defiant, cunning, unsubtle, sadistic.

♄ ♆

Functional needs: ♄ structure; ♆ refinement.

Focus on special need: regulation and control; sensitivity, subtlety and inspiration.

Outer planets: a ♄ ♆ aspect is only considered of personal significance if both planets aspect an angle of the chart.

Pertinent features: self-control, planning and endurance contribute to satisfaction through a sensitive and subtle interpretation of the environment; inspiration and idealism contribute to satisfaction through realistic methods of regulating and organizing the environment. Controlled inspiration and creativity; prepared to make sacrifices; ability to translate ideals into reality.

♄ ♆ + : *practical idealism, scrupulous, passive*. Introspective, perfectionist, finely discriminative, sober-minded, pensive, reflective, precise, reserved, retiring, sedate, devout, philosophical.

♄ ♆ − : *fastidious, melancholy, apprehensive*. Discontented, doubting, austere, shy, repressed, ill-judgement, moody, insecure, panics, anxiety.

♄ ♇

Functional needs: ♄ structure; ♇ transcendence.

Focus on special need: regulation and control; compulsive and extraordinary striving.

Outer planets: a ♄ ♇ aspect is only considered of personal significance if both planets aspect an angle of the chart.

Pertinent features: self-control, planning and endurance contribute to satisfaction through outdoing others and seeking to achieve the impossible; compulsive and extraordinary striving contribute to satisfaction through realistic methods of regulating and organizing the environment. In-depth study and research; dedication can be intensely serious; impatient to have control; deep-rooted depressions.

♄ ♇ + : *thorough, tenacious, tough-minded*. Dedication, endurance, immense strength, unyielding, ambitious, hardworker, persistent, courage, shrewd, hard-driving, a 'loner', industrious, manipulative, concentration, determination, penetrating, secretive, inscrutable, decisive, responsible, serious, lack of pretence, candour.

♄ ♇ — : *stubborn, autocratic, dominant*. Forceful, selfish, arrogant, merciless, authoritative, aloneness, cruel, rigorous (stern, severe, strict), standoffish, shy, uncompromising, isolation, reclusive, pugnacious, militant, muck-raking, ruthless, power-seeking, obsessive-compulsive.

♅ ♆

Functional needs: ♅ deviation; ♆ refinement.

Focus on special need: deviation from the normal; sensitivity, subtlety and inspiration.

Outer planets: a ♅ ♆ aspect is only considered of personal significance if both planets aspect an angle of the chart.

Pertinent features: originality, independence and surprise contribute to satisfaction through a sensitive and subtle interpretation of the environment; inspiration and idealism contribute to satisfaction through deviations from the normal. Desire to change conditions; unpredictable; hates inhibitions.

♅ ♆ + : *unrestrained, innovative, impressionable*. Dramatization, intuitive, controversial, foresight, unorthodox, originality, experimental, imaginative, unpredictable, inquisitive, impulsive, idealistic.

♅ ♆ — : *contrary, escapist, inconsistent*. Vacillating, moody, unreliable, touchy, unstable, excitable, restless, highly-strung, insecure, perverse, licentious, panics, cunning, hysterics, eccentric, indecisive, anxiety neuroses and phobias, nervous tension, hypersensitive, spasms.

♅ ♇

Functional needs: ♅ deviation; ♇ transcendence.

Focus on special need: deviation from the normal; compulsive and extraordinary striving.

Outer planets: a ♅ ♇ aspect is only considered of personal significance if both planets aspect an angle of the chart.

Pertinent features: originality, independence and surprise contribute to satisfaction through outdoing others and seeking to achieve the impossible; compulsive and extraordinary striving contribute to satisfaction through deviations from the normal. Do not 'stand on ceremony'; thrive on controversy and challenge; ability to see through things; seek to reform, transform, abolish; volcanic (capable of sudden and violently explosive activity).

♅ ♇ + : *to expose, revolutionary, explorative.* Dramatization, independent, loner, dedication, detached, venturesome, crusader, idealist, seeks a challenge, enthusiasm, outspoken, competitive, controversial, unorthodox, spontaneous, adventurous, progressive, innovative, curiosity, determination, reformative.

♅ ♇ − : *disruptive, rebellious, obsessive.* Extremist, restless, irritable, wilful, anarchist, impatient, excitable, fanatical, defiant, explosive temper, reckless, lawless, obstinate, gambler, divisive, impetuous, contrary, ruthless, moody, blatant, brusque, uncompromising, *enfant terrible*.

♆ ♇

Functional needs: ♆ refinement; ♇ transcendence.

Focus on special need: sensitivity, subtlety and inspiration; compulsive and extraordinary striving.

Outer planets: a ♆ ♇ aspect is only considered of personal significance if both planets aspect an angle of the chart.

Pertinent features: inspiration and idealism contribute to satisfaction through outdoing others and seeking to achieve the impossible; compulsive and extraordinary striving contribute to satisfaction through a sensitive and subtle interpretation of the environment. Powerful dramatization.

♆ ♇ + : *intensely sensitive, introspective, controversial.* Idealistic, insight, enigmatic, explorative.

♆ ♇ − : *self-indulgent, secretive, discontented.* Moody, excitable, restless, sensuous, permissive, acutely emotional, cunning, escapist, fastidious, confused, evasive, prejudiced, delusions, hallucinations, suicidal.

Summary of chapter

1 The aim of this chapter is to show that an aspect between two particular planets indicates the subject's need to experience a particular form of satisfaction; or, dependent on the subject's reaction to given circumstances, where a particular form of dissatisfaction may be experienced.

2 To experience satisfaction is a desire for self-fulfilment. It is fulfilment, pleasure, contentment. Dissatisfaction is disapproval, discontent, a feeling of being deprived of the gratification or fulfilment of a desire.

3 There are 3 basic groups of aspects:

    1 ♂   intenseness

    2 ✱ △   confidence

    3 ∟ ☐ ⊡ ♂° uneasiness

4 An aspect accentuates two particular (planets') functional needs and therefore indicates a significant feature of the psyche of potential stress, and of particular activity and behaviour associated with the search for satisfaction (with risk of acute dissatisfaction).

CHAPTER 20

Classification of Important Chart Factors

We are now ready to classify important features concerning Janet's chart. These need to be arranged systematically for quick reference, and to help one organize the interpretation of psychological patterns. We will need to refer to figure 1 (page xvi).

Aspects: focus on the satisfaction of special needs

In chapter 18, the aspects entered in the aspect grid, figure 16 (page 193) are for Janet's chart, and these are listed for you. Always make a particular note of planets linked by the ♂ ✳ □ △ and ☍, especially where they form an interesting pattern. In Janet's case we should list the following:

(♃ ♂ Asc.) ☍ (☿ ♂ ♅ ♂ Desc.)
(☽ ♂ Asc.) △ ♄ ♇, ✳ ♆
☉ □ ♂, △ ♆
♀ forming only one aspect, □ ♆

We will recall that an aspect focuses on the necessity to satisfy a special need.

Emphasis on signs occupied by Sun, Ascendant, Moon

The signs the Sun, Ascendant and Moon occupy will indicate traits that will be potentially prominent in Janet's psychological make-up. For Janet we should note:

⊙ ♊
Asc. ♐
☽ ♐

Traditionally, the sign each planet occupies is noted and interpreted, but in our system of personality interpretation we ignore these, as often the associated traits are over-emphasized in an analysis. An exception could be a cluster of three or more planets in one sign.

Polarities: attitude

In chapter 12 you learned about the division of the twelve signs into two opposing groups, each group representing a basic attitude of orientation. Here, we classify the planets according to whether each is in an odd-numbered sign (♈ ♊ ♌ ♎ ♐ ♒) implying an objective attitude, or in an even-numbered sign (♉ ♋ ♍ ♏ ♑ ♓) implying a subjective attitude. We do not necessarily classify every planet. We note ⊙ ☽ ☿ ♀ ♂, and and only note ♃ ♄ ♅ ♆ and ♇ if any of these forms a major aspect with an angle. In Janet's case there is a predominance of planets in odd-numbered signs, and only ♆ is unlisted because it does not aspect an angle. You should have found:

Odd-numbered: ⊙ ☽ ☿ ♃ ♄ ♅ ♇
Even-numbered: ♀ ♂

Quadruplicities: mental type

In chapter 12 you learned about the division of the twelve signs into three groups, each group representing a form of mental type. Here, we classify the planets according to whether each is in a Cardinal sign (♈ ♋ ♎ ♑), implying actuation; a Fixed sign (♉ ♌ ♏ ♒), implying concentration; or a Mutable sign (♊ ♍ ♐ ♓), implying dispersion. We note ⊙ ☽ ☿ ♀ and ♂, and only note ♃ ♄ ♅ ♆ and ♇ if any of these forms a major aspect with an angle. In Janet's case there is a predominance of planets in Mutable signs:

Cardinal: ♀
Fixed: ♄ ♇
Mutable: ☉ ☽ ☿ ♂ ♃ ♅

Triplicities: temperament

In chapter 12 you learned about the division of the twelve signs into four groups, each group representing a characteristic mode of temperament. Here, we classify the planets according to whether each is in a Fire sign (♈ ♌ and ♐), implying propulsion; an Earth sign (♉ ♍ and ♑), implying deliberation; an Air sign (♊ ♎ and ♒), implying interaction; or a Water sign (♋ ♏ and ♓) implying assimilation. We note ☉ ☽ ☿ ♀ and ♂, and only note ♃ ♄ ♅ ♆ and ♇ if any of these forms a major aspect with an angle. In Janet's case there is a predominance of planets in Fire and Air signs:

Fire: ☽ ♃ ♄ ♇
Earth: ♂
Air: ☉ ☿ ♅
Water: ♀

Angular planets: environmental relationships and potential distinction

In chapter 16 you learned about the angles of the birth chart representing four different sectors of environmental relationships. Even if no planet aspects a particular angle (and rarely is an angle unaspected) the environmental relationships associated with that angle will still be a sector of some activity and interest in the subject's life. But when an angle receives a major aspect from a number of planets, its associated environmental relationships will be of especial importance in the subject's life, most particularly where a ☌ and/or ☍ is concerned. If we refer to figure 16 (page 193), we will see that the Asc. (Me sector) is most prominent in Janet's case when we list those planets forming a major aspect to the angles:

Asc.   (Me sector):   ☽ ☿ ♃ ♄ ♅ ♇
IC   (Us sector):   ☿ ♃ ♅
Desc. (You sector): ☽ ☿ ♃ ♄ ♅
MC   (Them sector): ☿ ♃ ♅

In chapter 16 you also learned about the two distinctive zones around the angles of a chart. When a planet is positioned in ♂ with either of these zones, there is the potential for achieving some act or expression of distinction. In Janet's case we find:

Distinctive Zone 1: ☽
Distinctive Zone 2: ☿ ♃ ♅

This completes the entry of important features in Janet's chart. But this is only the first stage of preparing for the final interpretation of her psychological potentialities. The above listing pinpoints particularly significant features. In chapter 21 we will deal with the second stage of preparation, and you will learn the formula that will enable you to cover her chart's features in more detail; in chapter 22, the third stage, applying this formula to Janet's chart.

Summary of chapter

The theme of this chapter is the necessity of systematically classifying and listing the important features of a given chart. This is the first stage in the preparation for the chart's ultimate interpretation.

CHAPTER 21

Preparing for Interpretation (1): the Formula

The need to follow a formula

In this chapter we will learn a formula to apply not only to Janet's chart, but that can be applied to any other chart to ensure that the various factors are listed systematically and no important psychological feature is overlooked.

When you have several years' experience in interpreting charts for clients you will probably find you make fewer and fewer preparatory notes, and almost certainly you may have devised a formula of your own.

The formula you are being taught here is designed to guide the beginner-student through what may appear to be a confusing mass of chart factors. The task of selecting important features from the less important must be done systematically, hence a formula. With experience, the beginner will be able to look at a chart he or she wishes to interpret without the need to refer to this chapter.

In the next chapter we will use Janet's chart as an example application for the formula, and then explain how to use the data we have systematically listed.

Formula for the Ascendant (Asc.)

1 Enter sign on the Asc. (e.g. ♐)
2 Enter the following paragraph: 'The Me sector: a focal-point for all self-conscious expression with emphasis on a self-centred relationship with the environment; a feature particularly vulnerable to stress, and seeking a personal sense of uniqueness – of being different to anyone else.'

3 Sign's disposition (Chapter 13)
4 Sign's attitude (Chapter 13)
5 Sign's mental type (Chapter 13)
6 Sign's temperament (Chapter 13)
7 Sign's stimulus reaction (+) (Chapter 13)
8 Sign's stress reaction (−) (Chapter 13)
9 Sign's distinctive zone planets
10 List any planet's aspect to the Asc.

Formula for the Sun and Moon

1 Functional need (FN) (Chapter 11)
2 Focus on
3 ☉ or ☽ by sign. For ☉ enter: 'A predominant disposition, in terms of attitude, mental type and temperament, for directing purposeful activity.' For ☽ enter: 'A predominant disposition, in terms of attitude, mental type and temperament, for choosing successful adaptation to and equilibrium with the environment.'
4 ☉ or ☽ sign's disposition (Chapter 13)
5 ☉ or ☽ sign's attitude (Chapter 13)
6 ☉ or ☽ sign's mental type (Chapter 13)
7 ☉ or ☽ sign's temperament (Chapter 13)
8 ☉ or ☽ sign's stimulus reaction (+) (Chapter 13; ☽ also Chapter 14)
9 ☉ or ☽ sign's stress reaction (−) (Chapter 13; ☽ also Chapter 14)
10 –13 Aspects to angles (SERs) (☉ page 173, ☽ page 173). For each angle aspected, the information to be listed against points 10, 11, 12 and 13 is:

  (a) ☉ or ☽ aspect to angle
  (b) Aspect type (page 199) (e.g. for □ or ☍ you will simply note 'uneasiness'. Similarly for △ ✳ simply enter 'confidence/over-confidence'; for ∟ ⊡ enter 'uneasiness'; for ☌ enter 'intenseness, concentration'.
  (c) Enter for ☉: 'Purposeful activity, particularly through:' (page 173)

Stimulation + :

Stress − :

Enter for ☽: 'Sensitive and meaningful adaptation to the environment, particularly through:' (page 173)

Stimulation + :

Stress − :

(d) Distinctive Zone (1 or 2) (page 169)

10 ☉ or ☽–Asc. (Me Sector)

11 ☉ or ☽–IC (Us Sector)

12 ☉ or ☽–Desc. (You Sector)

13 ☉ or ☽–MC (Them Sector)

14 List ☉ or ☽ aspects to planets.

15* Deal with each ☉ or ☽ aspect in correct sequence, extracting the following information from chapter 19:

(a) Aspect with planet (e.g. ☉ □ ♂)

(b) Aspect type (page 199)

(c) Functional needs (FNs)

(d) Focus on special need

(e) Pertinent features (PFs)

(f) Stimulation (+)

(g) Stress (−)

*(Note: *all* traits given under (e), (f) and (g) need not be entered.)

Formula for each planet

1 Functional need (FN) (Chapter 11)

2 Focus on

3–6 Aspect to angles (SERs) (Chapter 16). For each angle aspected, the information to be listed against 3, 4, 5 and 6 is:

(a) Planet aspect to angle

(b) Aspect type (page 199) (see 10b above for ☉/☽ formula)

(c) Enter for each planet its relationship with the environmental sectors given in chapter 16, followed by:

Stimulation +

Stress −

        (E.g. ☿'s relationship is given as 'Communication and an inquisitive involvement with the environment, particularly through:')

   (d) Distinctive Zone (1 or 2) (page 169)

3 Planet–Asc. (Me Sector)

4 Planet–IC (Us sector)

5 Planet–Desc. (You Sector)

6 Planet–MC (Them Sector)

7 List planet's aspects to other planets.

8* Deal with each aspect in correct sequence, extracting the following information from chapter 19:

   (a) Aspect with planet (e.g. ♂ ☍ ♄)

   (b) Aspect type (page 199)

   (c) Functional needs (FNs)

   (d) Focus on special need

   (e) Pertinent features (PFs)

   (f) Stimulation (+)

   (g) Stress (−)

*(Note: *all* traits given under (e), (f) and (g) need not be entered.)

The other three angles (IC, Desc., MC)

We have already dealt with the Ascendant, and have listed the planets' aspects to these other three angles. All we need to do now is to jot down the complete list of aspects to these three angles so we can see them at a glance.

IC (Us Sector)
List planets' aspects to the IC (no need to enter other details).

Desc. (You Sector)
List planets' aspects to the Desc. (no need to enter other details).

MC (Them Sector)

List planets' aspects to the MC (no need to enter other details).

Summary of chapter

The theme of this chapter is the necessity of using a formula for methodically and systematically classifying the many and complex features in a birth chart, in preparation for the actual analysis.

CHAPTER 22

Preparing for Interpretation (2): Janet's Chart

We are now at the second stage in preparing to interpret Janet's chart, and are ready to list interpretations of the various chart factors using the formula explained in the previous chapter. Although these interpretations are already set out in this chapter, you should carefully go through each item, ensuring that you clearly understand where they have been extracted from. To do this you will need to refer to:

(a) Janet's birth chart.
(b) Chapter 11 for the planets' details.
(c) Chapter 13 for the signs' details.
(d) Chapter 14 for the Moon in signs details.
(e) Chapter 16 for the angles' and Distinctive Zones' details.
(f) Chapter 19 for the aspects' details.

The Ascendant (Asc.)

1 ♐

2 The Me Sector: a focal point for all self-conscious expression with emphasis on a self-centred relationship with the environment; a feature particularly vulnerable to stress, and seeking a personal sense of uniqueness – of being different to anyone else.

3 Disposition: to extend, be explorative. Reaching forth beyond normal limits, expanding and extending range or scope; characterized by exploration.

4 Attitude: objective; directing interest outside oneself; tending to extraversion.

5 Mental type: dispersion; changeable, flexible. Adaptable; varied and widespread interests.

6 Temperament: propulsion; eagerness. Forward and onward seeking; impatience; self-projection.

7 +: exploration, opportunism, competitiveness. Enthusiasm, adaptable, optimism, inquisitive, self-projection, sociable, frank, versatile, spontaneity.

8 −: impulsive, extremist, erratic. Impatient, extravagant, exaggerative, restless, unsubtle, moody, careless, unmethodical.

9 Distinctive Zone planets:

Zone 1: ☽ (see ☽ 10d).

Zone 2: ♃ (see ♃ 3d).

☽ ☌ Asc. (see ☽ 10).

☿ ☍ Asc. (see ☿ 3).

♃ ☌ Asc. (see ♃ 3).

♄ △ Asc. (see ♄ 3).

♆ ☍ Asc. (see ♆ 3).

♇ △ Asc. (see ♇ 3).

The Sun ☉

1 FN: purposeful activity.

2 Focus on: doing; releasing energy; purposefulness.

3 ☉ sign: a predominant disposition, in terms of attitude, mental type and temperament, for directing purposeful activity.

4 Disposition: ♊ to transmit, be volatile. Transmitting, passing on or spreading about, conveying; characterized by lightness, rapid movement, volatility.

5 Attitude: objective. Directing interest outside oneself; tending to extraversion.

6 Mental type: dispersion; changeable, flexible. Adaptable; varied and widespread interests.

7 Temperament: interaction; looseness. Elasticity; unrestrained action/feeling; desire for reciprocal activity, participation; accessibility.

8   + : flexible, communicative, inquisitive. Interactive, volatile, adaptable, versatile, gregarious.

9   − : restless, diffusive, inconsistent. Superficial, fickle, vacillating, impatient, lack of concentration, changeable.

14   ☉ □ ♂, △ ♆

15   (a) ☉ □ ♂

    (b) uneasiness.

    (c) FNs: ☉ purposeful activity; ♂ exertion.

    (d) Focus on special need: releasing energy purposefully; stimulation and acceleration of effort.

    (e) PFs: purposeful activity contributes to a satisfying mobilization and exertion of energy; stimulation and acceleration of effort contribute to satisfying purposeful activity. Active emotional release; readily aroused sex drive.

    (f) + : *irrepressibly active, vigorously influential, impulsive.* Determination, enthusiasm, competitive, hardworker, seeks challenges, spontaneity, intense, tireless effort, directness, outspoken, quickness, demonstrative.

    (g) − : *restlessly/uneasily energetic, power-seeking, combative.* Excitable, impatient, sensual, aggressive, forceful, hasty, risk-taking, quarrelsome, selfish, brusque, militant, fanatical, accident-prone, foolhardy, quick-tempered, irritable, impetuous.

16   (a) ☉ △ ♆

    (b) △ confidence/over-confidence.

    (c) FNs: ☉ purposeful activity; ♆ refinement.

    (d) Focus on special need: releasing energy purposefully; sensitivity, subtlety and inspiration.

    (e) PFs: purposeful activity contributes to satisfaction through a sensitive and subtle interpretation of the environment; inspiration and idealism contribute to satisfaction through purposeful activity. Idealistic; can live in disorder, muddle; reluctance to face problems or hard tasks 'squarely'; disappointments; seldom recognize own motives.

(f) + : *idealistic, subtly influential, subtle.* Sensitive, perfection-ist, creative, charm, unorthodox, easygoing, warm, soft-hearted, impressionable, imaginative, affable.

(g) − : *dramatization, extravagant, escapist.* Sensuous, evasive, disorderly, self-deceptive, unreliable, emotionally unsettled/confused, insecurity, vain, unstable, vacillat-ing, moody, impractical.

The Moon ☽

1 FN: adaptation.

2 Focus on: equilibrium; vulnerability, receptiveness; rhythm.

3 ☽ sign: a predominant disposition, in terms of attitude, mental type and temperament, for choosing successful adaptation to and equilibrium with the environment.

4 Disposition: ♐ (as for Asc. 3).

5 Attitude: (as for Asc. 4).

6 Mental type: (as for Asc. 5).

7 Temperament: (as for Asc. 6).

8 + : (as for Asc. 7); emotionally-charged reactions.

9 − : (as for Asc. 8); emotionally-charged reactions.

10 (a) ☽ ♂ Asc. (Me Sector).

(b) ♂ intenseness, concentration.

(c) Sensitive and meaningful adaptation to the environment, particularly through:

  + : the need to choose one's own environment.

  − : self-preoccupation, vulnerability, insecurity.

(d) Distinctive Zone 1: tendency to restlessness, risk-taking. Possible compulsive exposing of self to risk of danger, loss, hurt. May go to extremes of exertion. Could be advantageous through seizing opportunities for personal betterment and distinction.

11 (a) ☽ ⊡ IC (Us Sector).

(b) ⊡ uneasiness.

(c) Sensitive and meaningful adaptation to the environment, particularly through:

+ : sharing oneself with another person, participating in a mutual choice of environment.

− : possessiveness.

12 (a) ☽ ☍ Desc. (You Sector).

(b) ☍ uneasiness.

(c) Sensitive and meaningful adaptation to the environment, particularly through:

+ : the influence and stimulation of another person.

− : over-defensive or submissive reactions.

13 (a) ☽ ∟ MC (Them Sector).

(b) ∟ uneasiness.

(c) Sensitive and meaningful adaptation to the environment, particularly through:

+ : conforming to the influence and demands of society.

− : discontentment and anxiety.

14 ☽ △ ♄, ✶ ♆, △ ♇

15 (a) ☽ △ ♄

(b) △ confidence/over-confidence.

(c) FNs: ☽ adaptation; ♄ structure.

(d) Focus on special need: effective adaptation and receptiveness; regulation and control.

(e) PFs: effective adaptation and receptiveness contribute to satisfaction through realistic methods of regulating and organizing the environment; self-control, planning and endurance contribute to satisfaction through adaptation. Deep instinctive awareness to reality and to vulnerability; risk of emotional disappointments; strong or dutiful family links; rigid deep-rooted habits.

(f) + : *cautious, vigilant, security-conscious.* Defensive, protective, tenacious, hardworking, conscientious, patient, shrewd, concentration, realistic, acquisitive, discriminating, endurance, introspective, pride, passive, cool precision, disciplined, conforming, restrained.

(g) − : *apprehensive, self-pitying, distrustful.* Sense of inadequacy, emotionally vulnerable, obstinate, critical, hesitant, fastidious, indecisive, submissive, prejudiced, easily embarrassed, discontentment, self-conscious, selfish, emotionally cool, depressive, restrained, brooding.

16 (a) ☽ ✳ Ψ

(b) ✳ confidence/over-confidence.

(c) FNs: ☽ adaptation; Ψ refinement.

(d) Focus on special need: effective adaptation and receptiveness; sensitivity, subtlety and inspiration.

(e) PFs: effective adaptation and receptiveness contribute to satisfaction through a sensitive and subtle interpretation of the environment; inspiration and idealism contribute to satisfaction through adaptation. Vulnerability; seeks 'line of least resistance'; to seek enlightenment (in terms of awareness to something as yet only acutely sensed or experienced intuitively).

(f) + : *acute sensitivity, empathy, easygoing.* Perceptive, impressionable, imaginative, subtle, controversial, creative, unorthodox, romantic, tenderness, accessible, intuitive, sympathetic, idealistic.

(g) − : *unreliable, moody, escapist.* Vacillating, self deception, submissive, susceptible to feeling/emotional disturbance, sensuous, easily embarrassed, prejudiced, fastidious, restless, touchy, confused, anxious, unstable, alcohol/drug addiction.

17 (a) ☽ △ ♇

(b) △ confident/over-confident.

(c) FNs: ☽ adaptation; ♇ transcendence.

(d) Focus on special need: effective adaptation and receptiveness; compulsive and extraordinary striving.

(e) PFs: effective adaptation and receptiveness contribute to satisfaction through outdoing others and seeking to achieve the impossible; compulsive and extraordinary striving contribute to satisfaction through adaptation. Powerfully ruled by emotions; could be 'torn apart' by intense moods; concerned with social issues; deep-rooted, powerfully influencing habits.

(f) + : *intense, introspection, compulsion.* Determination, perseverance, enigmatic, enthusiasm, spontaneity, dedication, ability to change, quiet strength, imaginative, vigilant, reserved, controversial, strong opinions, informality.

(g) − : *obstinacy, self-absorbed, brooding.* Restless, self-centred, overly suspicious, indisciplined, moody, ill-tempered, explosively emotional, secretive, obsessional.

Mercury ☿

1 FN: communication.

2 Focus on: information exchange; co-ordination; interpretation.

3 (a) ☿ ☍ Asc. (Me Sector).

  (b) ☍ uneasiness.

  (c) Communication and an inquisitive involvement with the environment, particularly through:

    + : conscious and excitative projection of self.

    − : restlessness, nervous exhaustion.

4 (a) ☿ ✳ IC (Us Sector).

  (b) ✳ confidence/over-confidence.

  (c) Communication and an inquisitive involvement with the environment, particularly through:

    + : connective contact and co-ordination with another person.

    − : meddlesomeness and over-conscientiousness.

5 (a) ☿ ☌ Desc. (You Sector).

  (b) ☌ intenseness, concentration.

  (c) Communication and an inquisitive involvement with the environment, particularly through:

    + : acquisition and analysis of knowledge of another person.

    − : over-criticalness and nervous tension.

  (d) Distinctive Zone 2: Potential for distinctive activity. Urge to be active and self-expressive in terms of communication, with a controlled risk-taking, and likelihood of any restlessness being restrained.

6   (a) ☿ △ MC (Them Sector).

     (b) △ confidence/over-confidence.

     (c) Communication and an inquisitive involvement with the environment, particularly through:

        + : information exchange and acute mental and sensory awareness to the needs and demands of society.

        − : anxiety and instability.

7   ☿ ☌ ♃, ♂ ♅, ∟ ♇

8   (a) ☿ ☌ ♃

     (b) ☌ uneasiness.

     (c) FNs: ☿ communication; ♃ increase.

     (d) Focus on special need: information exchange, co-ordination and interpretation; opportunism and expediency.

     (e) PFs: connective involvement with and perceptive interpretation of the environment, contribute to a satisfying increase in benefits and improvement within oneself; opportunism and expediency contribute to satisfaction through communication with others and translation of experience. Abundant mental energy; exaggerated mental expression.

     (f) + : *broad-minded, diversification, emphatic.* Optimistic, witty, cheerful, open-minded, skilful debater, much nervous energy, versatile, discerning.

     (g) − : *misjudgement, dispersive, indiscriminate.* Indiscreet, highly-strung, compulsive talker, censorious, verbose.

9   (a) ☿ ☌ ♅

     (b) ☌ intenseness, concentration.

     (c) FNs: ☿ communication; ♅ deviation.

     (d) Focus on special need: information exchange, co-ordination and interpretation; deviation from the normal.

     (e) PFs: connective involvement with and perceptive interpretation of the environment contribute to satisfaction through deviation from the normal; originality, independence and surprise contribute to satisfaction through communication with others and translation of experience. Provocative or controversial ideas.

(f) + : *inquisitive, lucid, inventive.* Witty, unorthodox, independent, quick, spontaneous, curiosity, dramatic impact, changeable, diversity, flexible, perceptive, dexterity, originality, open-minded.

(g) − : *unsettled, edgy, eccentric.* Irregular, highly-strung, impulsive, excitable, impatient, restless, critical, irritable, nervous tension, tactless, brusque, rebellious, perverse.

10 (a) ☿ ∟ ♇

(b) ∟ uneasiness.

(c) FNs: ☿ communication; ♇ transcendence.

(d) Focus on special need: information exchange, co-ordination and interpretation; compulsive and extraordinary striving.

(e) PFs: connective involvement with and perceptive interpretation of the environment contribute to satisfaction through outdoing others and seeking to achieve the impossible; compulsive and extraordinary striving contribute to satisfaction through communication with others and translation of experience. Much nervous energy; risk of deep-rooted neurosis.

(f) + : *forthright, incisive, concentration.* Discerning, curiosity, enigmatic, persuasive, spontaneous, outspoken, enthusiasm, unorthodox, intense.

(g) − *obsession, cunning, brooding.* Mischievous, highly-strung, compulsive talker, piercingly critical, explosive outbursts, abrupt, acute nervous tension.

Venus ♀

1 FN: evaluation.

2 Focus on: feeling-evaluation; interdependent relationships; attraction.

7 ♀ □ ♆

8 (a) ♀ □ ♆

(b) □ uneasiness.

(c) FNs: ♀ evaluation; ♆ refinement.

(d) Focus on special need: evaluating and establishing relationships; sensitivity, subtlety and inspiration.

(e) PFs: sensitively and feelingly evaluated relationships contribute to satisfaction through a sensitive and subtle interpretation of the environment; inspiration and idealism contribute to a satisfying development of interdependent relationships. Given to sensuous delights; especially sensitive to music, harmony, rhythm, art; emotional disappointments due to unrealistic expectations.

(f) + : *sympathetic, idealistic, placid.* Equanimity (composure, calmness), romantic, sentimental, aesthetic tastes, elusive charm, conscientious, easygoing, tenderness, enticement, amiable, refined tastes, affectionate.

(g) − : *confused feelings, vain, fastidious.* Restless idealist, vulnerable through feelings, unreliable associations, self-indulgent sensuality, fickle, permissive, drug addictive.

Mars ♂

1 FN: exertion.
2 Focus on: impetus; stimulation; effort.
7 ♂ □ ☉, △ ♃
8 (a) ♂ □ ☉ (see ☉ □ ♂)
9 (a) ♂ △ ♃
  (b) △ confidence/over-confidence.
  (c) FNs: ♂ exertion; ♃ increase.
  (d) Focus on special need: stimulation and acceleration of effort; opportunism and expediency.
  (e) PFs: stimulation and acceleration of effort contribute to a satisfying increase in benefits and improvement within oneself; opportunism and expediency contribute to a satisfying mobilization and exertion of effort. Voracious sexual appetite; ability to actively enjoy life; abundant emotional energy; excessive excitability.
  (f) + *boundless energy, enthusiasm, venturesome.* Emphatic, ambitious, open directness, courageous, determination, intense,

competitive, enterprising, outgoing, adventurous, initiative, great sense of humour.

(g) − : *over-reaction, extremist, extravagant*. Forceful, boisterous, impatient, wasteful, reckless, dissipated energies,
aggressive, defiant, quick-tempered, uncompromising,
overbearing, compulsive gambling, fanatical.

Jupiter ♃

1 FN: increase.
2 Focus on: expansion; improvement; abundance.
3 (a) ♃ ♂ Asc. (Me Sector).
   (b) ♂ intenseness, concentration.
   (c) To achieve increase and improvement, particularly
       through:
       + : personal growth, maturity and making an
       impression.
       − : self-aggrandizement, extravagance.
   (d) Distinctive Zone 2: potential for distinctive activity.
       Urge to be active and self-expressive in terms of increase,
       with a controlled risk-taking and likelihood of any
       restlessness being restrained.
4 (a) ♃ △ IC (Us Sector).
   (b) △ confidence/over-confidence.
   (c) To achieve increase and improvement, particularly
       through:
       + : a generous and genial relationship with another
       person.
       − : exaggerated enthusiasm of oneself may conflict with
       another's less enthusiastic responses.
5 (a) ♃ ♂° Desc. (You Sector).
   (b) ♂° uneasiness.
   (c) To achieve increase and improvement, particularly
       through:
       + : benefiting from another person's advantages and
       influence.

−: over-optimism, inability to accept inferiority.

6 (a) ♃ ✳ MC (Them Sector).

(b) ✳ confidence/over-confidence.

(c) To achieve increase and improvement, particularly through:

+: an opportunist and optimistic involvement with society.

−: presumptuous status-seeking, exhibitionism.

7 ♃ ☌ ☿, △ ♂, ☌ ♅, ▱ ♇

8 (a) ♃ ☌ ☿ (see ☿ ☌ ♃).

9 (a) ♃ △ ♂ (see ♂ △ ♃).

10 (a) ♃ ☌ ♅

(b) ☌ uneasiness.

(c) FNs: ♃ increase; ♅ deviation.

(d) Focus on special need: opportunism and expediency; deviation from the normal.

(e) PFs: opportunism and expediency contribute to satisfaction through deviations from the normal; originality, independence and surprise contribute to a satisfying increase in benefits and improvement within oneself. Need for 'space'; strong sense of the dramatic.

(f) +: *freedom-loving, independent, open-minded*. Spontaneous, alert, outspoken, controversial, explorative, inquisitive, demonstrative, generous, good-humoured, enthusiastic, unorthodox, innovative, dramatization.

(g) −: *injudicious, disobedient, rebellious*. Careless, extremist, gambler, selfish, restless, fanatical, extravagant, exaggerative, disruptive, militant, impatient, excitable.

11 (a) ♃ ▱ ♇

(b) ▱ uneasiness.

(c) FNs: ♃ increase; ♇ transcendence.

(d) Focus on special need: opportunism and expediency; compulsive and extraordinary striving.

(e) PFs: opportunism and expediency contribute to satisfaction through outdoing others and seeking to achieve the impossible; compulsive and extraordinary striving contribute to a satisfying increase in benefits and improvement within oneself. Determined to prove one's superiority in some way.

(f) +: *optimistic, impressive, productive.* Unflappable confidence, hard worker, dedication, shrewd, flamboyant, abundant energy, intense, outspoken, determined, enthusiastic, insight, self-assured, idealistic, generous, conspicuous.

(g) − : *egotistical, exhibitionism, ruthless.* Showmanship, uncompromising, power-seeking, over-ambitious, exaggeration.

Saturn ♄

1 FN: structure.
2 Focus on: form; regulation; accuracy.
3 (a) ♄ △ Asc. (Me Sector).
   (b) △ confidence/over-confidence.
   (c) Self-control, regulation and organization of the environment, particularly through:
       + : self-discipline and responsibility.
       − : egotism, inhibition.
5 (a) ♄ ⁎ Desc. (You Sector).
   (b) ⁎ confidence/over-confidence.
   (c) Self-control, regulation and organization of the environment, particularly through:
       + : a commonsense desire to learn from the example of another person.
       − : inferiority feelings or being suspicious of others' motives.
7 ♄ △ ☽, ♂ ♇
8 ♄ △ ☽ (see ☽ △ ♄).
9 (a) ♄ ♂ ♇
   (b) ♂ intenseness, concentration.
   (c) FNs: ♄ structure; ♇ transcendence.
   (d) Focus on special need: regulation and control; compulsive and extraordinary striving.
   (e) PFs: self-control, planning and endurance contribute to

satisfaction through outdoing others and seeking to achieve the impossible; compulsive and extraordinary striving contribute to satisfaction through realistic methods of regulating and organizing the environment. In-depth study and research; dedication can be intensely serious; impatient to have control; deep-rooted depressions.

(f) + : *thorough, tenacious, tough-minded.* Dedication, endurance, unyielding, hard worker, persistent, shrewd, industrious, concentration, determination, secretive, decisive, responsible, serious, candour.

(g) − : *stubborn, autocratic, dominant.* Forceful, selfish, aloneness, rigorous, uncompromising, militant, obsessive-compulsive, power-seeking.

Uranus ♅

1 FN: deviation.
2 Focus on: originality; freedom, surprise.
3 (a) ♅ ♂ Asc. (Me Sector).
  (b) ♂ uneasiness.
  (c) Deviation from the normal and an uninhibited experience of the environment, particularly through:
    + : independence, originality.
    − : wilfulness, eccentricity.
4 (a) ♅ ✳ IC (Us Sector).
  (b) ✳ confidence/over-confidence.
  (c) Deviation from the normal and an uninhibited experience of the environment, particularly through:
    + : an unconventional and frank relationship with another person.
    − : contrariness, impetuosity.
5 (a) ♅ ♂ Desc. (You Sector).
  (b) ♂ intenseness, concentration.
  (c) Deviation from the normal and an uninhibited experience of the environment, particularly through:

+ : seeking exciting and unusual influences and stimulation from another person.

− : over-excitability, instability.

(d) Distinctive Zone 2: potential for distinctive activity. Urge to be active and self-expressive in terms of deviation from the normal, with a controlled risk-taking, and likelihood of any restlessness being restrained.

6 (a) ♅ △ MC (Them Sector).

(b) △ confidence/over-confidence.

(c) Deviation from the normal and an uninhibited experience of the environment, particularly through:

+ : an unorthodox and original contribution to and involvement with society.

− : rebelliousness, irrational behaviour.

7 ♅ ♂ ☿, ♂ ♃, ∟ ♇

8 ♅ ♂ ☿ (see ☿ ♂ ♅).

9 ♅ ♂ ♃ (see ♃ ♂ ♅).

10 (a) ♅ ∟ ♇

(b) ∟ uneasiness.

(c) FNs: ♅ deviation; ♇ transcendence.

(d) Focus on special need: deviation from the normal; compulsive and extraordinary striving.

(e) PFs: originality, independence and surprise contribute to satisfaction through outdoing others and seeking to achieve the impossible; compulsive and extraordinary striving contribute to satisfaction through deviations from the normal. Do not 'stand on ceremony'; thrive on controversy and challenge; ability to see through things; seek to reform, transform, abolish.

(f) + : *to expose, revolutionary, explorative.* Dramatization, independent, dedication, detached, venturesome, idealist, seeks a challenge, enthusiasm, outspoken, competitive, controversial, unorthodox, spontaneous, adventurous, innovative, curiosity, determination.

(g) − : *disruptive, rebellious, obsessive.* Extremist, restless, irritable, wilful, impatient, excitable, defiant, explosive, temper, reckless, obstinate, gambler, contrary, moody, brusque, uncompromising.

Neptune ♆

1 FN: refinement.
2 Focus on: sensitivity; subtlety; idealism.
7 ♆ △ ☉, ⚹ ☽, □ ♀, ⚹ ♇
8 (a) ♆ △ ☉ (see ☉ △ ♆).
9 (a) ♆ ⚹ ☽ (see ☽ ⚹ ♆).
10 (a) ♆ □ ♀ (see ♀ □ ♆).
11 (a) ♆ ⚹ ♇ (ignore, as ♆ does not aspect an angle).

Pluto ♇

1 FN: transcendence.
2 Focus on: exceeding limits; compulsion; power.
3 (a) ♇ △ Asc. (Me Sector).
   (b) △ confidence/over-confidence.
   (c) To exceed known limits and make an extraordinary impact on the environment, particularly through:
      + : self-confidence, enthusiasm.
      − : arrogance, selfishness.
7 ♇ △ ☽, ∟ ☿, ⌷ ♃, ♂ ♄, ∟ ♅, ⚹ ♆
8 ♇ △ ☽ (see ☽ △ ♇).
9 ♇ ∟ ☿ (see ☿ ∟ ♇).
10 ♇ ⌷ ♃ (see ♃ ⌷ ♇).
11 ♇ ♂ ♄ (see ♄ ♂ ♇).
12 ♇ ∟ ♅ (see ♅ ∟ ♇).
13 ♇ ⚹ ♆ (ignore, as ♆ does not aspect an angle).

IC (Us Sector)

Aspects: ☽ ⌷, ☿ ⚹, ♃ △, ♅ ⚹

Desc. (You Sector)

Aspects: ☽ ☍, ☿ ☌, ♃ ☍, ♄ ✶, ♅ ☌

MC (Them Sector)

Aspects: ☽ ∟, ☿ △, ♃ ✶, ♅ △

You now have a methodical listing of the complex features that comprise Janet's personality. How do we assess which of these are likely to be most evident in her behaviour and her responses to other people? To help us to ascertain the potentially most salient features, we must carefully take a few preliminary steps, and this will be done in chapter 24, prior to the final analysis in chapter 25. But first, in the next chapter, we will learn about the ethics and discipline of counselling others in the role of an astrological-consultant.

Summary of chapter

The aim of this chapter is to show how one can classify brief interpretations of all the features in Janet's chart that need to be studied before compiling the final analysis of her potentialities.

CHAPTER 23

Counselling and Professional Ethics

Counselling is to help and to guide

Much is written about counselling procedures for those working
in the fields of psychology, psychiatry and social welfare. Basically,
the ethics and guidelines these workers are instructed to follow
are the same as those practised by the trained and dedicated
astrological-consultant.

The astrologer has more than a 'head start' on other counsellors in the understanding of a subject's psychological make-up
because he has the subject's birth chart. Even in advance of the
consultation, he possesses a unique source of information about
the subject's potentialities, limitations, type of personality and
motivation. This, of course, is particularly valuable because one of
the basic needs of any client, whatever problem they may seek
advice on, is to increase their self-understanding.

Books on counselling may make it seem that there are
complicated procedures to be learned for the counsellor–client
relationship to be successful. But the essence of counselling is
really quite simple to understand, even if it is not exactly simple to
put into practice.

The essence of the counselling role of the astrological-consultant is similar in aim to that of any other counsellor in the
psychiatric or social welfare professions: to help and to guide
those who seek his services.

The guidelines given in this chapter stem from this basic aim.
Ultimately, if you have clients who consult you, you may develop
your own style of giving help and enlightenment in addition to
following the basic advice given here. Any constructive and
sympathetic approach to help clients resolve their problems will
be a move in the right direction.

For convenience, the astrologer is referred to in this chapter in the masculine gender (i.e. 'he'), and the client in the feminine gender (i.e. 'she').

Professional ethics

Whether you ultimately qualify to practise astrology as a part-time or full-time profession or just apply your knowledge as a hobby, whenever the analysis of other persons' charts is undertaken, there is a professional code of ethics to be strictly adhered to:

Confidential information: Much confidential information about herself will be imparted in trust to the astrologer by the client, apart from his having information revealed by her chart. The trained astrologer will disclose nothing about his client's identity or her chart to other persons without her consent. If her case were considered suitable for research purposes or for reference in an article or book, her identity would remain anonymous.

Negative or fatalistic interpretations: You should not see fearful disasters or severe psychological illnesses in every □ or ♂ aspect. Never, never try to predict anyone's death.

Tactfulness is essential, especially in a written analysis.

Never moralize.

To establish confidence and rapport

Effective counselling demands a good personal relationship, a caring relationship. Thus, in a consultation it is very important that the astrologer and his client establish a rapport. A good counsellor quickly achieves this by winning the client's confidence, by making her feel at ease. This way the astrologer secures her co-operation, so that together they may seek to understand her problems and to endeavour to resolve them. It is essential that the client feels fully involved in the discussion and investigation of her behaviour patterns and personality.

It is important for you to listen to the client, as well as for her to see that you want to hear what she wishes to tell you. Counselling has sometimes been defined as 'creative listening'. Often a client needs just to tell someone who will be sympathetic about her problems or anxieties.

Here again one can see how the astrological counsellor has a unique advantage over the non-astrological counsellor because, through the birth chart, he will be able to detect when the client is 'assuming a pose', how prone she might be to covering up her true feelings and nature, and any tendency to neuroticism and instability. Even before he has met the client in the flesh the astrologer will have a fair picture of the type of person he will be talking to and will have planned the best way to encourage her to relax and be her natural self.

When the contact is solely by correspondence there is no lessening of the need for the astrologer to quickly establish confidence and rapport. From the birth chart the trained astrologer will know the type of person he is writing to and his manner of writing will be adjusted accordingly. This will also depend upon the age and status of the client. An Aries teenager will be written to in a different manner to an Aries fifty-year-old, just as an Aries subject will be written to in a different manner to a Virgoan subject. The freshly launched and newly-qualified astrologer cannot expect to achieve outstanding success in this respect right away. But those who are dedicated and who have the right potential for counselling will always conscientiously do their best and this will naturally lead to success more quickly than average.

Counselling by correspondence

The ideal contact is, of course, that of the client consulting the astrologer in person. However, the astrologer who is widely and internationally known may actually meet only a small percentage of his clients personally, due to their living abroad or at inconvenient distances in his own country. All help and guidance for these distant clients is therefore given through a typed analysis and, occasionally, on the telephone. The utmost tact is needed to ensure that nothing in the analysis could offend, disturb or be misunderstood. When the client is not sitting opposite and is only represented by her birth chart and a handwritten letter, it could be all too easy for the inexperienced astrologer to present an impersonal, clinical type of analysis.

As has already been said, when the contact is solely by correspondence there is no lessening of the need for the astrologer to quickly establish confidence and rapport between the client and himself.

When giving advice and guidance by correspondence, the astrologer should always endeavour to put himself in the client's place by reading back over what has been typed as if he were the client. This way it is generally easy to note any passage that may not be clearly understood, or that does not fully convey what was intended to be said.

The client's role

We have seen that the counsellor must quickly establish confidence and rapport with the client to secure co-operation.

It is also vitally important that the client is encouraged to play a major role in resolving her problem, especially where this is of a psychological nature. Where decisions are to be taken for immediate or future action in her own interest, such decisions can only be taken by the client. The astrologer's role is that of guide and counsellor. The client, alone, decides on her subsequent course of action.

Of course, the client who has a personality problem cannot make fundamental changes in her behaviour merely by being told to do so. Likewise, if the client's material problem or personality problem stems largely from aggravating and disharmonious environmental conditions, she cannot resolve these simply by manipulating her environment or making fundamental changes (for example, moving home and changing employment – although in certain instances these are partial remedies) because the astrologer has told her to do so. She may well find that whatever new environment she moves to, the problem will be much the same – unless she has begun to resolve her problems through a deeper understanding and recognition of her psychological potential and limitations.

Occasionally it is clear that a client is determined to reveal as little as possible about herself. She conceals her reasons for contacting you. You may have to point out to her that she would not conceal information from her doctor if she wished him to give her the most accurate diagnosis of her condition. It is helpful to know what she has done with the potential shown in her chart, whether she has been working against major drives and so stemming or dissipating energies.

Consultation procedure

It is generally agreed that most counselling sessions follow a sequence of five stages, because in almost every case the client has consulted the astrologer with a particular problem or a decision that needs to be taken. These stages are:

1 To establish rapport: To put the client at ease, gain her confidence, let her see that she will be given space to express herself and that you are interested in her as an individual. She should be encouraged to speak about herself and gradually led into the next stage . . .

2 Her problem: At this point she does most of the talking and you do the listening, and at the same time you are quietly making notes with reference to her chart. 'Tick' any notes you had previously made about her which are confirmed as she is talking, and show these to her at some apt point. Sometimes what the client thinks is her problem is really masking a deeper issue that – perhaps subconsciously – cannot yet be faced.

3 Discussing the problem: This is not yet the point where you offer possible solutions to the problem or advise her how

best she might cope with or learn to live with it. Together you want to see the problem clearly, every detail of it. You may need to ask a lot of questions, sometimes with reference to her chart.

4   Finding solutions: She should be given first chance to suggest possible solutions to her problem. You will then offer your own suggestions, always bearing in mind that *she* must make the final decision and choice of action. This is now the time for the client and yourself to *explore* together her chart for a deeper understanding of her personality in relation to her problem/s, and to assess the options open to her for improving conditions and coming to terms with her real self. It is probable that you will need to encourage her to make changes to her present lifestyle.

5   Summarizing the discussions: This may be the most difficult part of the interview, dependent on the nature or severity of the problem. Your aim must be to give the client (and yourself) a clear picture of what has been discussed, of her potential (shown in her chart) for dealing with the problem, and of the course of action she has decided on – even if it was your suggestion. This must be presented clearly and concisely to her before there is any risk of the conversation drifting into mere chatter. If all has gone well the client will go away with the encouraging knowledge that there is a warm and caring person she can come back to at any time to discuss the existing problem further or to bring fresh problems to. And much of the encouragement she feels may be the result of the excitement that springs from the fact that her own birth chart can predict the probable best solution to her problem. This can be a very moving experience for someone who has never consulted an astrologer before.

Finally, after the client has left, make any further notes for future reference whilst things are fresh in your mind.

Vital points to remember

The astrologer must have a genuine interest in people.

The astrologer must see the client's situation objectively, but must not forget that the individual personally concerned with a problem is likely to be biased and probably emotionally so, and her statements are influenced largely by an inhibited subjective viewpoint.

From the information given by the client and from her behaviour, the astrologer must carefully assess how well she is expressing various major chart features, and where her potential may be as yet virtually 'untapped', due to inhibition or unawareness of these innate qualities that could be beneficially developed. Bear in mind therefore that, apart from specific problems she wishes you to help her resolve, you are aiming to help her realize her potential in important areas of her life as suggested by her chart. These areas are personal relationships, work, creative/active self-expression and recognizing a sense of meaning to life.

Equally, the astrologer must be frank in pointing out probable limitations shown in the client's chart. Advise her, for instance, to set goals for herself that are reasonably attainable and according to indications in her chart.

Realize your own limitations. For example, if a client wishes advice on business matters beyond just an explanation of the potentially favourable or difficult astrological trends she can adjust her plans to, and you know that you have an inadequate understanding of the intricacies of business and finance, be frank in this respect.

The age-group and status of the client must always be kept in mind.

Two-way experience. Remember that each counselling session is a new experience in relationships for both yourself and the client. It will make demands on you, and this is exactly what it should do if you are a dedicated professional astrologer who is conscious of learning with each fresh chart and client encountered. It is a shared process of educational activity.

Astrological jargon. Unless the client is a keen student of astrology and is interested to know which chart features relate to herself, you should avoid wherever possible including astrological factors (planets, signs, aspects, angles) in your conversation or typed analysis. These could only tend to confuse those unfamiliar with these technical terms.

Stressmanship

In chapter 5 we dealt with stress as a potential threat or challenge. Stress was seen as a principal determinant of behaviour, since stress is the way we feel about an environmental stimulus and the way we react to its happening to us.

Our method of interpreting astrological factors in individual charts focuses particularly on the individual's manner of coping with and utilizing stress.

It is important that the astrologer helps his client to understand the stresses in her life and suggests ways that she can better cope with them. She should be encouraged to learn to use those stresses that provide her with a challenge, a source of energy and a possible creative or constructive outlet.

In recent years methods of coping with stress have come under the general identification of *stressmanship*. The astrological-consultant should make himself familiar with everything that stressmanship offers as pointers to living more healthily and happily.

Here, briefly, are some observations of stressmanship. It is:
knowing how to control stress;
identifying stress; knowing why one has it and what to do about it;
coping with the environment;

believing in one's sense of control over stress;

being prepared to restructure one's lifestyle;

goal-setting; visualizing as clearly as possible a desired goal;

confronting one's problems directly;

standing up for one's rights without being aggressive;

clearly communicating to others one's needs;

learning to say what is on one's mind instead of suppressing it, without being aggressive or offensive;

developing more flexible and less rigid behaviour patterns;

to be able to choose not to get upset and relax instead;

relaxing into humour and laughter when one could easily get uptight;

the ability to let off steam or relieve tension occasionally, without hurting or offending others;

unwinding in a variety of ways;

recognizing one's sensible limit of working hours in a day;

practising conscious techniques to reduce unnecessary worrying;

avoiding obvious pressures, such as taking on too many commitments;

learning not to worry about past failures and embarrassments;

learning not to take on another's problems when they are another's responsibility;

developing contentment and meaningful energy outlets and friendships;

the ability to listen and relate to others;

sharing one's feelings with those one can trust;

developing increased sensuality and loving sensitivity in lovemaking;

learning about deep relaxation techniques;

learning and regularly practising a meditation technique suited to oneself;

learning deep breathing techniques;

cultivating a relaxing hobby;

becoming more attuned to one's body and any warning nudges;

avoiding junk food, overeating, excessive alcohol intake and smoking;

putting into practice as wide an understanding as possible of
    wholefoods and vitamin/mineral supplements;
developing time and space in which to be utterly oneself;
discovering new depths in oneself.

The above provides you with a fund of guidelines for drawing
on at appropriate moments during a counselling session or for
inclusion in a typed analysis.

Extreme psychological disorders

These are not normally listed when preparing notes for a client's
chart analysis or prior to a consultation, unless there is reason to
suspect a tendency to a psychological disorder. Sometimes a client
openly admits to rather severe neurotic tendencies, and in this case
a sympathetic discussion of relevant chart features can be of
immense help. Otherwise, great care must be observed not to
disclose to the client a suspected psychological illness, but guidance
can be given in regard to chart features you associate with the
illness or disorder.

For instance, as an oversimplified example, during a consultation, a client with ♂ □ ♃, ☉ ♂ ♂ talks about herself in such a
way that you suspect she has psychopathic tendencies (antisocial,
amoral, irresponsible). You will endeavour to encourage her to
apply and harness her fund of energies to constructive outlets that
demand unselfish enthusiasm and enterprise.

I have usually found that persons with obsessive and compulsive afflictions will not be offended or embarrassed if their
anxiety-based disorder is openly discussed and help offered.

Diet and relaxation

You should read and learn as much as you can about wholefoods
and alternative or holistic medicines and therapies. It was in my
early twenties, in 1946, that I first became interested in organic
gardening, wholefoods and alternative medicines. We who then
advocated these natural methods of building health in the soil and

in humans were labelled 'cranks' and 'muck and magic mystics'. Today, in the 1990s, there is a pleasing swing towards healthier eating habits, vitamin and mineral supplements, the avoidance of additives in foods, exercise, and various forms of relaxation and meditation as therapies to combat stress. Few can be unaware of this trend, and every astrological-counsellor should be conversant with the holistic approach to better health and the reduction of stress.

In very many cases I have personally found that recommending a change from 'junk foods' to a more balanced and wholesome diet, avoiding excess salt and sugar, stopping smoking and learning how to relax, brought about a remarkable improvement in a client's feeling of well-being and in their ability to cope with stressful situations. This taught me years ago that astrological counselling can achieve even greater benefits if employed hand in hand with a sensible and positive attitude towards attaining a healthy and wholesome lifestyle. The very best astrological counselling may achieve no lasting improvement in a person's ability to cope with day to day problems and their own psychological discords if their general lifestyle and eating habits are unhealthy and deficient in vital nourishment – both material and spiritual.

Summary of chapter

The theme of this chapter is the necessity of the astrological-consultant following certain procedures during a consultation to ensure that the utmost benefit is gained by his client, and for the astrologer to be satisfied with his own efforts. Whether the client is seen personally or receives a typed analysis, the astrologer adheres strictly to professional ethics in the presentation of his service as a counsellor.

CHAPTER 24

The Analysis of Janet's Chart: Preliminary Steps

The chart pattern only shows 'potential'

Compiling an analysis is a complex business if the end product is to be an accurate interpretation of the subject's unique patterns of psychological features. We have said that life means activity, and that the human organism is a dynamic system of complex energy exchanges motivating continual changes, inspired and directed by that spark of divine creativity at the very centre and nucleus of each of the billions of cells in a human body. The framework of the body is always changing: the pattern alone remains.

However fixed some of us may tend to be in our behaviour and habits, we each express the dynamic nature of our being through our complex emotional, mental and nervous energy exchanges, indicating the impossibility of our psyche ever becoming static and immune to change or development. Hence, the birth chart indicates the *potentialities*, and it is up to the individual concerned to become aware of this potential. The birth chart shows the basic psychological pattern that provides the flexible, adaptable, dynamic framework of potentialities.

When interpreting a birth chart, always bear in mind that the chart can only indicate potential behaviour. It is for the individual to choose how he or she develops this potential. Until he meets a client, the astrologer cannot be sure how much a particular trait or group of traits may have been developed and are being beneficially applied.

However, in writing the final analysis (and the brief preliminary assessments in this present chapter) we prefer to assess many of the features of the personality as though they have been developed and are evident in the subject's behaviour. It is suggested that you do likewise in any future analyses you undertake. The following note should therefore be included in the foreword to an analysis:

The use of the word 'will' may appear to imply habitual occurrence or traits that are clearly evident in your behaviour. But it may be that this particular behaviour is not yet very evident, or perhaps not at all. For example, if it were said, 'You will be adventurous and enterprising . . .' our use of the word 'will' is intended to emphasize *potential* traits likely to be of benefit to you if developed. You should not straightaway reject these as an exaggeration or even impossible.

What should we look for in a birth chart?

Some of the salient features we will probably find ourselves looking for in a chart will not necessarily be those the client would wish to know most about. A chart can also reveal previously unrealized and perhaps very subtle or latent (potential) features which should be of immense benefit for the client to know, and to recognize how they have influenced their behaviour at times and might prove productive in the future.

Presentation of significant features depends on the age, sex and status of the client, and whether they have consulted you for guidance during a crisis period involving business interests, emotional relationships or some other major activity. Particular requests concerning the client's interests, plans or certain psychological problems conveyed to the astrologer during an initial one-to-one consultation or by letter should be given special attention.

We have seen that a fundamental and powerful need in man is for perfection and wholeness. Whatever we choose to do with our lives and talents, whatever goals we set ourselves, even if in most of us this need is never consciously thought about, we hunger for perfection and wholeness. Denial of this need is a root cause of inner discord, anxiety, frustration, dissatisfaction. We experience the disturbing and harmful effects of stress. There is disequilibrium within the psyche.

Stress is a principal determinant of behaviour, since stress is the way we feel about an environmental stimulus and the way we react to its happening to us. Hence the astrologer's need to locate those features within a client's personality structure most likely to be associated with stress. Here the client is potentially vulnerable to stress.

To achieve equilibrium, harmony and stability, both within oneself and in one's relationships with others, one must learn to adapt to the constantly changing and complicated environment (which includes other people). Once we discover how to manage and use stress to advantage for ourself and for others, the constructive use of stress can be seen as a challenge and not a threat.

Reference to the relevant chapters where the planets, signs, angles and aspects have been interpreted will provide you with invaluable pointers to potential stress reactions. For Janet these have already been listed in chapter 23.

Personality versus character

Psychologists vary considerably in their definition of 'personality'. It is therefore necessary that you understand how we prefer to define this concept.

Personality refers to the whole person, the total of one's behaviour as it is revealed in characteristic habits of thought and expression, attitudes and interests, emotional responses, values and one's philosophy of life. It is that which characterizes one as an individual and determines one's unique adaptation to the environment. It refers specifically to how one differs from other individuals.

Personality must not be confused with character. We prefer to define 'character' as the measure of *organization* of one's personality and its complex features. Thus, a strong character would be very much in control of their motives and behaviour; whereas a weak character would be lacking in self-control, with motives and behaviour disorganized. A common misuse of the concept is to refer to a 'strong character' as someone who is very forceful or influential. Nothing, perhaps, could be further from the truth!

By 'characteristic' we mean distinctive, typical. 'Characterize' means, of course, to be characteristic of.

A preliminary assessment of important facets of the personality

No single factor in the chart (e.g. a planet, aspect, Ascendant) may be seen as an isolated feature when composing the final analysis, any more than an organ or a physiological process of the body can be thought of as functioning entirely separate from the whole organism. All are interdependent and interacting parts of the whole.

But, prior to compiling the final analysis, we should attempt to assess the quality (disposition and capacity to express its function) of each planet and angle, activated by aspects which produce significant relationships or stimulations with other chart features. We need to simplify and clarify such an assessment by working within a particular meaningful framework.

This framework is based on the profound human need for equilibrium, in the sense that it is a major goal of the psychological function represented by a planet or angle. This framework, therefore, must allow for evidence of *satisfying* forms of expression (i.e. traits indicative of an effort to experience equilibrium) and evidence of *unsatisfying* forms of expression (i.e. traits indicative of disequilibrium). The former will include the subject's (almost certainly unknowing) attempts to use stress to advantage. The latter will include stress-aggravated reactions and behaviour that are unlikely to lessen the stress. For example, with ☉ ☌ ♂, a stressful situation could be seen as a challenge to apply determination and enthusiasm to focus energy on achieving an objective through hard work and tireless effort. Or, the subject's reaction to the stressful situation may be self-defeating and create further stress through irritability, aggression and restlessness when the stress-activated energies remain unharnessed and thus denied a constructive or creative outlet.

Don't worry if you feel that it may be confusing to think in terms of 'equilibrium' and 'disequilibrium' when interpreting a chart. We have felt it necessary for you to understand the subtle influence of this powerful and basic human need. Now that you realize this, it will only be necessary to convey to the client that she possesses the potential to respond to any stimuli in either a satisfying or unsatisfying way. The choice is hers. This is what is meant by 'behaviour' – and the astrologer has the unique advantage over non-astrological psychologists and counsellors of being able to indicate the complex variations of an individual's potential behaviour, and to encourage the exercise of those traits most likely and most naturally to prove beneficial.

Some may suggest that *all* behaviour satisfying to a person may not reasonably be 'beneficial'. For example, it is known that certain types will derive pleasure and satisfaction from hurting others physically or mentally, stealing from others, vandalizing others' property. How can these forms of 'satisfying expression' be indicative of 'an effort to experience equilibrium'? Such satisfaction, and any satisfaction derived from harmful perversions, antisocial and hate-instigated activities, is misdirected energy and feeling, an abnormal form of pleasure – misdirected because the psyche is engaged in activities it may be deceived into believing give 'satisfaction', but which cannot give true satisfaction when these focus on imbalance, leading inevitably to disequilibrium. The need for equilibrium springs from a natural (and spiritual) law; just as the need to love is the greatest of spiritual laws for achieving satisfaction and equilibrium.

As you will see presently when we work on Janet's chart, this is a relatively simple framework to employ. Interpreting any person's complex behaviour patterns and attempting to understand motives instigating particular behaviour can never be entirely simple. It is, without question, a work of art, requiring patience, concentration and thorough training on the part of the student and astrologer.

We will first look at the Ascendant and what this represents for Janet according to the rising sign, the Me Sector and aspects to this angle. We will bear in mind that behaviour associated with the Asc. is frequently more in evidence than that of the Sun sign. This is because self-conscious awareness of one's uniqueness in relation to other people is significantly influenced by this angle. This produces an emphasis on self-centred interests and affects the ways by which one needs to prove what one is capable of achieving on one's own. One must look carefully at the Asc. as it represents a vitally important orientation of the psyche, focussing on self-conscious adjustment and identification.

We will next study the Sun, Moon and each planet in turn, and the contribution of each to the personality. Each represents a specialized form of energy expression and psychological activity that we have named a functional need (FN), and that is instrumental to the working of the psyche as a whole organism; each is a specialized adaptive response to the environment.

Finally, we will assess the other three angles in terms of their representing basic forms of environmental relationships or ways of relating to other people, and their having a significant bearing on the subject's uniqueness, vulnerability and adaptation to the environment.

The following assessments are concise interpretations of each chart factor, based on, rather than mentioning in detail, all the traits related to each. In the final analysis we will be free to draw on any of the listed traits. The opening paragraph for each planet or angle briefly describes their function within the psyche and may be used as a standard introduction in future 'preliminary assessment notes' for your own reminder and reference.

The Asc. (Me Sector): to be self-conscious in adjusting to the environment (page 167)

Asc. ♐, ♂ ☽ ♃, △ ♄ ♇, ♂ ☿ ♅, ☽ DZ1, ♃ DZ2

The focus with the Asc. is on the Me Sector, and therefore on relationships where for Janet the critical factor is that she needs to benefit from a recognition (by herself and others) of what she can achieve on her own, largely through her own choice of interest and activity. The other person in the relationship is necessary to help Janet focus on her own unique abilities. Each should inevitably give and take in producing the experiences resulting from the relationship.

Janet should be conscious of a desire to be outgoing (♐, ☌ ♃) and independent (♐, ☍ ♅); to have wide-ranging interests, enjoying communication with others and seeking to satisfy inquisitiveness and a need to explore (♐, ☍ ☿ ♅, ☌ ♃). It will be natural for her to express an uninhibited spontaneity and enthusiasm (♐, ☌ ☽ ♃, ☍ ♅, △ ♇). This will be a feature of restlessness (♐, ☌ ☽, ☍ ☿ ♅, △ ♇), as will be an enjoyment in making changes, taking risks (♐, ☽ DZ1, ☿ DZ2, △ ♇). Restlessness and intenseness will be particularly evident in expressing emotional energies (☽ DZ1, △ ♇), and she will tend to be very sensitive and impressionable to her immediate environment and to other people (☽ DZ1). Even so, there will be an innate desire – at times, a passion – to find her true identity through being venturesome and opportunistic (♐, △ ♇, ☌ ♃), most strikingly in unorthodox directions (☍ ♅, △ ♇).

This side of her personality will love making an impression on others (☌ ♃, △ ♇), and this will not be difficult to do with her outspokenness, controversial ideas and sociableness (☌ ☽, △ ♇, ☍ ☿ ♅). She will be a hard worker and will show great resilience when things go wrong (☌ ☽ ♃).

Care should be taken to avoid over-impulsiveness, impatience, extravagance (♐, ☌ ♃). This self-conscious side of her personality will burn up much nervous energy (♐, ☍ ☿ ♅), and stress will be evident when she becomes uncompromising (☌ ♃, △ ♄ ♇), critical (☍ ☿, △ ♄ ♇) or self-indulgent (☌ ☽ ♃). At times she will be subject to quickly-changing emotional moods (♐, ☌ ☽, △ ♇), contrariness (☍ ♅) and over-excitability (☍ ☿ ♅).

⊙: to express activity purposefully and objectively (page 99)

⊙ ⊓, □ ♂, △ ♆

Life is continual activity but, for an individual's life to have meaning and identity, a very basic need is provided. In response to this need the individual feels the urge to be active, to be releasing energy and to be doing things especially in *purposeful* ways, with effort directed to the attainment of an objective.

With Janet, this need will tend to be evident in her love of activity and exerting herself (□ ♂). She will delight in challenge and stimulation to satisfy restless, inquisitive, communicative, imaginative and enthusiastic qualities (⊓, □ ♂, △ ♆). She desires quick results, as reflected in a tendency for impatience, impulsiveness, risk-taking (⊓, □ ♂). Care should be taken to avoid over-excitability, quick temper and irritability (⊓, □ ♂).

Determination and enthusiasm to achieve objectives (□ ♂), coupled with idealism and perfectionism (△ ♆), will imbue her with the ability for hard work. Quite contrary to this is a potential weakness for unreliability, vacillation, moodiness, extravagance (△ ♆). This may seem something of an enigma, but her irrepressible activeness and idealism, demanding quick and worthwhile results, could have a contrary reaction when frustrated and under stress (□ ♂, △ ♆).

Emotionally, Janet will be sensitively (△ ♆) communicative and adaptable (⊓), with a tendency to dramatization and sensuousness (□ ♂, △ ♆).

☽: to be susceptible and accessible in adapting to the environment (page 101)

♐ , Me Sector DZ1, ♂ Asc., ⊡ IC, ♂° Desc., ∟ MC, △ ♄ ♇, * ♆

A critically important activity in making a success of one's life, let alone for survival, is that of maintaining an effective *adaptation* to the environment, particularly with other people. To this end, there is in each one of us a powerful need to be susceptible and accessible to others. Susceptibility means to receive from and be affected or influenced by other people and our environment, especially through sensitivity and impressionability, where the experience could be of benefit to our own personal growth. To be accessible means to be open to the approach of others, to make ourselves able to be reached by others more deeply than just to the surface or superficial mien we mostly employ in our daily activities. Both 'susceptibility' and 'accessibility' involve the emotions and feelings, and here we are inevitably referring to the feminine principle in both men and women. These emotional features are vital activities for the achievement of that essentially feminine need to belong to another person.

In Janet's case, this basically emotional and sensitive side to her personality is likely to be extremely restless and active, ready to spontaneously adapt to new conditions and interests, indeed welcoming change and fresh experiences that might temporarily quell her inquisitiveness and desire to explore (DZ1, ♐, △ ♇). Clearly Janet will be very sensitive and impressionable (✶ ♆), which will tend to make her vulnerable to emotional disturbance and upsets (DZ1, ✶ ♆). She will have her share of moodiness (✶ ♆, △ ♇). At times she may be self-absorbed, brooding, apprehensive, critical (△ ♄ ♇), but this will be a negative reaction stemming from an underlying necessity for introspection (△ ♄ ♇), defensiveness and discrimination (△ ♄). In contrast, a sudden change of mood could find her aglow with enthusiasm and restless socializing (♐, △ ♇).

There will be a deep-rooted fear of emotional insecurity (DZ1, △ ♄).

☿: to be communicative through mental, nervous and sensory faculties (page 104)

You sector DZ2, ☍ Asc., ✶ IC, ♂ Desc., △ MC, ☍ ♃, ♅, ∟ ♇

Being sociable is an essential human activity and this necessitates *communicating* oneself through the mental, nervous and sensory faculties.

With Janet, communication will require no effort. She will readily seek this form of self-expression. Being connectively involved with others exercises her inquisitive and discerning traits (DZ2, ♂ ♅). She should have an abundance of nervous energy to draw on, evident in restlessness and a tendency to quickly become highly-strung, excitable and impatient (♂° ♃, ∟ ♇). Inevitably there will be a risk of nervous tension (DZ2, ♂° ♃, ♂ ♅, ∟ ♇). She could develop keen perception and original and unorthodox ideas. These latter will be associated with a need to maintain a feeling of independence even when she is relating intimately with others (♂ ♅).

♀: to evaluate experience through the feelings (page 106)

□ ♆

Vital to one's understanding of the environment and other people is the capacity to *evaluate* experience through the feelings. This is an essential feature in achieving equilibrium and harmony. In this way one learns to relate to other people and to attract those one feels could be of most value and most in harmony with oneself.

In Janet's case she will tend to be extremely sensitive through her feeling-reactions to other people and to external conditions. This will be associated with the capacity for sympathy, conscientiousness, a refined taste and subtle forms of expression. There will be an easy-going, affectionate and tender side to her nature (□ ♆).

However, she will be vulnerable to some uneasiness and stress through the feelings, possibly as the result of confused and unreliable evaluation of other people, being deceived or taken advantage of in love relationships (□ ♆).

♂: to stimulate and quicken action, exert emotionally (page 109)

□ ☉, △ ♃

All psychological and bodily processes involve action and move-ment of some kind, but one particular function within the psyche can stimulate an *acceleration* and *excitation* of action when an occasion demands a strenuous exertion of energy.

This function within Janet will be evident in her seemingly boundless energy and enthusiasm, especially when involved in activities she enjoys or that have a definite objective and can benefit her. Thus, she will be capable of showing much determina-tion and intenseness, ideal for expressing an innate competitiveness (□ ☉, △ ♃).

Stress, however, could also be much in evidence if care is not taken to control impulsiveness and impatience. These restless and excitable reactions could provoke risk-taking, irritability and quick temper. She may be prone to tackling arguments through aggres-sion rather than diplomatic reasoning. There will be proneness to over-reaction (□ ☉, △ ♃).

♃: to achieve increase in personal growth and material benefits (page 110)

Me Sector DZ2, ♂ Asc., △ IC, ♂° Desc., ✳ MC, ♂° ☿ ♅, △ ♂, ⛶ ♇

A basic feature in life is desire for improvement: success, advan-tages, growth and maturity, enrichment materially and spiritually. To expand, develop one's potential, achieve increase.

This need for Janet will be a significant objective (Me Sector DZ2). Satisfaction in this direction may be achieved particularly through her ability to: communicate and involve herself with others (♂° ☿) while retaining a necessary independence and indi-viduality (♂° ♅); and make great efforts mentally and physically to complete a task (△ ♂), even to the extent of striving for what might appear to others to be 'the impossible' (⊡ ♇). Opportunism and expediency will be keywords for improving herself and her circumstances (Me Sector DZ2).

Behaviour associated with this powerful need to improve herself will be expressive of optimism, enthusiasm (♂° ☿ ♅, △ ♂) and an intense determination (⊡ ♇). At appropriate times she will enjoy 'making an impression' (Me Sector DZ2, ⊡ ♇) and she will be especially liked for her open-mindedness and generosity (△ ♂, ♂° ♅, ⊡ ♇).

Care, however, should be taken to avoid over-reaction and impatience (△ ♂, ♂° ♅). Under stress she could easily become highly-strung, portray potential weaknesses of indiscretion and exaggeration and prove uncompromising – to her possible detriment (♂° ☿ ♅, △ ♂, ⊡ ♇).

♄: to develop self-control and realistic methods of regulating and organizing the environment (page 113)

△ Asc., ✳ Desc., △ ☽, ♂ ♇

The achievement of stability, security and a responsible attitude to life demands that the individual learns to *control* and *regulate* his or her behaviour and energy expenditure. Normally one has to learn to adhere to an acceptable code of conduct within the social structure.

With Janet, success in terms of self-control is likely to be achieved particularly through a sensitive and realistic adaptation to exterior conditions (△ Asc. ☽, ♂ ♇) and by a cautious and discriminating receptiveness to the influence of other individuals (△ ☽). Also, self-control will be developed through a desire to be naturally thorough and tenacious in attaining goals (△ Asc. ☽, ♂ ♇), and at times through the potential to exercise persistence and industry to satisfy a compulsive and extraordinary striving towards what may be only an ideal (♂ ♇).

Typical behaviour attributable to this powerful need is likely to be conscientiousness, endurance, dedication, determination. Janet will not be afraid of hard work (△ Asc. ☽, ♂ ♇).

Stress will inevitably result in attempting to master self-control and to be organized, and this could manifest itself in behaviour such as obstinacy, discontentment, selfishness, depression (△ Asc. ☽, ♂ ♇).

♅: to deviate from the normal, be uninhibited and original (page 116)

You Sector DZ2, ☌ Asc., ✶ IC, ♂ Desc., △ MC, ♂ ☿, ☍ ♃, ∟ ♇

Man's potential could never be fully realized without a powerful need to express himself freely and originally and through *deviating from the normal*.

In Janet's case, she will be particularly likely to achieve a satisfying sense of freedom and independence and be successful in unorthodox pursuits through being an opportunist (☍ ♃) and having enough confidence in her own ability for exceptional striving to try and attain even the most improbable objectives (∟ ♇). Close involvement with certain individuals will be necessary for encouraging the development of original ideas (♂ Desc. ☿).

This very strong attraction towards the unconventional in pursuits and self-expression will make her inquisitive, innovative, open-minded. There will be spontaneity and flexibility, and she may tend to be changeable and venturesome (You Sector DZ2, ♂ ☿, ☍ ♃, ∟ ♇).

Janet should endeavour to control her nervous and emotional energies, which are likely to cause stress by being dissipated through restlessness, impulsiveness and over-excitability (You Sector DZ2, ♂ ☿, ☍ ♃). Another possible manifestation would be contrariness and rebelliousness (∟ ♇).

♆: to seek perfection through refinement and sensitivity (page 118)

△ ☉, ✳ ☽, □ ♀

Personal growth and enlightenment, as well as improved adaptation to the environment, necessarily depends on a continuous elevation and revaluation of experience in an endeavour to achieve *perfection* in all that one does. This is a need to seek a standard of excellence and requires in particular the qualities of refinement and sensitivity.

This need is a strong feature in Janet's make-up, and a sensitive and subtle understanding of and reaction to other people would be advantageous in personal and business relationships (□ ♀); also, in successfully adapting meaningful activities to changing environmental circumstances (△ ☉, ✳ ☽).

This will be a very likeable side to Janet's personality – easy-going, impressionable, sympathetic, accessible (△ ☉, ✳ ☽, □ ♀). The perfectionist (△ ☉) in her will be evident, as will idealism (△ ☉, ✳ ☽, □ ♀) and an urge for a creative (△ ☉, ✳ ☽) outlet for her keen imagination (✳ ☽) and romantic streak (✳ ☽, □ ♀).

A potential weakness may be a tendency, when faced with a tricky problem, to be evasive. This is linked with an underlying fear of insecurity and resultant moodiness and risk of self-deception and escapism (△ ☉, ✳ ☽).

♇ : to exceed the limits of what might be expected of oneself (page 120)

△ ☽, ∟ ☿ ♅, ⊡ ♃, ♂ ♄

Within each human being there is not simply a 'wish' that they might be able to draw on a hidden reservoir of power to enable them to achieve great feats, but there is a deep-rooted need for this, albeit on a subconscious level and not consciously realized by most individuals. A typical manifestation of this need is a sense of compulsion.

Janet's best chance of satisfaction through outdoing others and seeking to achieve the impossible will be through effectively adapting herself to the environment ($\triangle$ ☽). This will produce self-confidence by developing communication and involvement with others while retaining independence, and by self-control coupled with opportunism and expediency ($\triangle$ ☽, ♂ ♄, ∟ ☿ ♅, ▢ ♃). Self-control and the ability to adapt and to communicate with others will be essential qualities.

This need could provide quite powerful features to her personality, which could be usefully developed though necessarily kept under control. Typical would be intenseness, determination and dedication ($\triangle$ ☽, ▢ ♃, ♂ ♄, ∟ ♅), combined with enthusiasm and spontaneity ($\triangle$ ☽, ∟ ☿ ♅).

Stress, however, may easily be experienced when such powerful energies are expressed, and this could result in reactions productive of a self-centred obstinacy ($\triangle$ ☽, ♂ ♄, ∟ ♅), restlessness and irritability ($\triangle$ ☽, ∟ ☿).

The angles: basic ways of relating to other people

The angles provide a dimension of uniqueness according to their positions in the birth chart relative to the whole chart pattern and to individual planets. They correspond to powerful areas of energy potential within the psyche, particularly focussing their activity on relating to other people.

It is important to know the nature of these powerful areas in Janet's case, and which planets (FNs) will tend to be enhanced and more keenly activated (by aspects to angles), and so contribute to qualities of uniqueness or distinctive self-expression.

A planet or planets in a Distinctive Zone (DZ) of an angle grants an additional importance to that sector of environmental relationships (SER). This conjunction (of planet–angle) highlights this sector as of immense significance for providing necessary experience for the subject's development in this area of his or her relations with other people. For example, ☿ in DZ2 of the You Sector suggests that of much importance to Janet would be learning from and being influenced by another person on a one-to-one basis. Traditionally, astrologers would have said this means through the marriage partner. We do not confine this sector to experience through the marriage partner alone or, as is increasingly appropriate these days, to the live-in boy- or girlfriend. It applies to any relationship on a one-to-one basis where one needs to receive from and learn through what the other can give to oneself. This can apply equally to a loving relationship, or one of conflict and hate. In Janet's case, her contribution to stimulating, encouraging or aggravating this relationship will be especially through the ☿ function in her own personality. Through the experiences brought about, her ☿ functional need will receive vital lessons for development. And as ☿ is in DZ2, if Janet exerts herself in a controlled manner in terms of communication, there will be the potential for achieving acts or expression of distinction.

No one person in Janet's life is necessarily associated with just one of the four areas. As an example, if we were able to give a 'rating of importance to Janet' for a particular male friend, with 10 as a maximum of importance, her need of him through the You Sector may be rated 8, through the Us Sector rated 6, through the Me Sector rated 5, and through the Them Sector rated 0. In other words, one or even all four angles can indicate Janet's interest in and need of a particular individual. The only way the astrologer could assess the relative importance of Janet's 'relationship needs' where a particular person in her life was concerned, would be through discussion during a consultation.

Because of the powerful energies associated with the angles, they are seen as areas where Janet is likely to be particularly vulnerable to stress. The greater the pressure of energy expenditure, the greater the risk of stress reactions. This applies especially to the Ascendant, the Me Sector, where Janet needs to project herself, expose herself, to achieve recognition of what she can be and do entirely by her own efforts. The sign on the Ascendant, planets in the Ascendant's Distinctive Zones and aspecting planets to this angle will suggest the likely nature of any stress reaction.

The Ascendant or Me Sector has already been dealt with in this chapter. Now we will assess the Us, You and Them sectors in Janet's chart.

Us Sector (IC): to develop joint yet interdependent interests with another person (page 167)

ꀬ ☽, ✶ ☿, △ ♃, ✶ ♅

The critical factor in this type of relationship is that Janet needs to benefit from sharing herself jointly and yet interdependently in a you-and-me-together process of development. Satisfaction must be achieved through mutual interest and benefit. A 'give and take' attitude is vital.

Predominant will be Janet's flexibility (✶ ☿ ♅), sensitivity (ꀬ ☽) and generous enthusiasm (△ ♃) in endeavouring to achieve satisfaction through sharing herself with another person. She will tend to launch herself into this type of you-and-me-together relationship with confidence (✶ ✶ △). Of much importance will be a meaningful (ꀬ ☽) and genial (△ ♃) situation, providing an uninhibited (✶ ♅) experience with the excitement of unconventionality and frankness (✶ ♅) allowing a free flow of communication (✶ ☿). Necessary, too, will be a basis for improvement (△ ♃), both in the relationship and in herself.

She could be particularly vulnerable to stress due to her sensitivity (ꀬ ☽) towards the other person. Potential behaviour associated with stress reactions could be meddlesomeness and over-conscientiousness (✶ ☿), contrariness and impetuosity (✶ ♅). This points to Janet's need for such an intimate relationship being activated by emotions (ꀬ ☽) and a keenly responsive nervous system (✶ ☿ ♅). Care should be taken to avoid the risk of exaggerated enthusiasm (△ ♃) and possessiveness (ꀬ ☽).

You Sector (Desc.): to receive from and be influenced by another person (page 167)

☍ ☽ ♃, ☌ ☿ ♅, ✶ ♄, ☿ ♅ DZ2)

The critical factor in this type of relationship is that Janet needs to benefit through receiving from and being influenced by another person on a one-to-one basis. Experience gained through the other person may often compensate for a certain lack in Janet's personality. Although here the predominant need is for Janet to take and receive, she will inevitably be giving of herself to help stimulate and sustain the relationship for the time her need requires her to. Thus, this sector suggests how Janet could handle a relationship on a one-to-one basis where she needs to receive from and learn through what the other person can give to her. This can apply equally to a loving relationship, or one of conflict and hate.

Significant relationships of this type will be formed by Janet quickly and probably unexpectedly (☌ ♅), and will be necessary opportunities for her to exercise her need to communicate (☌ ☿) and to be excited and stimulated by someone she feels is different from normal (☌ ☿ ♅). Janet's own approach in forming such relationships or in dealing with conflicts that arise will very much tend to the unorthodox (☌ ♅). This type of learning-through-relationship, where she seeks the intimacy of someone who is in many ways very different to herself, could bring her important opportunities to develop her self-expression in distinctive ways (☿ ♅ DZ2).

These relationships, from which Janet needs to receive and to feel the influence of other individuals, and through which she may learn significant details about herself in needing to relate in this way to others, will tend often to make her feel intense and uneasy (2 × ☌; 2 × ☍).

She will need to learn to relax with other people, especially as she enjoys excitement and activity, if she is to lessen nervous tension and the risk of instability (☌ ☿ ♅). Potential weaknesses likely to disrupt this type of relationship are over-criticalness (☌

☿), being suspicious of other's motives (∗ ♄), mixed feelings about experiencing inferiority (∗ ♄, ♂ ♃), and being over-defensive or submissive with particularly powerful personalities – reactions she could despise herself for (♂ ☽).

This area of Janet's life – especially of her emotional and love life – is likely to significantly affect her own personality, spiritual growth and maturity, as well as bring her heartache and critical turning-points in her life pattern of activities. Changes there will certainly be, unexpected and disruptive changes, as well as those of her own choosing (☿ ♅ DZ2).

Them Sector (MC): to develop contacts and interests within society generally (page 169)

∟ ☽, △ ☿ ♅, ∗ ♃

The critical factor in this type of relationship is that Janet needs to benefit from contacts and interests in society generally. This covers business and financial interests, work involving others and indeed any activity or interest where she feels herself to be a functioning part within the structure of society – in work or play. In this area pressures can be on performance, co-operation, the ability to conform conventionally or as the majority dictates. The criteria here demand that Janet contributes to others, even in an impersonal way, if she is to receive any beneficial experiences within society and 'the world at large'. In this area of her life the relationships Janet seeks are really of two distinct types: those resulting from direct contact with individuals through which her socializing or business activities can be developed to her advantage; and those resulting from projecting herself through the image she feels is that of the public or business or social structure her work or play provides her with. In the latter relationships the feedback is essentially in terms of success or failure on Janet's part.

In these social and business areas of her life, Janet will tend to sense considerable confidence (3 × △ ∗) in her own potential. This will be due largely to a natural attitude of opportunism and optimism ($*$ ♃); a powerful urge to communicate with others and to be inquisitively involved with her social and business environments ($\triangle$ ☿); and the need to realize her unique qualities through an unorthodox and original contribution to society ($\triangle$ ♅). She may fall prey to over-confidence ($_3$ × $\triangle$ $*$), especially if she sought to attract advantages to herself by presumptuous status-seeking or exhibitionism ($*$ ♃).

Although it has been said that she may seek to contribute to society in unorthodox and original ways, there may also on occasions be a willingness to conform to the influence and demands of society ($\llcorner$ ☽), which would be beneficial for her.

Care will definitely be required to cope with an instinctive anxiety ($\llcorner$ ☽, $\triangle$ ☿) that could undermine her social and business relationships. She could be prone to discontentment ($\llcorner$ ☽), instability ($\triangle$ ☿) and rebellious and irrational behaviour ($\triangle$ ♅) when frustrated or under much pressure.

What is our overall impression of Janet's personality?

We have assessed each planet and angle in Janet's chart, and have shown the role of each within her psyche and its contribution to the growth and activity of her personality.

Dominant factors in Janet's chart are:

Asc. ♐.
☽ and ♃ in Me Sector Distinctive Zones 1 and 2 respectively.
☿ ♂ ♅ in You Sector Distinctive Zone 2, σ^{o} ♃.
☉ in ♊, □ ♂, $\triangle$ ♆.

In a 'nutshell' our impression of Janet's personality is as follows:

Essentially she is an extraverted woman with an abundance of energy, loving activity and communicating with others. She is inquisitive and forever restless, readily able to try to adapt to changing environments and circumstances. If there is a sense of power in her, it is that of enthusiasm and determination to be an active and interested participant in life. Her love of independence and unorthodoxy may lead to conflict and expose her emotional vulnerability. She will be very prone to stress through her impatience, impulsiveness, over-reacting, excitability. This will be evident in her potential for a highly-strung disposition, moodiness and on occasions a quick temper and aggressive behaviour – quite a contrast from the sensitive and affectionate person she can be.

In the next chapter we must combine and arrange the varied and contrasting features so that as accurate an interpretation as possible of Janet's personality is presented. The main purpose of an astrological analysis is not to describe these complex features as if one were able to portray them in a painting or a photograph, but so that Janet may understand her personal needs and behaviour more clearly. In this way she may see how to improve her adaptation to and relationships with other people and the environments of her work and leisure activities, and learn how best she can reduce the stress-inducing reactions of her own behaviour.

Summary of chapter

The aim of this chapter is to show how helpful it is to prepare brief preliminary interpretations for each functional need (FN) and angle prior to the final analysis, to clearly indicate the role of each within the psyche.

CHAPTER 25

Janet's Character Analysis

Accurately interpreting a chart is an art

Now we come to the 'end product' of our studies. This analysis of Janet's birth chart is an example of what astrology is all about. Preparing and writing an analysis is an art. The skill and craft of interpretation may take several or even a great many attempts to achieve satisfactorily, most particularly if your objective is to do this counselling work professionally. Even if you only want to compile analyses as a hobby for friends and relatives, and to study the charts of interesting persons, you will still want to make accurate and methodically presented interpretations. It normally takes much experience of consultations, studying and discussing charts, keeping a methodical record of your own experience of astrological factors related to observed behaviour in others and writing analyses before a confident professional standard is attained.

There is no fixed way of compiling an analysis. The method used by an astrologer depends upon the sequence in which he or she prefers to present the varied features of the client's personality. Whatever the method used, there must be a sound reason for its choice, otherwise, with no sound method for presenting the chart and personality features, the inevitable outcome will be chaos, the subject concerned will almost certainly be confused – and the astrologer could well have missed out vital facets of the personality.

After the opening foreword to Janet's analysis, I have chosen to begin with a concise summary of her personality, created from the major complex and contrasting features. For a reason that by now should be apparent to the reader of this book, we follow a sequence in detailing the psychological aspects or basic needs of the personality beginning with the Ascendant, the Sun, Moon, and so on through the order of planets to the other three angles (or areas of environmental relationships). It would be totally wrong to simply interpret each function (e.g. the Sun or Venus) as an *isolated* feature of the psyche. An accurate interpretation of each function or chart factor can only be given by indicating how behaviour associated with it is reinforced by or merged with psychological activity or expression from other areas of the psyche or chart. This is made clear by the 'significators' (planetary and angular symbols) appropriately placed in the left-hand margin. These significators would not appear on the client's top copy of the analysis, but on your carbon copy for future reference.

You should read through the analysis several times, noting the significators in the margin. Refer to Janet's chart, chapters 22 and 25 and the chapters detailing interpretations of the planets, signs, angles and aspects. You should soon be able to understand how the analysis was constructed.

Correct presentation of the analysis

The analysis will, of course, be addressed to Janet. As has been said, the significators are entered in the left-hand margin of your copy only, for your instruction and reference. A cluster of significators in brackets indicates that they refer to a particular paragraph or portions of it, where it would be awkward to try and place individual significators in line with the interpretation they apply to. Always keep a carbon copy of an analysis (or anything you write to a client) with the letters they write to you for your own records in the client's file. Each client's file, containing letters, your notes, calculations, a copy of the analysis and any other relevant material, may be a stiff folder or, as I always used, a suitable sized envelope.

The analysis must always be typed, on A4 good Bond typewriting paper. If you have a word processor, this is ideal! It is ideal to put an analysis inside a good-wearing cover, front and back, and either join these together with two evenly spaced staples on the left side or with two evenly spaced split pins. This way, the analysis opens like a book if you do not use too stiff a cover. You could then choose a title for the front cover, perhaps like this:

Character Analysis
for
John Smith
by
(your name)

In the bottom right-hand corner it would be as well to type in the date the analysis was compiled. On the last page of the analysis, in the bottom right-hand corner, you should enter your name and address, signature and again the date the analysis was compiled.

Here is the analysis, just as it was prepared for Janet, commencing with a foreword (which you may copy for other analyses of your own).

A Character Analysis . . . for Janet

A human being is an incredibly complex organism. We each have the common driving force to survive, and survival means successfully adapting to the environment and its constant pressures and demands. Human beings have another basic characteristic in common: each is unique. No two of us are alike in the way we behave and choose to express thoughts and feelings. It could be said that uniqueness arises because individuals differ in degree rather than in kind. This means that we can each experience emotion in its variety of forms – anger, amusement, happiness, fear and so on. But some react emotionally to stimuli and situations more keenly than others. Similarly, we all have imagination, but some exercise this more frequently and powerfully than others.

This analysis will attempt to describe the potentially

dominant qualities and traits that contribute to your unique personality. It gives prominence to two vitally important features of your life: the environment and stress. Successful adaptation to the environment can go hand in hand with successfully coping with stress. It should be of immense value for you to understand your potential for handling the environment and stress successfully and to identify those reactions that are most likely to produce conflict and dissatisfaction.

Just as the physical body needs food and liquid for sustenance, so will the individual that is you have certain powerful psychological needs. The effective and balanced functioning of you as a person depends upon the satisfactory fulfilment of these needs. Each is a vital adaptive response to the environment. This analysis takes into account these needs and how your unique personality has been moulded to cope with them.

The use of the word 'will' may appear to imply habitual occurrence or traits that are clearly evident in your behaviour. But it may be that this particular behaviour is not yet very evident, or not at all. For example, if it were said, 'You will be adventurous and enterprising ...' our use of the word 'will' is extended to emphasize potential traits likely to be of benefit to you if developed. You should not reject these as an exaggeration or even impossible.

Dear Janet,

(☉ ♊ □ ♂, ☽) ♐   Essentially you are a person who will see the
Asc. ♐, ♃ ☌ Asc.,   environment (especially the people in it) as a
♂ △ ♃)   challenge and a source of stimulating activity and interest. You enjoy expressing yourself in extraverted ways, with your abundance of energy and love of communicating with others. Forever restless, inquisitive and ready to adapt to changes, your personality must surely exude its enthusiasm for activity and delight in being an interested participant in life instead of a mere bystander.

But why this restlessness? Why must you forever be active, doing things, communicating and projecting your ideas, energies and feelings? Is there another side to you, essentially introverted, happy to sit back and relax and quietly contemplate achievements and thoughts on life? There certainly needs to be if a satisfying equilibrium is to be a healthy reward for your constant striving to actively participate in and contribute to life.

In your letter you asked if, in this analysis, I could tell you why you behaved 'in the bloody way you do sometimes'. If by 'bloody way' you mean being awkward or bloody-minded, this is something most of us can admit to at times, and it is hardly a critical weakness to have specifically interpreted from your chart. But the fact that you pose this question implies a more deep-rooted reaction to other people at times, which could cause you some concern. Probably you are
(☿ ♂ ♅ DZ2, ♂⚶ ♃   acutely aware of the intensity and spontaneity
♇ △ ☽, ∟ ☿ ♅   of your energetic personality that may some-
Asc. ♐)   times 'get out of control' and even surprise
you with its behaviour. I am sure that your special question will be answered by this analysis.

Whether we realize it or not, in our own individual way we each strive to recognise who we are, that we should be somebody different and separate from all other human beings. It has to be an inescapable quest of our inner spiritual being. Perhaps we can never know exactly who we are, but a particularly self-conscious side of your personality needs to pro-
Asc. ♐ ♂ ♃, ♂⚶ ☿ ♅   ject yourself as outgoing and independent, with wide-ranging interests, enjoying communication with others and seeking to satisfy inquisitiveness and a desire to explore. It will be natural for you to express an un-
Asc. ♐ ♂ ☽ ♃, ♂⚶ ♅ △ ♇   inhibited spontaneity and enthusiasm. This is important to how you see yourself and want others to see you.

Asc. ♂ ☽ (DZ1), △ ♇   Sometimes you may wonder why you
♆ ⚹ ☽, △ ☉, □ ♀   are so sensitive, impressionable, intense.

Inevitably this stimulates you emotionally and activates restlessness. These traits express your need to understand yourself and your environment. You find it hard to tolerate doing anything you have no interest in and that you consider has

Asc. ♐, ☽ DZ₁, Asc. △ ♇,   no purpose for you. This would

☉ ♊ □ ♂, ☿ DZ₂   account to some extent for your need to experience change and tread new ground, to vary your activities, even if it entails taking risks.

Asc. ♂° ♅ (DZ₂), △ ♇   Not for you a conventional or restrict-

Asc. ♐ ♂ ♃   ing lifestyle, and this seeking to experience unorthodox activities and relationships, and to express yourself in venturesome and opportunistic ways is probably part of the process of seeking where you may come closest to finding your true identity.

(Asc. ♂ ☽ ♃, △ ♇   At apt moments you may enjoy making an

♂° ☿ ♅)   impression on other people, and this will not be difficult to attempt with your outspokenness, controversial ideas and sociableness.

(Asc. ♐, ♂ ☽ ♃, ♂° ☿ ♅,   This is very much a part of the self-

△ ♄ ♇)   conscious side of your personality, which tends to be particularly vulnerable to stress; hence you should try to avoid over-impulsiveness, impatience, extravagance, over-excitability and excessive expenditure of nervous energy. Stress could be evident when you become uncompromising, critical, self-indulgent, contrary, with quick-changing emotional moods.

☉   Life is an expression of activity, and you would be acutely aware that yours lacks meaning and identity if you were active without purpose and objective. This will be a power-

☉ □ ♂   ful need to satisfy in your case and another source of restlessness.

(☉ ♊ □ ♂, △ ♆   There will be a delight in challenge,

♂ △ ♃, Asc. ♐ △ ♇)   stimulation and exertion to satisfy your inquisitive, communicative, imaginative qualities. An important ingredient for activity and exertion will be your natural enthusiasm and determination once you have an objective in

view. There is no doubt that you will be a hard worker and something of a perfectionist and idealist.

☉ ♊ □ ♂ But, you require quick results and will sometimes tend to 'jump into action' too impulsively, with the probability that you must fight others when opinions differ, rather than try to see their viewpoint. This is where many problems and conflicts are likely to occur. Indeed, this is a major source of – as you mention in your letter – the 'bloody way you behave sometimes'. This will be a powerful feature of your personality, a fund of energy, and stress-vulnerable if care is not taken to avoid impatience, impulsiveness and spontaneous risk-taking. Frustration and opposition could provoke quick temper and irritability.

It is when you are under stress and don't feel that you are making headway in an activity or with life in general, that you may suddenly lose control of your normally apparent self-confident display of energy and enthusiasm and a sort of ☉ △ ♆, ☽ ☌ Asc. ✶ ♆ 'disintegration' sets in. You may then become moody, vacillating, unreliable. What was perhaps over-confidence is suddenly lack of confidence. ☉ □ ♂, Asc. ♐ ☌ ♃ You must always endeavour to recognize physical and mental 'warning signs' that you may be 'burning up' too much nervous energy.

☉ ☽ The psyche of each one of us functions in both masculine and feminine roles. Normally, for a female the feminine needs are most apparent; with a male the masculine. What I ☉ □ ♂ have just described concerning purposeful activity and a tendency to fight others applies to the more masculine impulse within you.

☽ ♐ ☌ Asc., ☽ DZ1, ✶ ♆ With you, the feminine aspect will be a very distinctive expression of your personality, accentuating sensitivity and restlessness. Despite the fact that this means you will be susceptible to the influence of other people and the environment, your instinctive desire for independence ☽ ☌ Asc., DZ1 will make you keenly and shrewdly aware of the need to choose your own environment and close friends.

Easygoing and sympathetic, this is an extremely attractive and appealing part of you. Here is tenderness, the romantic,
☽ (DZ1) ⚹ ♆ and a sensitive, fertile ground for creativity. This is a part of you that needs to feel accessible and open to others, to belong to someone. It is vital that you cultivate this important side of your personality. But beware: here also, accentuated by such sensitivity and impressionability, you may be prone to an underlying, subtly pervasive anxiety. It may be that you conform to the classic scenario of being so intent on projecting yourself into the environment and scattering your interests and energies in diverse directions, that the more feminine receptive and impressionable aspect of your psyche is left very vulnerable emotionally. This spells emotional insecurity.

☽ △ ♄ Yet such is the complexity of human nature, that even this gentle, easygoing and accessible expression of need is emotionally linked with a discriminating and defensive impulse that demands a realistic and disciplined control of the emotions and feelings. The message here is that you need to make yourself accessible to others, but that you must exercise a goodly measure of control in relationships where the emotions and feelings are uppermost. This feminine side to your nature is vitally important in achieving effective adaptation to other people and the environment, and satisfaction will be experienced if you couple this sensitivity with realism and self-control – qualities you should be capable of applying.

However, regulating your emotions and feelings will not be easy when they are sufficiently aroused, for another facet of this dynamic feminine nature will add intensity and compulsiveness
☽ △ ♇ to emotional expression. This is excellent in terms of intense enthusiasm and dedication, but suggests a risk of obstinacy and brooding discontentment if intentions are frustrated.

It is vital that you endeavour to identify and understand these needs and the potential within the powerful emotional and feeling content of your essentially feminine nature, and realize that here is a key for improved adaptation to other people and the environment.

(☽ ♂ Asc., △ ♄ ♇, ✶ ♆) A crucial part of this understanding is learning to avoid the stress that may arise should there be moodiness, brooding, self-preoccupation, obstinacy, criticalness, discontentment, touchiness, or spontaneous explosive emotional reactions.

☿   Being sociable is an essential human activity, and a vitally important factor is the ability to communicate through the

☿ DZ2 ♂ ♅   mental, nervous and sensory faculties.

☉ ♊, Asc. ♐, ☽ ♐ ⎫ Communication through words and ideas

☿ DZ2   ⎭ should be no effort for you. You will readily seek this form of self-expression. Being connectively involved with others exercises your inquisitive and discerning traits and is an intellectual challenge as well as being a stimulating means of 'information exchange'. For you, it will not be enough simply to 'be in touch' with others and to accept a conventional programme of social activities. Real satisfaction will come through interpreting meaning and reality from your experiences involving others, through exchange of ideas and thoughts on life, through applying your

(☿ DZ2 ♂ ♅   mind and senses in original and unorthodox

♂ Asc. ♃, ∟ ♇) ways. Apart from your deep-felt pleasure in acquiring knowledge and furthering your understanding of yourself and life, actively and meaningfully communicating yourself should contribute to an increase in benefits and satisfaction in the material sense.

(☿ DZ2 ♂ ♅   Qualities likely to be developed are versatility,

♂ Asc. ♃, ∟ ♇) a cheerful and optimistic attitude, broad-mindedness, flexibility and a great sense of humour. You will be known for being forthright, emphatic in opinions, keenly perceptive and at times intensely persuasive – and capable of having a dramatic impact on others!

But this area of your psyche's contact with the environment is likely to generate a highly-strung condition if care is

Asc. ♐, ☉ ♊ □ ♂ ⎫
♃ ♂ Asc.   ⎭   not taken. You may feel able to draw on a
boundless source of energy, but inevitably
an imbalance will be experienced if regular relaxation periods
or an easing of activities are not observed, resulting in
(☿ DZ₂ ♂ ♅, ♂ Asc. ♃,   nervous exhaustion. Stress signs could
∟ ♇)   be indiscretions, annoying misjudge-
ments, edginess, over-excitability, irritability, criticizing, rebelliousness or acute nervous tension and anxiety.

♀   Vital to one's understanding of the environment and of
other people is the capacity to evaluate experience through
the feelings. This is an essential feature in achieving equilibrium and harmony and in learning to avoid disharmony and
unpleasant situations. In this way one learns to relate to other
people and to attract those one feels could be of most value
and be most in harmony with.

☿   We have just seen how necessary to you communication
with others is. But communicating and relating are not
quite the same thing. When it comes to establishing and
♀ □ ♆ putting a value on a relationship with another person, it
may well happen that your feelings do not always impart to
you an accurate assessment of that person.

☉ □ ♂, ☽ DZ₁ ♂ Asc. ⎫   Why is this? There could be several
☽ * ♆, △ ♇   ⎭   reasons. You are capable of spontaneous emotional expression, and your behaviour is easily
activated and charged with a depth of emotion that could
liven up any relationship. But emotional reaction alone cannot
provide a true evaluation of the other person. To do this,
your *feelings* have to be involved in the relationship. Emotion
is largely an objective process, whereas feeling is subjective
and we begin to like or dislike points about the other person
and find these pleasant or unpleasant, to put it very simply.
With you, the emotions could well influence your evaluation
☉ △ ♆, ☽ * ♆, ♀ □ ♆ of a person. Another reason is that,
where the opposite sex is concerned, in terms of an intimate
relationship, you will tend to be very much of an idealist and
thus may often be inclined to underrate someone's good points.

♀ □ ♆ But perhaps the main reason for the likelihood of your feelings giving you an inaccurate evaluation of a person is that your feelings can become confused. All too easily you can experience self-deception or be deceived by the other person. This may happen because you have acutely sensitive ☽ ↑ DZ₁ ♂ Asc., △ ♇ ⎱ feeling-reactions to other people, have ♂ □ ☉, △ ♃ ⎰ the capacity for sympathy, conscientiousness, are easygoing and affectionate, and also because, where a relationship invites intimacy, you have a very healthy and virile appreciation of sex.

Physical sex will be important to you and, with your fund of energy, keenly expressed emotions and powerful feeling-reactions for anyone you are attracted to, the frustration or deprivation of a sexual outlet may have a stressful effect emotionally and on the nervous system. For you, real sexual (☉ □ ♂, △ ♆ satisfaction will not be achieved through ☽ DZ₁ ♂ Asc., ✷ ♆ physical lovemaking that lacks the sensitiv-☽ △ ♇, ♀ □ ♆) ity the 'mystical' experience of two souls in love can bring to it. It may well happen that, however beautiful sexual experience can be for you, you will always feel that you have never quite reached the ultimate height of ecstasy that your restless feelings reach out for.

♀ □ ♆ From what has been said it is clear that you may be vulnerable to stress through the feelings. You may be taken advantage of, so be careful.

Your chart has clearly enabled me to indicate a personality that delights in activity, evident in restlessness, excitability and excessive expenditure of nervous energy. This is evident too, in impulsiveness and impatience, and in a refreshing expression of natural enthusiasm to tackle tasks and enjoy a challenge. The very survival of the human species has necessitated the development of a capacity for accelerated action and ♂ aggressive exertion. This is basically the need to strive against others, to be competitive.

In your case, this particular capacity for exertion and effort can be a significant feature of your personality. If applied constructively, your innate accompanying enthusiasm and determination will benefit you through being a hard (♂ □ ☉, △ ♃) worker, adventurous, venturesome, with a flair for enterprise and initiative. You will have much to gain through your ability for spontaneity, quickness, directness. The intensity of emotional and intellectual expression you can apply to a commitment will be enhanced by this capacity for making that extra exertion and effort when needed.

But if this special energy need is not used constructively, you may create problems for yourself and others. The restless, (♂ □ ☉, △ ♃) impatient traits already referred to will be accentuated, producing combative and quarrelsome behaviour with resultant stress. There will at times be a risk of extremism and extravagance or overreaction. This is a feature of your psyche where there may be an above average accident-proneness.

(☉ □ ♂, ♂ △ ♃,   A salient feature, however, will be
☿ ♂ ♅ DZ2 ☍ ♃ DZ2,   competitiveness, applied as a healthy,
Asc. ♐, ☽ ♐ DZ1)   exciting, stimulating challenge of sheer exertion of your whole personality striving against others for the same object – especially when your unconventionality matches the orthodoxy of others. Competitive outlets will provide you with opportunities to feel free to be yourself.

♃   A basic feature in life is desire for improvement: to achieve success, advantages, personal growth and maturity, enrichment materially and spiritually. There is a need to expand through the development of one's potential.

With you, this need for improvement will be an important determinant in your choice of activities and interests. It will be evident in your seeking to increase your knowledge and understanding of life, of yourself and of your role and (♃ ♂ Asc. ♐ DZ2,   purpose in life. With you, it will not be
♆ △ ☉ ✳ ☽, ♃ ☍ ☿ ♅,   sufficient satisfaction to lead a lifestyle
☿ ♂ ♅ DZ2)   based essentially on building a conventional home and family structure and holding a 'nine to five' job. Always there will be this need to seek beyond the

material and to get the very best from every feature of your
$\Psi \triangle \odot, \ast\ \mathbb{D}$ psyche. If perfection must ever be unattainable,
at least you will do your utmost to approach it. Life would
be intolerable for you if you could not improve yourself.

$(\mathcal{4}\ \sigma^{o}\ \male\ \text{♅}, \triangle\ \sigma, \ \square\ \text{♇})$ Personal improvement and maturity,
even apart from material benefits, can in your case be achieved
especially through communication and involvement with
others, while retaining your independence and individuality;
and making great efforts mentally and physically to complete
a task, even to the extent of striving for what might appear
$\mathcal{4}$ Me Sector D Z2 to others 'the impossible'. Opportunism and
expediency should be keywords for improving yourself and
your circumstances.

$(\mathcal{4}\ \sigma\ \text{Asc.}\ \nearrow, \triangle\ \sigma,$ Behaviour associated with this need to im-
$\square\ \text{♇}, \sigma^{o}\ \male\ \text{♅})$ prove yourself will be expressive of optimism, enthusiasm and an intense determination. You will
enjoy seeking new horizons, varying your interests and activities, deviating from normal and well-trodden paths both
physically and intellectually. Spontaneity, inquisitiveness,
shrewdness, an element of surprise and at times a flamboyant
attitude when desiring to make an impression may be typical
behaviour. You will be liked for your open-mindedness,
frankness and generosity.

$\mathcal{4}\ \sigma^{o}\ \male\ \text{♅}, \triangle\ \sigma, \ \square\ \text{♇}$ Under stress you could easily become
highly-strung, portray potential weaknesses of indiscretion
and exaggeration and prove uncompromising. Overreaction,
impatience and extravagance may be symptoms of imbalance
and stress.

It will not be easy for you to achieve stability in your life
with such a restlessly energetic and active personality. I
rather think that you will not give much thought and con-
$\hbar\ \triangle\ \triangle\ \ast$ sideration to it. It may be that you have an instinctive
confidence in a 'stabilizing factor' in your psyche acting for
you and keeping a check on any tendency to excesses.

$\hbar$ This would be unwise. Humanity's very survival has depended on the development of self-control and the regulation and organization of the environment for the establishment of stability and security. This demands from the individual a responsible attitude to life with he or she learning to control and regulate behaviour and energy expenditure. This

☿ ♂ ♅ DZ2 ♂ ♃ normally means learning to adhere to an acceptable code of conduct within the social structure. Again, not easy for you to do!

(☉ □ ♂, ♂ △ ♃,   I have already shown that a strong fea-
Asc. ♐ △ ♄ ♇)   ture of your personality is dedicated to and enthusiasm for a task or objective; that you are capable of endurance, persistence, hard work. This demands self-control, but it will not necessarily achieve stability and a sense of security.

(☉ ♊, Asc. ☽ ♐,   Adaptability is a keynote of your personality,
☽ DZ1, ☿ ♂ ♅)   together with versatility and a need to make changes, to vary your interests and activities, to avoid stagnation and restricting yourself to a routine type of lifestyle. This may bring a nagging sense of insecurity. However, you will no doubt feel most in control of yourself and your life by a means of a sensitive and realistic adaptation to exterior

♄ △ Asc. ☽ ♂ ♇   conditions and by a cautious and discrimin-
♆ □ ☿, △ ☉, ✳ ☽   ating receptiveness to the influence of
☽ ♂ Asc.   others. It would be wise to learn not to
♄ △ Asc. ☽, ♂ ♇   accept strangers on face value and first impressions. Self-control will also be developed through thoroughness and tenacity, persistence and industry in striving for what you want from life and experience.

Endeavouring to master self-control and to regulate and organize yourself and your environment will probably aggra-
♄ △ Asc. ☽, ♂ ♇ vate a measure of stress manifesting itself in obstinacy, discontentment, bouts of depression and indecision.

It will be clear from what has just been said that for you, a conforming and regulated lifestyle with emphasis on self-control will be far harder to achieve or even desire to achieve than an urge to deviate from the normal and be uninhibited

♅   in self-expression and choice of activities. This important
need, necessary for the release of your potential, will be
♅ ♂ ☿ DZ2, ⚼ Asc. ♃ powerfully evident in your personality.

You are likely to achieve a satisfying sense of freedom and
Asc. ☽ ♐, ♃ ♂ Asc. ⎱ independence and be successful in unortho-
♅ ⚼ ♃, ∟ ♇   ⎰ dox pursuits through being an opportunist
and having confidence in your ability to attain even the
most improbable objectives. You should have a flair for
originality, and close involvement with particular individuals will be necessary for encouraging the development of
original ideas.

♅ DZ2 ♂ ☿, ⚼ ♃, ∟ ♇   This strong attraction towards the unconventional could gift you with innovation, and emphasizes
again traits already referred to: inquisitiveness and open-mindedness, as well as those of spontaneity and flexibility.

This exciting and stimulating need that will attract you so
keenly calls for control of your nervous and emotional energies, which could produce stress by being dissipated through
restlessness, impulsiveness, excitability. Lack of control could
♅ DZ2 ♂ ☿, ⚼ ♃, ∟ ♇   manifest itself as contrary or rebellious
behaviour, even perversity, and occasional delight in shock-
ing people.

Personal growth and enlightenment, as well as improved
adaptation to the environment, necessarily depend on a con-
♆   tinuous elevation and revaluation of experience in an endeavour to achieve perfection in all that one does. This is a need
to seek a standard of excellence and requires in particular the
qualities of refinement and sensitivity.

♆ △ ☉, ⚹ ☽   This need is another strong feature in
♆ △ ☉, ⚹ ☽, □ ♀ ⎱ your make-up, drawing on the perfection-
☽ ♂ Asc.   ⎰ ist and idealist in you, encouraging sensitivity and subtlety. It will be a very likeable side to your
personality – easygoing, impressionable, sympathetic, accessible and very feminine. It will be such a contrast to the
restlessly active and at times quite forceful extraverted
features.

♆ △ ☉, ✳ ☽, □ ♀ If you can allow yourself time and space to relax and be quiet, this may encourage release of the creative potential within you. Outlets should be discovered for your keen imaginative faculty. Music is likely to provide much enjoyment and could prove of particular value therapeutically. Indeed you should possess the potential for an above average appreciation of the artistic and aesthetic in life.

Asc. ♐, ☉ ♊, ♃ ♂ Asc. ⎱ You will apply your intellectual facul-
☿ ♂ ♅ DZ₂, ☍ Asc. ♃ ⎰ ties mostly to interpret and under-
☽ DZ₁ ♂ Asc., ✳ ♆ stand life and its complexities, contradictions and problems and, although you could develop a keen intuitive gift, it may not always be too reliable, especially (as has already been noted) in your evaluation of other people. This need to seek perfection may have a subtle effect on you at times and be linked with an underlying fear of insecurity. However, I do not think this will in any way deter you from taking risks and projecting yourself energetically and

Asc. ♐, ☉ ♊ □ ♂, ♃ ♂ Asc. adventurously into life. It could, however, create stress and this may influence you to take evasive or escapist action when faced with tricky emotional

♆ △ ☉, ✳ (☽ DZ₁ ♂ Asc.) ⎱ problems. Other symptoms could
♆ □ ♀ ⎰ be moodiness, instability, vacillation. Do take particular care with regard to alcohol and drugs. This area of the psyche, involving the need to be sensitive, imaginative and relaxed will tend to be one where you are emotionally vulnerable.

♇ Have you ever wished you possessed a deep reservoir of power to enable you to achieve great feats, to exceed the limits of what would be expected of you? This would not be mere fantasizing, but responding to a normal need. A typical manifestation of this need is a sense of compulsion. Most of us may never realize this exists or will ever achieve any worthwhile benefit from its expression.

☉ □ ♂, ♂ △ ♃ ⎱ I think with you, however, there is a
Asc. ♐ ♂ ♃ DZ₂ ⎰ strong possibility that in response to this need you may gain satisfaction through outdoing others,

especi-ially as you have this strong competitive spirit. Also, I would not be surprised if you experience at times a compul-

Asc. ♐ ☌ ♃ DZ2, ☍ ☿ ♅ ⎫
☽ ♐ DZ1 ☌ Asc., △ ♇ ⎭ sive urge to seek to achieve feats of endeavour or even the impossible.

You are definitely capable of compulsive and extraordinary striving, energized by your basic qualities of dedication and

☽ △ ♇ endurance. Probably the most benefit and satisfaction to
☿ ∟ ♇ be gained through this striving will be its contribution to effectively adapting yourself to other people and the environment. This depends so much on developing confident communication and involvement with others and on a shrewd and intelligent translation of experience that you can learn from. For you, effective adaptation should involve developing self-

♄ ☌ ♇ control and stability. This will not come easily, particu-
♅ ∟ ♇ larly because of your nervously active temperament and your need to deviate from the normal. This will seem a far more natural and satisfying expression of the urge to outdo others or to achieve something you would not have been thought capable of. Success in this way would indeed be pleasurable.

Responding to this need and its potentially powerful energies may involve the risk of stress. This may result in

♇ △ ☽, ☌ ♄, ∟ ☿ ♅ reactions that produce a self-centred obstinacy, increased restlessness and irritability. Stress is most likely to arise when frustration is encountered.

Asc. ♐, ☉ ♊, ☽ ♃ ☌ Asc. ⎫
☿ ☍ Asc. ⎭ I have already given you some indications of how you are likely to relate to other people. Your chart gives further insight. For you, other people are vital to your interest in life and for your own personal development and exchange of ideas and thoughts. However, possibly more important than anyone else is the necessity to recognize and develop your own poten-

☽ ♃ DZ1/2 Me Sector tialities; to achieve benefits from what
Asc. ♐, ☿ ☌ ♅, ☍ Asc. you are able to accomplish entirely on
☽ DZ1 ☌ Asc. your own and to have your individuality

recognized by others; to have the space and freedom to be yourself. This is a particularly self-conscious side to your personality and suggests a sensitive and alert adaptation to your environment.

)) DZ1 ♂ Asc. Despite the critical factor of recognizing and developing your personality, you will be unable to ignore your need to belong to another person, to make yourself accessible to others, most particularly on the emotional level. This emphasizes how much you need to be on intimate terms with and making yourself open to another person. Even though

)) ✳ ♆ you are sensitive and alert to your environment, you will also be emotionally vulnerable, especially if your emotions influence your reasoning judgement.

You Sector   Significant relationships may occur that will be very much based on the need for you to benefit through receiving from and being influenced by the other person. Learning through others is very important for you, even through a relationship where there is conflict. Important relationships

☿ ♅ DZ2 ♂ Desc. are especially likely to be formed quickly and probably unexpectedly, and will be stimulating exercises in communication. In this sense you are likely to be attracted to and excited by a person, especially of the opposite sex, who is distinctly different from normal and shares with you an

☿ ♂ ♅ DZ2 interest in unconventional activities and behaviour. It is in this area of socializing that you could receive opportunities for developing your self-expression in distinctive ways.

☿ ♂ ♅ ♂ ♃   You will need to learn to relax with other
Desc. ♂ ☿, ✳ ♄ people, particularly as you enjoy excitement and activity, if you are to lessen nervous tension and risk of instability. Avoid being over-critical of others, or suspicious of their motives.

Clearly this powerful need to learn through others (even if you are not always consciously aware of it nor the reason you persist with a certain friendship or disharmonious contact) can significantly affect your personality, spiritual growth and
(You Sector Aspects) maturity. This may also bring heartache

and critical turning-points in your life. You will have your full share of changes, unexpected and disruptive, and could learn much about yourself through broken relationships.

☽ DZ1 ♂ Asc.   It has already been said that there will be the strongly felt need to belong to another person, making yourself accessible, especially emotionally. This means sharing yourself with another person on a give and take basis, jointly (Us Sector Aspects) and yet interdependently in a you-and-me-together process of development. This aspect of a relationship could bring much satisfaction through mutual interest and benefit. It would provide scope for your flexibility and sensitivity, and encourage the generous enthusiasm you are capable of. A relationship would not succeed if you felt inhibited or lacking in the excitement of unconventionality and frankness, stemming a free flow of communication.

(Us Sector Aspects,   Sharing and fully exposing yourself in a
☉ ♊ □ ♂)   relationship may make you vulnerable to stress, due to your sensitivity, producing reactions of contrariness, over-excitability. One of your greatest tests will be learning to accept that you are highly unlikely to find anyone who can satisfy you in all respects, emotionally, physically, intellectually.

Them Sector   There is yet another need to be satisfied through relationships, and that is for you to contribute to others in society generally and in the workaday world, and to benefit from such contacts. In this area, you will tend to have a
♃ ✳ MC   natural attitude of opportunism and confi-
(☉ ♊ □ ♂, Asc. ♐,   dence. It will be a challenge to your power-
☿ ♅ △ MC)   ful urge to communicate with others to exchange information and gain knowledge. Your enquiring mind and zest for unorthodoxy and originality will seek to find stimulating openings for your energetic personality. It will make for restlessness; hence you may find difficulty in holding a job. This is not because you may soon lose interest in your work, but due to another interest or objective suddenly holding greater attraction.

You are likely to choose active, energetic and challenging pursuits socially. A similar choice in regard to vocational pursuits would be very much to your advantage. Your intellect, keen imagination, flair for originality and innovation, inquiring attitude, adaptability, communicative ability and aptitude for intense and enthusiastic industry are qualities that should attract to you an appropriate vocation benefiting your personality.

You will have noted that in this analysis many potential traits are mentioned several times. This is not due to unnecessary repetition. It is because certain traits will be associated with more than one psychological need, as well as being sufficiently distinctive features worthy of mention several times. Instances are inquisitiveness, originality, unconventionality, enjoying a challenge, activity and enthusiasm, adaptability, urge for communication, independence and freedom-loving, spontaneity, perfectionism, sensitivity, accessibility, over-excitability, restlessness. Here are clear pointers to your personality.

Here, too, are pointers to why you behave in 'the bloody way you do sometimes'. You are restlessly active and this energy and enthusiasm for constantly doing things, communicating, projecting yourself into the environment, must inevitably encounter frustrations, restrictions, opposition. You love a challenge, and everything you set yourself to do must be 'meaningful' and give you yet further insight and understanding of life and of yourself. Your particular restlessness implies a very active mind, sensitive feelings, powerful emotions. If you do not allow yourself adequate relaxation periods, this must impose stress on your nervous system, involving mental strain and emotional aggravation. Resultant behaviour may well be impatience, irritability, quick temper, criticizing others – instinctive reactions as if preparing to fight the source of frustration.

You should gain valuable insight into the cause of particular behaviour and the strong desires, impulses and compulsions that may seem to dictate your choice of activity and lifestyle by carefully considering the various basic needs mentioned in this analysis.

Stressmanship   Methods of coping with stress come under the
Page 264.   general identification of stressmanship. Here are some helpful guidelines applicable to your psychological make-up. These will be aimed at helping you especially with these potential stress-inducing features:

> excessive activity; restlessness.
> diversity of interests and activities.
> unorthodox; a rebel.
> impatience; ready for a fight.
> nervous tension/exhaustion.
> emotionally vulnerable.

You need to identify stress, and know why you have it and what can be done to prevent or relieve it. This analysis will be invaluable in this respect. Communication is vital for you, but maybe you can more clearly communicate your needs to others. Learn how to be able to *choose* not to get upset and to relax instead. Take a deep breath and count to ten, rather than reacting on impulse! Learn about deep relaxation and deep breathing techniques and thus give yourself a chance to become more attuned to your body and any warning nudges of an imbalance or excess. Above all, develop time and space in which to be utterly yourself.

This analysis has shown how important it is to you to 'know who you are'. Excessively diversifying your interests and activities could be depriving you of those magical quiet and restful moments when you could look inwards and meditate. It is true that it will be quite natural for you to seek a variety of experiences, but perhaps more will be gained from such variety if you can also learn to unwind in a variety of ways. Avoid obvious pressures, such as taking on too many commitments. You know that you have deep and easily motivated emotions, so develop the ability to 'let off steam' or relieve tension occasionally, but without hurting or offending others. Finally, you possess a goodly sense of humour, so it shouldn't be too difficult to relax into humour and laughter at times when you could otherwise easily get uptight.

This completes your character analysis and I trust that you will benefit considerably from the indications given. If at any time you feel that I may be able to help you further or to elucidate points, please do not hesitate to contact me.

Potential ill health indications

Traditionally, a character analysis included a section on 'health'. This dealt with the birth chart's indications of areas of the physical body likely to be most vulnerable to ill health. At the time I prepared the analysis for Janet, I had stopped including this section unless it was specifically requested. For the reader's interest, indications for Janet are given in chapter 28.

CHAPTER 26

Janet's Comments on Her Analysis

In mid-January 1979, a month after I had completed Janet's character analysis, she typed a very long letter to me, commenting on the analysis and herself. She was thrilled with it and ended her letter by asking me to send the Mayo School of Astrology's prospectus so that she might enrol for the basic course. 'I am really excited about astrology,' she wrote – but she never did get round to enrolling.

'Oh! how I've always needed other people to project myself onto,' she wrote, 'and how correct you are about me being a poor judge of others. I get taken advantage of, but I don't really blame the men – after all, I'm partly taking advantage of their being the opposite sex! I haven't really got many friends, though I know hundreds of people very well. Yes, true, I'm too much of an idealist, and such a bloody perfectionist! I've had so many love affairs, and I go through periods when sex is like a drug to me, but after all these affairs (I began at sixteen) I'm not sure now exactly what I want in an ideal man. Yes, I suppose I'm very much an intellectual, but when the emotions take over in a close relationship I either get confused or just love wallowing in the emotions and feelings. I really feel excited about being a woman then – this feeling is almost as good as having an orgasm! What am I looking for in a man? I know I've got to have *love*. I like the excitement of discovery and a man I'm attracted to discovering me. Yes, I love making myself 'accessible' as you put it. That's the real woman in me.

'There's something you never mentioned in the analysis, unless you avoided this out of politeness. It might be useful in your research work. I've engaged in what some might call "sexual perversions". Nothing disgusting. Just variations on an old theme! I expect it's because I love experimenting, doing things differently. I'm not bothered if I never do those things again. My introduction was a beach swimming party. About twelve of us all swam in the nude one evening, and it ended in a free for all love-in. I love swimming in the nude, especially on my own and at night. I'm told I'm a very strong swimmer.'

When Janet was seventeen (in 1965), she began living with a man ten years her senior. Her family practically disowned her. A year later, because she was pregnant, they married. She lost the baby by miscarriage. Then, when she was nineteen (1967), they separated. The following year he was killed in a car accident.

Janet said that her life has been a series of ups and downs and unexpected changes. In her letter she wrote, 'How right you are when you say I'm likely to have my full share of changes, unexpected and disruptive.' In 1971, at the age of twenty-three, she suffered a nervous breakdown. Janet went on, 'I can feel quite fit and healthy for longish periods and then suddenly things go wrong. It's as if I'm trying to constantly run a car at 80–110 mph and forget that the oil might dry up and parts get overheated. I'm then forced to admit – yet again – that I never really give my body and brain a chance to maintain good health. When I assumed I was fit, warning noises in the engine did occur fairly regularly.' She said the basis of all her health troubles was her nerves and, probably; her strong emotional reaction to things going on around her. She mentioned cramps, especially when swimming, poor circulation, irregular periods, anaemia and headaches. 'That sounds as if I'm actually a nervous wreck,' she continued, 'but how I loathe myself when I'm unwell.'

She apparently did well to get to grips with her breakdown and was only off work for three months. In 1972, when she was twenty-four she was driving her car when it careered off a country road and scythed down several small trees in a spinney. She had taken a sharp bend too fast. She was extremely fortunate to receive only facial cuts and bruises to her body. Hence the scar I had seen on her face.

Between 1973–77 she enjoyed increasing success in her work. Since leaving school she had been in a variety of jobs. During the 1973–77 period she had five different jobs, four secretarial with a considerable increase in pay each time, plus a 'steamy affair' with a top executive at each of the three offices! She even experimented with being self-employed, setting up her own typing agency. She said, 'Astonishingly I was doing too well, didn't want to take on an assistant and so, after nine months of typing all hours like a maniac, I packed it in.' Her most interesting employment was in 1976. She successfully applied for a position as a courier with a major overseas holiday tour company. She felt she had found her perfect vocation – travel, variety, sunshine, totally in touch with people, learning all the time. She had taken a 'crash course' in Greek and was amazed how well she was learning the 'cock-eyed language'. She added, 'But after only six months I buggered it up and got fired. They were such beautiful men in Rhodes . . .'

'Yes,' she wrote, 'it is forever a conflict between needing my independence and needing to be influenced by and to belong to someone gentle yet strong. I suppose my independence always wins. But sometimes I do get tired and have sudden black depressions and feel terrifyingly lonely. I don't think I could ever kill myself. I simply turn to heavy drinking when I'm really depressed. I'm not an alcoholic. I've never taken drugs. I want to be alert, I want to be *me*, not a zombie or a corpse. Sometimes I feel trapped. I crave to know all I can about life and people, but I yearn to break out of myself and *really* know the truth within all things. I get so frustrated, and it's sometimes then that I mentally and emotionally fight people who disagree with me; sometimes I try to shock them.'

Janet wondered whether I had sufficiently emphasized in the analysis how anxiety-prone she can be. 'Outwardly,' she wrote, 'the extravert me really does feel full of bounding optimism and will joke about set-backs. But the "inside me" is a sod of a worrier. It's my stupid sensitivity and perfectionism. I'm quite positive my being a perfectionist is a phobia. I desperately need to adapt to my environment *perfectly*. Do you know what I mean? I feel perfectly in harmony out in the country. But with other people I'm so often aware of the imperfections in my relationships. Maybe it's a lot to do with me loathing convention and polite orthodox behaviour. I do not mean I enjoy being rude to others, but I can so easily be if someone's a hypocrite.' She admitted being a born rebel.

'I think it's great, your mention of basic needs,' she wrote. 'These give an exciting and sensible structure to the analysis and to your portrayal of my personality. It's fascinating to know the reasons and sources within the psyche for my behaviour.'

Eventually – after twelve pages – Janet apologized for writing so much about herself. She had to, the analysis was so uncannily accurate that she felt I already knew her 'naked psyche', so she wanted to share other intimate details that might aid astrological research, which she knew I am so intensely interested in.

Farewell, Janet: and so you broke out at last

Discussing various interesting birth charts and their subject's case histories in confidence with a psychology colleague, I mentioned Janet. This colleague lives on the south coast of England. One evening in October 1980 he telephoned me. Did I know Janet was dead? He had read in the local newspaper of a swimming tragedy.

The naked body found washed up on the shingle beach had been identified, from the clothes found neatly folded on a beach about a mile away, as that of Janet.

'I love swimming in the nude,' she wrote, 'especially on my own and at night. I'm told I'm a very strong swimmer . . . I get cramps, especially when swimming . . . sometimes I do get tired and have sudden black depressions and feel terrifyingly lonely. I don't think I could ever kill myself . . . Sometimes I feel trapped . . . I yearn to break out of myself and *really* know the truth within all things . . .'

We will never know why this happened to Janet that night in October 1980, at the age of thirty-two.

CHAPTER 27

Extreme Psychological Disorders

It would be no exaggeration to say that at certain times everybody can experience mental and nervous strain, times when our ability as an individual to cope with worries and stress, conflicts and frustrations, bring us to what may seem the verge of breakdown. It is possible that each one of us has within our psyche's make-up a latent vulnerability to one or more of the major recognized psychological disorders; although for most of us the disturbing or 'out of character' symptoms may never prove to be more than a temporary upset.

For most of my professional life as an astrological counsellor and teacher, I have had a special interest in extreme psychological disorders. This chapter deals with the results of my study and research, and direct personal contact with the case histories and charts of those suffering from these disorders.

One can never stress too strongly that an astrologer interpreting a client's birth chart must never suggest that the client could be suffering from one of the major disorders. He can make notes (strictly for his own confidential reference) of planetary patterns in the client's chart suggestive of a root cause for particular neurotic or antisocial behaviour, which might suggest a mild link with one of the disorders. His awareness of these patterns of behaviour and symptoms of an imbalance in the personality structure would help him in his counselling.

The extreme psychological disorders

Depression: an emotional disorder or attitude, sometimes definitely pathological, involving a feeling of inadequacy and hopelessness, characterized by anxiety, guilt feelings, self-deprecation and withdrawal of interest from the outside world.

Neuroticism: a mental or personality disorder in which a person is unusually anxious, miserable, troubled or incapacitated, due to an inadequate or faulty response to the demands of life.

Hysteria: an illness resulting from emotional conflict, generally characterized by immaturity, impulsiveness, attention-seeking, dependency and the use of the defence mechanisms.

Manic-depressive: a condition in which the primary disturbance is a severe change of mood and emotional responses, exhibiting over-enthusiasm when life goes well and extreme rejection when it does not go well.

Paranoia: a condition in which a person persistently has delusions that he or she is being persecuted, characterized by extreme suspiciousness, bizarre behaviour, delusions of grandeur, aggression.

Psychopathic: behaviour that is predominantly amoral or antisocial and characterized by impulsive, irresponsible actions, with little or no sense of right or wrong.

Psychotic: behaviour characterized by some degree of personality disintegration and failure of the ability to correctly evaluate external reality. The most severe psychoses are the insanities.

Obsessive-compulsive: irrational, useless acts that constantly intrude into a person's behaviour, characterized by repetitive and often ritualistic behaviour, and a preoccupation with the need to control the self and the environment.

Schizophrenia: a condition characterized by withdrawal from reality and entry into a world of bizarre fantasy; a splitting from or break with reality, of detachment and emotional isolation.

Diagnosing a psychological disorder through a chart

The planets, and aspects between planets and the angles, are more reliably associated with extreme psychological disorders than are the signs, although, as will be seen, each sign has a potential for certain types of extreme behaviour.

With experience, an astrologer can recognize a potentially balanced and well-integrated personality from the subject's chart. It is vitally important to recognize balance and imbalance in the overall chart pattern as these are generally strong clues as to the potential occurrence or absence of behavioural problems. In the general sense, one cannot rely too strictly on hard and fast rules for trying to pinpoint a major disorder – or the potential for it that would appear to be developing by way of symptomatic behaviour. It is advisable to accept that never less than *four* planets are likely to contribute to a major psychological disorder. In most cases *each* of these planets are in ♂ or □ with an angle.

In looking now at each planet and sign, we are indicating their contribution to each psychological disorder. When interpreting a planet's aspect to an angle, the features associated with the disorder or abnormality that will be emphasized will tend to be those of the planet. When interpreting an aspect between two planets, one assesses the contributions attributed to each planet for each extreme psychological disorder. For example, for a major Sun–Moon aspect, for depression, one could consider a particular emphasis on withdrawal into self, self-preoccupation, self-reproach, guilt feelings, great tension, discontentment.

The Sun's contribution

Emphasis on: self-preoccupation, great tension, discontentment, restlessness, insufficient self-control, attention-seeking, aggression, constantly driving oneself. Associated particularly with the manic-depressive, psychopathic, obsessive-compulsive, and with paranoia and hysteria.

Depression: self-recrimination, self-preoccupation, great tension, discontentment, restlessness, self-reproach.

Neuroticism: strive excessively for satisfactions and perfections, obsessiveness, insufficient self-control, hysterical symptoms.

Hysteria: self-absorption, selfish, excitable, impulsiveness, attention-seeking, needs to be centre stage.

Manic-depressive: self-demanding, self-critical, very confident, energetic, aggressive, constantly drive oneself, over-activity.

Paranoia: conceited, inflated idea of own abilities, crave praise and recognition, aggressive, delusions of grandeur.

Psychopathic: egocentric, selfish, impulsive, defiant, cannot tolerate frustration.

Psychotic: self-centred, over-excitement, aggressive, tough-mindedness.

Obsessive-compulsive: self-exacting, insistency, persistency, excessive obstinacy, uncompromising.

Schizophrenia: megalomania (delusions of grandeur), exhibitionism, desire for power.

The Moon's contribution

Emphasis on: withdrawal into self, guilt feelings, phobias, anxiety, discontentment, restlessness, instability, maladaptation, insecurity, disorientation, dependency, disturbed emotional responses, severe mood swings, hypersensitive. Associated particularly with depression, neuroticism, hysteria, schizophrenia, the manic-depressive and psychotic.

Depression: withdrawal into self, self-preoccupation, self-reproach, guilt feelings, great tension, discontentment, apprehensiveness, anxiety, inferiority feelings, restlessness, disturbed emotional responses.

Neuroticism: disequilibrium, maladaptation, instability, emotional disorders, anxiety, phobias, insecurity, hypersensitive.

Hysteria: self-absorption, instability, emotional conflict, attention-seeking, dependency, submissive reactions, shifting emotional feelings, insecurity, anxiety.

Manic-depressive: self-critical, severe mood swings, disorientation, restlessness, hypersensitive, severe emotional responses, anxiety, intense guilt.

Paranoia: moody, touchy, sensitive, extremely suspicious of others' motives.

Psychopathic: selfish, egocentric, emotionally unstable, drug/drink addictive.

Psychotic: disorientation, maladaptation, self-centred, extreme defence mechanisms, severe emotional disturbance.

Obsessive-compulsive: perfectionism, worry over trifles, emotional tension, over-conscientious, defensive.

Schizophrenia: disorientation, rapidly alternating moods, hypersensitive, highly suspicious, over-possessive, shy, emotional distortion.

Mercury's contribution

Emphasis on: anxiety, indecision, restlessness, great tension, instability, excitability, functional nervous disorders, disorientation. Associated particularly with neuroticism, the manic-depressive, psychotic, obsessive-compulsive, schizophrenia.

Depression: apprehensiveness, anxiety, indecision, restlessness, agitation, confusion, discontentment, great tension.

Neuroticism: maladaptation, instability, excessive anxiety, indecision, functional nervous disorders, apprehensiveness.

Hysteria: excitable, instability, anxiety.

Manic-depressive: flight of ideas, acceleration of thought, alertness of sensory perception, wildly talkative, over-activity, irritability, restlessness, anxiety.

Paranoia: irritability, overly zealous in attention to detail, critical.

Psychopathic: tantrums, bored by routine.

Psychotic: disorientation, over-excitement, fragmented thought, maladaptation.

Obsessive-compulsive: worry over trifles, indecision, over-conscientious.

Schizophrenia: disorganized thinking, confusion, rapidly alternating moods, over-anxious.

Venus's contribution

Emphasis on: inferiority feelings, self-preoccupation, disturbed emotional responses, emotional instability, hypersensitive, attention-seeking. Associated particularly with depression, neuroticism, hysteria, the psychopathic and psychotic.

Depression: low morale, feelings of extreme unworthiness, inferiority feelings, inadequacy, self-preoccupation, loss of interest in others, disturbed emotional responses, sense of isolation.

Neuroticism: strive excessively for satisfactions and perfections, socially inadequate, emotional disorders, inadequate emotional adjustment, emotional instability, hypersensitive.

Hysteria: emotional conflict, attention-seeking, self-absorption, selfish, shifting emotional feelings.

Manic-depressive: hypersensitive, severe emotional responses, promiscuity, increased interest in sex, self-pity.

Paranoia: sensitive, conceited, has few friends, hypersensitive to criticism.

Psychopathic: selfish, promiscuity, emotional instability.

Psychotic: severe emotional and feeling disturbance, self-centred, incorrect reality evaluation.

Obsessive-compulsive: emotional tension, extreme tidiness, perfectionism.

Schizophrenia: hypersensitive, perfectionism, emotional abnormality.

Mars's contribution

Emphasis on: restlessness, agitation, compulsiveness, excitability, emotional conflict, aggressiveness, constantly driving oneself. Associated particularly with hysteria, the manic-depressive, paranoia, psychopathic and psychotic.

Depression: restlessness, agitation, disturbed emotional responses, irritability, discontentment.

Neuroticism: hysterical symptoms, emotional disorders, compulsiveness.

Hysteria: impulsiveness, instability, excitability, emotional conflict, emotionally tempestuous.

Manic-depressive: frenzied activity, aggression, reckless, constantly driving oneself, severe emotional responses, irritability, excitability, restlessness, extremely quick, increased interest in sex.

Paranoia: aggressive, irritability, difficult to live with.

Psychopathic: impulsiveness, explosive, violent outbursts, promiscuous, tantrums, emotionally unstable.

Psychotic: over-excitement, tough-minded, aggressive, severe emotional disturbance.

Obsessive-compulsive: emotional tension, insistency, persistency.

Schizophrenia: extreme elation, desire for power, emotional abnormality.

Jupiter's contribution

Emphasis on: great tension, overacts, dramatization, exaggeration, extravagance, over-demanding. Associated particularly with neuroticism, the manic-depressive, paranoia, psychotic and obsessive-compulsive.

Depression: great tension, overreacts to minor upsets or losses, inability to accomplish tasks, restlessness.

Neuroticism: strive excessively for satisfactions and perfections, hysterical symptoms, insufficient self-control.

Hysteria: attention-seeking, multiple personality, dramatization, exaggeration, over-demanding.

Manic-depressive: exaggerated behaviour, overestimates, optimism, boastful, extravagance, grandiosity of mood, exuberant drive, restlessness, reckless, elevation of mood, overextend self.

Paranoia: inflated idea of own abilities, craves praise and recognition.

Psychopathic: egocentric, continually demanding, cannot tolerate frustration.

Psychotic: self-centred, over-excitement, inflated emotional responses, over-enjoyment.

Obsessive-compulsive: over-conscientious, excessive tension, extreme tidiness.

Schizophrenia: megalomania (delusions of grandeur), exhibitionism, extreme elation.

Saturn's contribution

Emphasis on: depressive moods, pessimism, low morale, inferiority feelings, sense of isolation, insecurity, anxiety-prone, self-pity, critical. Associated particularly with depression, neuroticism, hysteria, schizophrenia, the manic-depressive and obsessive-compulsive.

Depression: sense of helplessness, hopelessness, pessimism, despondency, despair, low morale, feelings of extreme unworthiness, guilt feelings, inferiority feelings, inadequacy, fatigue, sense of isolation.

Neuroticism: irrational fears, feelings of inadequacy, insecurity, apprehension, excessive anxiety.

Hysteria: frigidity, selfish, anxiety.

Manic-depressive: self-critical, anxiety, intense guilt feelings, feels unworthy and a failure, self-pity.

Paranoia: suspicious of others' motives, critical, has few friends, aloofness, zealous in attention to detail.

Psychopathic: egocentric, defiant, selfish, cannot form close relationships, antisocial.

Psychotic: self-centred, tough-minded, extreme defence mechanisms, depression.

Obsessive-compulsive: ritualistic, excessive orderliness, excessive obstinacy, uncompromising, self-exacting, preoccupation with correctness, worry over trifles, inhibited, defensive, conformist, over-conscientious, precision.

Schizophrenia: highly suspicious, depression, seclusionist, secretive, cautious, emotional blunting, shy, avoids intimacy, apathy, social isolation.

Uranus's contribution

Emphasis on: great tension, discontentment, restlessness, irritability, instability, excitability, eccentricity, uninhibited, disorientation, antisocial, severe mood swings. Associated particularly with neuroticism and schizophrenia, the manic-depressive, psychopathic and psychotic.

Depression: great tension, discontentment, restlessness, agitation, irritability.

Neuroticism: instability, maladjustment, functional nervous disorders, no established way of life, hysterical symptoms, emotional instability.

Hysteria: excitability, instability, dramatization, dissatisfied with real world, dissociation symptoms, emotional extremes, impulsiveness.

Manic-depressive: severe mood swings, bizarre behaviour, restlessness, reckless, irritability, promiscuity, intense excitement, uninhibited, gambling, disorientation.

Paranoia: irritability, difficult to live with, moody.

Psychopathic: antisocial, unable to conform, individualistic, explosive, tantrums, defiant, bored by routine, promiscuity, impulsive.

Obsessive-compulsive: indecisiveness, irrational, emotional tension.

Schizophrenia: bizarre behaviour, eccentricity, emotional abnormality, rapidly alternating moods, detachment.

Neptune's contribution

Emphasis on: anxiety, instability, hypersensitive, apprehensiveness, withdrawal into self, restlessness, confusion, phobias, dissatisfaction with real world, escapism, emotional insecurity, disorientation, excitability. Associated particularly with depression, neuroticism, paranoia, the psychotic and schizophrenia.

Depression: purposelessness, self-denigration, neurotic, apprehensiveness, anxiety, withdrawal into self, self-reproach, inadequacy, restlessness, delusions, confusion, affective disorder, disturbed emotional responses.

Neuroticism: disequilibrium, instability, feelings of inadequacy, strive excessively for satisfactions and perfections, self-denigration, emotional disorders, phobias, irrational fears, apprehensiveness, excessive anxiety, hypersensitive.

Hysteria: shifting emotional feelings, anxiety, fantasy, idealization, dissatisfaction with real world, imaginative elaboration, escapism, instability, excitability.

Manic-depressive: delusion, hallucination, disorientation, irrational, ecstasy, hypersensitive, severe emotional responses, flight of ideas, alertness of sensory perception, restlessness, intense excitement, self-pity, self-critical.

Paranoia: hypersensitive to criticism, touchy, delusions, hallucinations, feels persecuted, sensitive, moody.

Psychopathic: antisocial, irresponsible, emotionally unstable, drug/drink addictive, unreliable, fantasy, promiscuity, unable to conform.

Psychotic: misinterpretation of reality, fantasy, delusions, hallucinations, disorientation, over-excitement, severe emotional disturbance.

Obsessive-compulsive: irrational, perfectionism, emotional tension.

Schizophrenia: delusions, hallucinations, bizarre behaviour, perfectionist, withdrawal from reality, hypersensitive, disorientation, confused thinking, emotional abnormality, over-anxious, extreme elation.

Pluto's contribution

Emphasis on: great tension, obsessiveness, compulsiveness, self-absorption, dramatization, constantly drive oneself, aggressive, uncompromising, perfectionist. Associated particularly with the manic-depressive, psychopathic and obsessive-compulsive.

Depression: great tension, discontentment, withdrawal into self, restlessness, self-preoccupation, self-recrimination, sense of isolation.

Neuroticism: obsessiveness, strive excessively for satisfactions and perfections, compulsiveness.

Hysteria: self-absorption, dramatization, selfish, obsessional, emotional extremes, attention-seeking.

Manic-depressive: do extraordinary and harmful things, nothing seems impossible, pathological preoccupation, promiscuity, offensively frank, severe emotional responses, constantly drive oneself, restlessness, aggressive, elevation of mood, self-demanding, overextend self.

Paranoia: aggressive, inflated idea of own abilities, craves praise and recognition.

Psychopathic: antisocial, egocentric, selfish, defiant, promiscuous, explosive, emotionally unstable, outbursts of violence.

Psychotic: self-centred, aggressive, severe emotional disturbance, tough-minded.

Obsessive-compulsive: self-exacting, uncompromising, excessive obstinacy, obsessiveness, compulsiveness.

Schizophrenia: perfectionist, desire for power, megalomania (delusions of grandeur).

The Signs: extreme psychological disorders

Here is the behaviour associated with each sign that could contribute in extreme cases to the major psychological disorders.

Aries ♈
Monomania, instability, stress neuroses, violence, outbursts of destructive anger, hysteria.

Taurus ♉
Severe obsessiveness, fixity, possessiveness, resentfulness, broodiness.

Gemini ♊
Anxiety and nervous disorders, instability, restlessness.

Cancer ♋
Morbid touchiness, hypersensitivity, excessive moodiness, masochism, inferiority complex, self-dramatization.

Leo ♌
Self-dramatization, self-aggrandizement, power-complex, exhibitionism, powerful deep-rooted habits, aggressiveness.

Virgo ♍
Anxiety, hypochondria, inferiority complex, obsessiveness, extreme perfectionist complex, obsession with cleanliness, Les-
bian tendency, nerves.

Libra ♎
Vacillating moods, anxiety, depression.

Scorpio ♏
Obsessiveness, extreme emotional reactions, self-dramatization,
sexual neuroses, acute self-consciousness, severe temper or
rages.

Sagittarius ♐
Extravagance, exaggeration, fanaticism, restlessness.

Capricorn ♑
Pessimism, extreme seriousness, emotionally inhibited, materialistic and cynical, sadism, homosexuality.

Aquarius ♒
Fanaticism, eccentricity, extreme emotional detachment, antisocial,
perversity, insensitivity to others' feelings.

Pisces ♓
Confusion, emotionally vulnerable, anxiety, instability, withdrawal, sense of inadequacy, extremes of elation and depression, alcohol/drug addiction.

CHAPTER 28

Physiological and Anatomical Correlations

Centuries ago the ancient astrologers realized there was a connection between the planets and signs and the human body, and the individual's predisposition to particular ailments and diseases. Much of their knowledge, which has been handed down to us, still forms the basis of the modern astrologer's prediction of a client's potentially vulnerable physical features.

However, the study of the correlation of physical and psychosomatic ailments and diseases with astrological factors is still very much in its kindergarten stage and must be seen as a specialized area of astrological prediction. With the advent of computers, there is no reason why trained astrologers and the medical profession should not co-operate in an intensive research programme to establish the most reliable techniques for predicting astrological patterns and their correlation with potential sickness and disease. The benefit to mankind would be inestimable. Months or years before symptoms of a particular type of ill-health an individual is advised he or she could be prone to might appear, the necessary change of diet or lifestyle could be made to prevent this condition materializing. Or, when symptoms appear for which a doctor may not be too sure of the source through orthodox diagnosis, the chart could pinpoint the most probable seat of the developing imbalance.

As I always told my students, one is strongly advised to exercise the utmost caution when interpreting types of illness a particular subject may be prone to. Even an astrologer with medical training and qualifications should exercise caution when diagnosing sickness and disease through a birth chart, although in this case there should be a high probability of a correct diagnosis.

Disease is disequilibrium

'Disease' should be written as 'dis-ease', implying disequilibrium; lack of ease, of body harmony. There is a deficiency in the body, probably of specific nutrients or vitamins. Most diseases are aggravated by prolonged physical and mental stresses, which create biochemical and metabolic disorder. Stress has been defined as any condition that harms the body or damages or destroys a few or many cells. In chapter 5 we have also shown that stress is adaptation to one's environment and that it can become a valuable human response. But the stress that can cause ill-health and may lead to a specific disease is that which produces harmful effects in the body and the psyche: anxiety, faulty nutritional patterns, overwork, excessive intake of tobacco or alcohol, drug addiction, inadequate diet, lack of sleep or exercise, emotional upsets and so on.

The emphasis in this book is on the prediction of potential stress-related behaviour. In this present chapter we indicate how the planets and signs correlate with human bodily functions and because these planets and signs also correlate with specific forms of behaviour, how the study of them can lead to the prediction of potential stress-induced illnesses and disease.

Basic framework: the body systems

Traditionally, astrologers have tended to link an anatomical feature or organ and a physical ailment with a planet or sign. Mostly, these correlations are correct, but this method does not give a too clear picture of a planet's or sign's potential as a predictive factor.

For the first time in astrological literature I am presenting each planet and sign correlated with a particular body system. In this way one can then detail those parts of the body, organs, physiological functions, ailments and diseases connected with the particular body system, and thus with the relevant planet/s and sign/s. Reference to a reliable medical book from the Public Lending Library will provide this anatomical/physiological data.

Although each planet and sign does have a specific link with certain organs or functions, other planets or signs may also be seen to have an important connection with these same features. This is evident in the interrelationship of all organs and physiological functions, just as the functional needs of the psyche are interrelated.

The body systems are:

Musculo-skeletal system: (1) muscular, (2) skeletal. Together, the skeleton (bones), joints or articulations and the muscles constitute the locomotor system. The extensive distribution of muscle masses over the skeleton provide power for movement and give form and substance to the extremities. The general functions of bones are (a) provision of framework and support for the body, (b) points of attachment for muscles, (c) protection of internal organs, and (d) formation of blood cells in the bone marrow.

Vascular system: (1) heart and circulatory, (2) spleen and lymphatic. The heart governs and regulates the equilibrium of the whole body; its controlling influence integrates every feature and each cell; its function is life-sustaining and energizing. The circulation is the body's transport system. It brings essential substances to the cells and carries away waste products of cellular activity. The spleen, among other functions, is concerned with the elaboration of immune bodies in response to infection. The function of the lymphatic system, apart from drainage of excess tissue fluid and fat absorption, is the cleansing from the tissues of particles of foreign material, particularly when dealing with infection.

Respiratory system: the lifeline carrying oxygen and food to every cell.

Alimentary system: its function is feeding, nutrition, digestion, maintenance. Commencing at the mouth and ending in the lower bowels, this system is basically a tube with a series of specialized regions, such as the stomach, liver, small and large intestines.

Reproductive system: (1) male, (2) female. Those organs and physiological functions that reproduce the human species.

Excretory system: (1) urinary, (2) bowels, (3) skin, (4) lungs. The elimination of waste and indigestible material from the organism.

Central nervous system: (1) motor, (2) sensory, (3) special senses. The means by which various bodily activities are co-ordinated and by which we respond to changes in our environment. The special senses of sight, speech, hearing, smell, taste.

Autonomic (sympathetic) nervous system: responsible for automatic and spontaneous reflexes that do not come under the influence of the will or consciousness. It has to do with nutrition, elimination and protection of the organism, with emotions, affections and desires, and influences glandular secretions.

Endocrine system: the endocrine glands discharge their secretion directly into the blood stream and not through a duct into a body cavity. They are the great chemical regulators of bodily function, working together with the autonomic nervous system in maintaining a homeostatic balance.

Immune system: the body's natural defence system; a mechanism for protecting the organism against harmful viruses, bacteria and 'foreign bodies'.

The planets and physiological functions

The Sun ☉
Functional need: purposeful activity.
Physiological actions: vitalizing, integrating, doing, mobilizing, energy outflow.
Body systems: vascular, central nervous, immune.
Vital links with: heart and circulatory system; organic disorders; type of metabolism (the process of building up nutritive

material into living matter, and that of breaking down proto-
plasm into simpler substances to perform special functions);
structural alteration of tissue.

Health risk: lack of purposeful engagement with the environment,
intenseness, dominance, self-centredness, uncompromising.

Moon ☽

Functional need: adaptation.

Physiological actions: pliant, receptive, absorbent, secreting, rhythmic, fertilizing, fluidic, mediating, equilibration.

Body systems: alimentary, autonomic nervous, vascular, endocrine,
reproductive.

Vital links with: digestive system (feeding, nutrition, digestion,
maintenance); cerebellum (concerned with the automatic regulation of posture and the balance and co-ordination of movement); autonomic nervous system (nutrition, protection of
organism, emotions, affections, desires, glandular secretions);
heart and circulatory system (equilibrium, maintenance); lymphatic system (fluids); thymus gland (regulates rhythms of
growth); female reproductive system; osmosis (the percola-
tion and intermixture of fluids separated by porous mem-
brane); fluids and secreting functions; growths and tumours;
functional (as opposed to organic) disorders.

Health risk: faulty adaptation to and lack of a meaningful connection with the environment, emotional vulnerability, acute
sensitivity, restlessness, moodiness, self-indulgence,
instability.

Mercury ☿

Functional need: communication.

Physiological actions: nervine (acting on the nerves), exciting,
activating, restless, changeable, connective, co-ordinating,
irritating.

Body systems: central nervous, autonomic nervous, respiratory,
endocrine, vascular.

Vital links with: cerebellum (co-ordination and synchronization of muscle performance, and the sensations of touch, sight, hearing and thought processes); autonomic nervous system (communication and co-ordination of its auxiliary nerve network); respiratory functions (transmission of oxygen to all parts of the body); thyroid gland (control of the rate of body metabolism and combustion of air in breathing); circulatory system (transmission of blood); lymphatic system (co-ordinating function between capillaries and cells).

Health risk: frustrated or unsatisfying communication with the environment, nervous restlessness; hence, dissipation of nervous energy, excitability, hypercriticalness, anxiety-proneness, vacillation.

Venus ♀

Functional need: evaluation.

Physiological actions: centripetal, fermenting, congesting, fertilizing, lethargic, pustular, relaxing, rhythmical, cohesive, harmonizing.

Body systems: endocrine, central nervous, vascular, reproductive, excretory.

Vital links with: thymus gland (regulates rhythms of growth); parathyroid glands (productive of warmth of feeling, passivity, steadiness, serenity); cerebellum (balance and co-ordination of movement); venous circulation (the centripetal process of blood through the veins); genito-urinary system (especially female); kidneys (their essential activity of maintaining a constant composition of circulating blood); glandular disorders; growths and tumours.

Health risk: disharmony and unsatisfying relationships, self-indulgence, perfectionism, acquisitiveness, hypersensitivity, excessive eroticism.

Mars ♂

Functional need: exertion.

Physiological actions: centrifugal, inflammatory, forcing, combustive, disruptive, energizing, exciting, expulsive, stimulating.

Body systems: musculo-skeletal, excretory, reproductive, endocrine.

Vital links with: muscular system (manipulation and activation of the skeleton and functional processes through which energy and power is expressed); genito-urinary systems and sex glands (expulsive and centrifugal actions, emotional excitation); adrenal glands (the 'fight and flight' glands).

Health risk: misdirection or frustration of the desire for energetic activity, aggressiveness, over-activity, impatience, restlessness, over-excitability, emotionality, insufficient relaxation.

Jupiter ♃

Functional need: increase.

Physiological actions: healing, harmonizing, preservation, restoration, growth and expansion, filtration, nourishing, enrichment, enlargement.

Body systems: alimentary, endocrine.

Vital links with: liver (growth through fat production/storage of energizing glycogen); thyroid gland (growth production and regulation); posterior lobe of the pituitary gland (regulation of uniformity of growth); excessive weight; tumours; enlarged organs; surfeit or excess of fluids and secretions.

Health risk: inadequate improvement of one's relationship with the environment, extremism, dogmatism, fanaticism, self-indulgence, dissipation, nervous exhaustion.

Saturn ♄

Functional need: structure.

Physiological actions: binding, cooling, crystallizing, hardening, depleting, limiting, obstructing, retarding, suppressing, coagulating, condensing, constricting, emaciating, retentive, stabilizing, protecting.

Body systems: musculo-skeletal, endocrine.

Vital links with: skeletal system (framework of support, basis for form, protection of internal organs, points of attachment for muscles); thymus gland (regulates rhythms of growth); parathyroid glands (regulate the metabolism of calcium and phosphorous indispensable for the building of the skeleton framework that gives form and holds together the organism); anterior lobe of pituitary gland (where concerned with structural formation of bones and muscles); skin (protective agent, necessary boundary, structural limit); chronic and deficiency diseases; hardening of the arteries; arthritis.

Health risk: lack of a stable and controlled relationship with the environment, inhibition, pessimism, repression, fixity, fastidiousness, stubbornness, fear of insecurity, anxiety, depression.

Uranus ♅

Functional need: deviation.

Physiological actions: deviating, exciting, disrupting, separating, convulsive, cramping, distorting, erratic, freak-producing, inco-ordinating, irregular, shock-producing, spasmodic, stricturing.

Body systems: autonomic nervous, endocrine.

Vital links with: autonomic nervous system (association with disruptive and excitable emotional conditions); pineal body (sexual development and mental precocity); gonads or sex glands (abnormal activity of secretions); epilepsy; cramps, spasms; convulsions; disorders of nervous origin.

Health risk: lack of freedom to deviate from the normal and express originality, impatience, eccentricity, perversion, explosiveness, excitability, being erratic, nervous tension, irritability.

Neptune ♆

Functional need: refinement.

Physiological actions: dispersive, refining, comatose, relaxing, disintegrating.

Body systems: central nervous, endocrine.

Vital links with: sensory system (refinement and sensitizing of the various senses); spinal canal and cord (fluid and nerve fibres); thalamus (disturbed conditions giving rise to anxiety and intense excitement); toxic conditions; debilitation; fainting; addictions; asphyxiation; wasting diseases; allergies.

Health risk: too hypersensitive to the environment, instability, touchiness, vacillation, anxiety-prone, drug/alcohol addictiveness, excitability, excessive emotionalism, lowered vitality.

Pluto ♇

Functional need: transcendence.

Physiological actions: eliminatory, purgative, erupting, expulsive, inflammatory.

Body systems: autonomic nervous, endocrine.

Vital links with: autonomic nervous system (deep-rooted and long-term unconscious processes likely to produce chronic and virtually incurable diseases); gonads or sex glands (reactions upon from emotional pressures and deep-rooted frustrations); skin eruptions/boils; sexual excesses and venereal diseases; chronic conditions.

Health risk: frustrated power-complex, restlessness, moodiness, aggressiveness, criticalness, sexual excesses, discontentment, over-intenseness, obsessions.

Traditional sign relationships with the body

Traditionally, each sign has been related to a specific area of the physical body, beginning with Aries and the head and ending with Pisces and the feet, as follows:

♈ head	♎ lumbar region
♉ throat	♏ genitals
♊ chest	♐ thighs
♋ breasts	♑ knees
♌ heart	♒ ankles
♍ abdomen	♓ feet

Although this arrangement is conveniently simple, the ancient astrologers are to be congratulated for their discovery of this orderly arrangement, particularly as the above relationships still do apply. However, as we have already shown with the planets, the signs too are now to be related to body systems.

The signs and physiological functions

Aries ♈

Physiological actions: initiatory, activity, quick-reacting, exciting, inflammatory.

Body system: autonomic nervous.

Vital links with: head ailments, adrenal glands, neuralgia, fevers, insomnia, nervous disorders.

Health risk: over-activity, restlessness, intensity, impatience, risk-taking, self-centredness, over-excitability, emotionality, insufficient relaxation, instability.

Taurus ♉

Physiological actions: sustaining, enduring, productive, intensifying, restraining, rigid.

Body system: alimentary.

Vital links with: nutrition and digestion, throat and ears, thyroid gland and goitre, biliousness.

Health risk: inflexibility, holding grievances and worries within, insecurity, self-indulgence, jealousy, brooding, routine-obsessed, resentfulness.

Gemini ♊

Physiological actions: transmitting, volatility, adaptability, flexibility, versatility, connecting, changeable, restlessness.

Body systems: central nervous, respiratory.

Vital links with: nervous system, lungs and bronchial tubes, neck, upper limbs, catarrh, rheumatism, bronchial afflictions, asthma, pleurisy, pneumonia.

Health risk: nervous restlessness, excitability, dissipation of nervous energy, frustration and 'in a rut', loneliness, lack of repose and relaxation, anxiety, instability.

Cancer ♋

Physiological actions: containing, defensive, assimilative, retentive, receptive.

Body system: alimentary (upper).

Vital links with: stomach, chest, breasts, ductless glands, pancreas, gastric catarrh.

Health risk: moodiness, powerful emotionality, acute sensitivity, touchiness, self-indulgence, nervous/emotional exhaustion.

Leo ♌

Physiological actions: projective, persevering, organization.

Body system: vascular (cardiac).

Vital links with: cardiac, circulatory and spinal afflictions.

Health risk: intenseness, uncompromising, self-centredness, self-indulgence, over-exertion, aggressiveness.

Virgo ♍

Physiological actions: discrimination, flexibility, preciseness, assimilative.

Body system: alimentary (lower).

Vital links with: duodenum, ulcers, appendicitis, colitis, faulty intestinal functioning.

Health risk: hypercriticalness, perfectionist, anxiety, emotional suppression, irritability.

Libra ♎

Physiological actions: relating, communicative, adaptability, harmonizing.

Body system: excretory.

Vital links with: kidneys, lumbar region, anaemia, diabetes mellitus.

Health risk: weakness of nature – 'giving in' attitude to avoid conflict, emotional reaction to injustices, hurt feelings, inhibited mental/emotional expression, vacillation, nervous exhaustion, anxiety.

Scorpio ♏

Physiological actions: intensiveness, penetrative, perseverance.

Body systems: reproductive, excretory.

Vital links with: genito-urinary systems, colon, prostate gland (male).

Health risk: over-intenseness, unforgiving, powerful emotions, acute worrying, nervous/emotional depletion due to excesses, aggressiveness, jealousy, stubbornness.

Sagittarius ♐

Physiological actions: extensive, adaptability, flexibility, projective, spontaneity, changeable.

Body system: central nervous (motor).

Vital links with: nervous system, hips and thighs, expiratory function of the lungs, sacroiliac and sciatic nerves.

Health risk: nervous exhaustion, highly-strung, frustration, impatience, restlessness, extravagance.

Capricorn ♑

Physiological actions: constructive, persevering, productive, discriminative.

Body system: skeletal.

Vital links with: bone structure and joints, lower limbs, skin infections, rheumatics.

Health risk: niggardly worrying, inadequate relaxation or light-heartedness and buoyancy, fear of insecurity, inhibitions.

Aquarius ♒

Physiological actions: innovative, separating.

Body system: vascular (circulatory).

Vital links with: circulatory system, lower limbs, especially ankles, anaemia, varicose veins, nervous disorders.

Health risk: contrariness, nervous tension, rebelliousness, excitability, perversity.

Pisces ♓

Physiological actions: absorption, sensitivity, assimilative, receptivity.

Body system: vascular (lymphatic).

Vital links with: glandular and lymphatic systems, feet.

Health risk: excessive emotion, acute sensitivity, anxiety, nervous/ emotional exhaustion, instability, drug/alcohol addiction, restlessness, moodiness.

Janet's potential vulnerability to physiological imbalance and illness

Janet's birth chart presents the following factors, which are likely to indicate where she could be most vulnerable to potential ill-health:

Asc. ♐

☽ ♐, ☌ Asc.

♃ ☌ Asc., ☍ (☿ ☌ ♅)

☉ ♊, □ ♂

☿ ☌ ♅, ☍ (Asc. ♃)

♀ □ ♆

The Asc. and ☽ always indicate potential vulnerability to ill-health. Angular planets – especially any in ☌ with the Asc. – also suggest potential physiological imbalance, as do any □ aspects to the Asc. and the ☉'s interrelationship with the chart pattern. These should be carefully studied. We can see how the above chart factors came to be listed in Janet's case. ♀ forming only one contact with the whole chart pattern may also provide a 'weak link' through its □ ♆.

As an exercise, you should list the body systems and health risks associated with the above chart factors. The emphasis will be seen to suggest that Janet will tend to be especially vulnerable through the central nervous system, also the endocrine, vascular and autonomic nervous systems.

In her letter to me after she received her character analysis, we recall that (page 312) she mentioned she could feel quite fit and healthy for longish periods and then suddenly 'things would go wrong'. It was as if she had been trying to constantly run a car at 80–110 mph and forgot that the oil might dry up and parts get overheated. She would realize then that she never really gave her 'body and brains' a chance to maintain good health and, when she assumed she was fit, warning noises in the engine did fairly regularly occur. She mentioned cramps, especially when swimming, a poor circulation, irregular periods, anaemia, headaches and a severe nervous breakdown.

Your list of behaviour likely to aggravate a health risk for Janet will show a distinct emphasis on restlessness, dissipation of nervous energy leading to nervous exhaustion, over-excitability and activity, instability, impatience, intenseness, anxiety, emotional vulnerability, moodiness. A sensitive, restless creature, forever denying herself sufficient relaxation.

Summary of chapter

The theme of this chapter is to show that anatomical features and physiological functions can be related to the planets and signs. It follows, therefore, that it is possible to predict from an individual birth chart where the subject is likely to be most vulnerable to potential ill-health.

CHAPTER 29

Forecasting Future Trends in One's Life

As well as indicating a person's potential qualities, based on their chart pattern at birth, astrology can also 'project' that chart into the future. It is possible to calculate the varied trends (e.g. those bringing opportunities for growth and benefit or those marking a period of caution and self-discipline) for as many years ahead as are required.

It is not possible within the limits of this book to instruct you in the techniques for calculating future trends. This chapter will give brief and yet concise information regarding the interpretation of the Sun, Moon and each planet in terms of the forecasting systems known as *progressions* and *transits*.

Progressions

There are various methods of progressions (the name derives from the progression of planets from their positions in the birth chart) and each is of a symbolic nature. The most commonly used is the 'one day = one year' method. Each day after the day of one's birth symbolically represents a whole year of one's life. Even the Bible mentions this method for prophesying: 'I have appointed thee each day for a year' (Ezekiel: 4.6). A progressed planet can form an aspect with a natal planet or with another progressed planet. An aspect is likely to be of little value in terms of significant developments in the life concerned if the same two planets do not aspect each other natally.

From personal experience I have found that progressed

aspects are of most value if they occur simultaneously with transiting aspects of similar nature.

Transits

Progressions can only be calculated from the ephemeris for the year of one's birth. Aspects from transiting planets to natal planets are calculated from the ephemeris for the year under review. For example, if one wants to know the aspects formed by transiting to natal planets during 1986, one needs to consult the 1986 ephemeris.

Transits, therefore, are planets' positions in the ephemeris for whatever year one wants to calculate their aspects for.

Trends are shown far more clearly by transits than progressions. But, as with progressed aspects, a transiting aspect is likely to be of little value in terms of significant developments in the life concerned if the same two planets do not aspect each other natally.

What do we mean by a 'trend'?

When an astrologer speaks of a *trend* he is referring to a particular period, usually in the future, when circumstances or conditions (e.g. business or financial interests, health, personal relationships) are likely to change, advantageously or otherwise, to take a new direction, perhaps developing into a potential crisis point in one's life. A trend occurs when an aspect is formed by two planets by progression or transit.

More than one aspect may be 'operating' around the same time and, as a result, it is often clear why there are two or more contrasting trends affecting one's life simultaneously. We can indicate approximately how long a particular trend may be effective – for several days, weeks, months and even for a few years.

Orb of significance

When we speak of a 'trend being operative', we are usually referring to the period during which the aspect or aspects associated with the trend will be within an 'effective orb'. There is no fixed orb one can adhere rigidly to. It is best to make a note of the date a progressed or transiting planet comes to within 1° orb of exact aspect with a natal planet or angle; the date when the aspect is exact; and the date when the aspect has 'separated' by 1°. This period is most likely to correspond with significant developments (psychologically or in terms of events). Periods when the slower-moving planets ♃ ♄ ♅ ♆   ♇ are applying to an aspect will inevitably embrace more time than transits of ☉ ☿ ♀, which relate to only two or three days of effectiveness. Transiting ☽'s aspects will be even more fleeting.

The importance of a subject's reactions to trends

Only possibilities or potentialities can be indicated according to the two planets involved in an aspect. What the subject may accomplish within the scope offered by a particular trend depends upon her ability and efforts to make fullest use of the opportunities arising. The astrologer can but advise when to proceed with caution or encourage initiative when an opportune trend for expansion and constructive action is at hand. Opportunities may be wasted if one just sat back and waited for beneficial 'hand-outs' during a ♃ transiting ☌ ☉ period. *Constructive reaction* promotes growth and development of character; *negative reaction* is regressive and disintegrating. The astrologer has also to take into account a client's circumstances and lifestyle, and her capacity for projecting herself into life. A teenager with only average education, a young mother struggling to bring up three children on Social Security benefit, a retired clergyman and a business tycoon would each react to a similar aspect and trend quite differently – although the basic nature of the trend would be identical for each.

Astrology is certainly a unique system for making one aware

of opportunities for improvement in life, both materially and spiritually. Each aspect – even, for example, a seemingly severely afflicting ♄ transiting □ ☉ – indicates a type of opportunity and the area within one's range of experience and environment where this will most probably develop or become evident. Instead of predicting dire misfortunes that might befall a subject when this aspect occurs, one must offer the subject constructive advice as to how she may best utilize and adapt herself to the conditions likely to prevail during the period of effectiveness. The aspect offers a unique opportunity to try to avoid possible losses, illness and other afflictions. One must still advise the subject of the risks associated with the difficult aspect, though not implying that adversities must happen and the subject can do nothing to avoid these.

Trends corresponding to planets' aspects

Briefly, here are some types of development likely to be encountered during trends associated with major aspects formed by each planet. Not every contact a planet can make (e.g. prog. Venus aspecting the Moon, each planet and the angles) has been dealt with here.

The Sun

By progression: Developments of possibly major and critical importance, with emphasis on the Sun's functional need of purposeful activity. The time could be ripe for beginning new ventures (especially with the ♂). Any type of aspect will mark an opportune period for making important adjustments. All major aspects by the Sun (or to the Sun by another progressed or transiting body) should correlate with a vitally important stage in the subject's psychological development, and this invariably means opportunities must be seized for making major decisions concerning personal or business matters.

The Moon

By progression: Emphasis will be on the Moon's functional need of adaptation, marking critical periods for adjusting to other people and to the environment. Sensitivity will be keen and emotional reactions to stress may make one vulnerable to disturbance in this respect. The emotional side of life will tend to be highlighted. Progressed or transiting aspects to the natal Moon will be interpreted similarly, according to the other planet involved.

Mercury

This is the most important planet for indicating a period when significant changes and readjustments are likely to occur, or could be planned. This is because the functional need of Mercury is avoidance of static and restrictive conditions, the achievement of wider and diverse experience for the acquiring of knowledge and fresh interests – all distinctive motives stemming from the need to communicate with the environment. Hence, a period of above average restlessness, when one could be constantly 'on the go'. A great deal of nervous energy could be expended. A similar interpretation is given for a progressed or transiting aspect, except that the period of a transiting aspect may only cover two or three days (though, when near a stationary point, the period will be longer). Progressed or transiting aspects to natal Mercury will be interpreted similarly, according to the other planet involved.

Venus

Basically an opportune period for developing *social* interests, a period when feelings may well be intensified and lead to varied emotional and creative outlets. An important stage in a love affair or in the emotional–sexual area of marriage. A period when there is often an increasing need to receive love and affection, and when a lack of this could be keenly felt. It will mark a trend when the value of one's relationship with others will be tested and should be better understood by making an effort to do so. Difficult aspects suggest the risk of social problems or emotional stresses and important engagements should be chosen carefully. A similar interpretation is given for a progressed or transiting aspect, except that the period of a transiting aspect may only cover two or three days (though, when near a stationary point, the period will be longer). The interpretations can also apply when natal Venus is aspected by another progressed or transiting planet.

Mars

By progression or transit: Likelihood of increased activity and an urge for energetic forms of self-expression. An opportune period for taking the initiative, for developing one's potential for enterprise and constructive self-assertion and for tackling matters requiring plenty of energy and drive. A time when energies must be sensibly controlled and harnessed, and impulsive action avoided. There will tend to be an above average risk of accidents and conflict with others, so due care and forethought should be taken. Similar developments can apply when natal Mars is aspected by another progressed or transiting planet.

Jupiter

By progression: Jupiter will not often form an exact aspect by progression during an average lifetime, but aspects by progressed ☉ ☽ ☿ ☿ to natal Jupiter will occur more frequently. When an aspect does occur, it marks a highly significant period when every opportunity should be taken to expand one's interests, to seek ways of increasing material assets and to improve one's status. Much benefit can be gained through deeper participation in life.

By transit: these aspects occur quite frequently and similar indications apply as given for a progressed Jupiter period.

Special note: due to retrograde motion Jupiter usually forms the same aspect to a natal planet three times, and this means that almost a whole year can be coloured by this trend. A ♂ is a particularly apt time for launching a new venture or for forming new and influential relationships. When Jupiter is involved in a difficult aspect great care will be needed to avoid extravagant or exaggerative behaviour and the taking of unnecessary risks – especially where financial and business affairs are concerned. Similar developments can apply when natal Jupiter is aspected by another transiting planet.

Saturn

By progression: Saturn will not often form an exact aspect by progression during an average lifetime, and a period within 1° orb applying and 1° separating may last more than twenty years. However, aspects by other planets to natal Saturn will occur more frequently. A period of eight years, covering five years applying by Saturn to exact aspect and three years separating, would be of most importance for consideration. These aspects will always mark a period when the utmost caution must be exercised regarding health and material interests. Whatever the aspect, this will also be a period when stability and self-discipline must be sought, and when one needs to accept a probable slower pace of progress, annoying frustrations and restrictions.

By transit: similar developments as given for progressed aspects, also when natal Saturn is aspected by another transiting planet.

Special note: due to retrograde motion, Saturn usually forms the same aspect to a natal planet three times, and this means that a whole year can be influenced by this aspect.

Uranus

By progression: Uranus will not often form an exact aspect by progression during an average lifetime, and a period within 1° orb applying and 1° separating may last for more than forty years. But aspects by ☉ ☽ ☿ ♀ to natal Uranus will occur more frequently. A period of about ten years, covering six years applying by Uranus to exact aspect and four years separating, would be of most importance for consideration. Likely to mark a trend of unsettlement, sudden and possibly dramatic major changes and developments. An opportune time for developing one's potentialities and a need to deviate from the normal in some constructive, creative, self-fulfilling form. Outlets for originality and inventiveness should be encouraged. Likely to be an increasing desire for personal freedom and the breaking down of inhibiting and restricting features in the life pattern.

By transit: the above features are likely to be much more

evident than with the progressed aspect, particularly during the period of a year or more covering the three-times occurrence of an aspect due to retrogradation. Similar developments can apply when natal Uranus is aspected by another transiting planet.

Neptune

By progression: Neptune will not often form an exact aspect by progression during an average lifetime, and a period within 1° orb applying and 1° separating may last an entire lifetime. But aspects by ☉ ☽ ☿ ♀ to natal Neptune will occur more frequently. Due to such relatively slow motion of Neptune by progression, it will be difficult to ascertain any distinctive influence by Neptune on the psyche and life pattern.

By transit: due to retrograde motion, an aspect usually occurs three times and these will extend for over a year. A period of increased sensitivity to other people, the environment and to one's own inner needs and desires. Often an opportune time for developing a special form of creative expression. A keynote is given by Neptune's functional need: refinement. Much can be gained psychologically and materially by seeking perfection. Risk of involvement in woolly-headed or escapist activities. Risk, too, of confused conditions, deceit by others and one's own vulnerability to self-deception and over-indulgence in emotional and sensation-seeking activities. Another keynote could be disintegration of some feature or form-structure in one's life pattern or health. Need to maintain a stable and commonsense attitude to life and its problems. May be an inspired period or one of disillusion and chaos, or simply one of high sensitivity with resultant strange developments intermittently. Similar interpretations can apply when natal Neptune is aspected by another transiting planet.

Pluto

By progression: Pluto will rarely form an exact progressed aspect during an average lifetime and therefore these indications apply more or less entirely to what might be expected when ☉ ☽ ☿ ♀ aspect natal Pluto by progression, when transiting Pluto forms a major aspect with a planet or angle, or its natal position is aspected by another transiting planet. Due to retrograde motion, an aspect formed by transiting Pluto usually occurs three times and these will extend for over a year. It marks a period when some kind of transformation within the life pattern or of a psychological nature may occur. This may be scarcely evident, or it may result as one or a series of dramatic or even catastrophic developments. One may feel compelled to act and express oneself in a determined and single-minded way; to extend one's accepted capabilities further than ever before. Sometimes one becomes aware of an inescapable need to eradicate an existing discordant feature from the life pattern, or circumstances force such drastic action to be taken. Developments can often be seen as the 'ending of a chapter of experience so that a new chapter can inevitably begin'.

Summary of chapter

The theme of this chapter is that the Sun, Moon and planets can indicate trends in one's life for any number of weeks, months or years ahead, based on the planets' transiting and progressed positions related to the planetary pattern in the birth chart.

Mayo–Eysenck Research

In 1969 I decided to confirm the ancient astrological theory that, of the twelve zodiacal signs (when occupied by the Sun), the six odd-numbered signs tend towards extroversion, whilst the six even-numbered signs tend towards introversion.

I constructed a questionnaire of seventy-four items. My astrological school's heavy daily mail from all over the world was an ideal source for obtaining samples. Astrology students and non-student correspondents were invited to answer the question-naire and return it with their birth data. Extra copies were sent for relatives and friends. Between 1969–70, 1,794 samples were regis-tered. I contacted Professor Hans Eysenck of the Institute of Psychiatry in London. The Institute's analysis of the data showed a highly significant result in favour of the hypothesis; odds against this result being arrived at by chance were over 10,000–1. In graph form, a clear sawtooth pattern was shown, with *all* six odd-numbered signs *above* the mean line, and *all* six even-numbered signs *below*.

In an endeavour to replicate these results, I gathered another 2,324 samples from subjects born in seventy-four different coun-tries using Eysenck's Personality Inventory (EPI). The pilot study's results were perfectly replicated. Also, on the neuroticism scale, the Water signs showed, as expected, a highly significant tendency to neuroticism and instability. A paper jointly written by Eysenck and myself was published in the American Journal of Social Psychology in 1978. Chapter 18 of my *Teach Yourself Astrol-ogy* (Teach Yourself Books, Hodder & Stoughton, 1979) is devoted to a report on these studies.

Using Eysenck's Personality Questionnaire (EPQ), a third study was arranged and between 1977–78 I again invited the Mayo School of Astrology's correspondents to help with the study, collecting 2,284 samples. Coincidentally these also came from subjects born in seventy-four countries. Again the same significant results for extroversion/introversion and neuroticism/stability were obtained.

News of these remarkably successful studies went around the world but, alas, the deserved acclaim was relatively short-lived; clearly shock waves had hit orthodox psychology circles. Unfortunately, due to misinformation received by influential psychologists who sought to replicate the studies, the validity of my research and results was not just doubted but rejected by the majority. One objection was that the samples used 'do not represent a random selection but had all previously consulted an astrologer'. This was totally incorrect. Another objection was, that if someone knew even a mere fragment of astrology, they would attribute to themselves the knowledge of their Sun sign characteristics whether or not these fully applied in their case!

Taking just the EPQ study, it is hardly feasible that 2,284 subjects from all walks of life, with the varied national characteristics of seventy-four different countries of birth, should *all* be biased 'due to prior knowledge of astrology'. This is even less likely when it is known that two-thirds of the subjects stated that they knew nothing about astrology. If bias were the case, one would expect each of the twenty-four questions relating to extraversion to have an odd-numbered sign most prominent (a higher percentage of samples for the sign than for even-numbered signs correlating with extroversion). Yet, for females, we find an even-numbered sign tends most strongly to the particular extraverted trait in only ten out of the twenty-four questions; and for males, a mere nine of the questions have even-numbered signs most prominent. Clearly this is because they answered truthfully, and not every extraverted trait applied to themselves.

One of the latest groups to replicate my study consisted of Rooij, Brak and Commandeur of the Department of Psychology at the University of Leiden, the Netherlands, who stated: 'We successfully replicated the result found by Mayo *et al.* (1978) that persons born with the sun in an odd sign of the zodiac tend to be extraverted, and that persons born with the sun in an even sign tend to be introverted.'

Calculating the Birth Chart

As I said in chapter 1, this book is planned to deal essentially with the interpretation of a birth chart and not with its calculation. However, for those readers who have never calculated a chart, we will very briefly indicate the procedure involved. For a step-by-step guide with examples and exercises, my *How to Cast a Natal Chart* (published by L. N. Fowler, 1201 High Rd, Chadwell Heath, Romford, Essex RM6 4DH, England) is recommended, as it was written specifically for beginner-students.

Information and tools required

(a) The birth data of the individual concerned.
(b) Blank chart form.
(c) Ephemeris for year of birth.
(d) Tables of Houses.
(e) Gazetteer.
(f) Book/s giving variations in Standard and Daylight Saving (Summer) Times.
(g) Acceleration Table.
(h) Tables for conversion of arc to time.
(i) Writing tools and accessories.

If you have a personal computer, for which you can buy specially programmed discs, you should only need to enter the birth data, and the computer will do the work for you and print off the chart.

The birth data: Birth data required are the date, time and place of birth. Check for accuracy. The kind of time must be clearly stated. Depending on the country of birth, it may be given as local mean time, Zone or Standard Time, Daylight Saving or Summer Time, or Greenwich Mean Time.

Chart form: A chart form is necessary to plot the calculated positions of the Sun, Moon, planets, angles and aspects for a given time and place. You may quite easily design your own chart, similar to that shown for Janet in figure 1. Printed charts can be obtained from L. N. Fowler at the address given above, although the chart will not be exactly as presented in this book.

Ephemeris for year of birth: An ephemeris is a book, published either annually or to cover several years, containing the daily positions of the Sun, Moon and planets, usually for noon Greenwich Mean Time for Greenwich in England for a given year or years. These can be bought from Foulsham, Yeovil Rd, Slough, Berks SL1 4JH, England.

Tables of Houses: This is a booklet necessary for the calculation of the important angles of a birth chart as well as house cusps, if you wish to experiment with houses. The two booklets most used are *Raphael's Tables of Houses for Great Britain* and *Raphael's Tables of Houses for Northern Latitudes*. They are published by and can be obtained from Foulsham (address above).

Gazetteer: A good gazetteer containing co-ordinates (latitude and longitude) for thousands of places throughout the world is available from any reputable bookseller.

Books giving variations in Standard and Daylight Saving (Summer) Times: Because ephemerides give planets' positions based on GMT, the first step in calculating a chart, if the time is not given in GMT, is to convert the given time to GMT. L. N. Fowler (address above) should be able to advise you.

Acceleration Table: Acceleration on the interval is a step in the calculation of local sidereal time at birth. These tables are given in my *How to Cast a Natal Chart*. This is a necessary adjustment because we are converting mean time into sidereal time. A sidereal day is completed faster than is a mean (solar) day, and acceleration on the interval refers to the difference between mean (solar) time and sidereal time during the interval that has just been calculated.

Tables for conversion of arc to time: Another step in the conversion of local sidereal time at birth is the conversion of degrees and minutes of terrestrial longitude into longitude equivalent in time. These tables are given in my *How to Cast a Natal Chart*.

The basic calculations for Janet's chart

We will use Janet's birth data as an example of the basic natal chart calculations which, as with all natal charts, will follow two main stages: to convert the given time, if necessary, to GMT; and to find the local sidereal time at birth.

Name:	Janet
Birth date:	23 May 1948
Birth time:	10.25 p.m. BST
Birth place:	Welwyn, England
Latitude:	51°49′ N
Longitude:	0°11′ W

Stage 1: Time Conversion

	H	M	S	
Birth time as given	= 10	25	00	p.m.
Zone Standard (E −, W +)	= 0	00	00	
Summer (or Double) Time (−)	= 1	00	00	
GMT	= 9	25	00	p.m.

GMT date = 23 May 1948

Janet was born when British Summer Time was operating, so one hour has to be subtracted from her given birth time to convert to GMT.

Stage 2: Finding Local Sidereal Time At Birth

	H	M	S
Sidereal time noon GMT	=	4	04	01
Interval from noon (p.m. +)	=	9	25	00
Result	=	13	29	01
Acceleration on interval[1] (p.m. +)	=		1	33
Sidereal time Greenwich at birth	=	13	30	34
Longitude equivalent in time[2] (W −)	=		0	44
Local sidereal time at birth	=	13	29	50

[1] see page 354.
[2] see page 63.

The sidereal time at noon GMT is taken from the 1948 Ephemeris for Janet's birthdate, 23 May. As birth was *p.m.*, the nine hours twenty-five minutes is added to the sidereal time at noon GMT. We add to this result the acceleration on this nine hours twenty-five minutes interval. This adjustment is necessary because we are converting mean time into sidereal time. We speak of an acceleration by sidereal time on mean (solar) time due to a sidereal day being completed by about three minutes fifty-six seconds *faster* than a mean (solar) day. The final step in stage 2 is to make an adjustment called longitude equivalent in time. This refers to the difference in time between the meridian of Janet's birthplace and the Greenwich meridian, determined by their difference in terrestrial longitude. Time is related to terrestrial longitude in terms of the Sun's apparent movement around the Earth, which is produced by the Earth's rotation on its axis from west to east.

Why is it so necessary to know Janet's local sidereal time at birth? Sidereal time and local sidereal time are directly related to the Earth's axial rotation. In setting up Janet's birth chart it is as if we have been able to stop the Earth rotating at the moment she was born, and by also knowing her exact place of birth, we have been able to determine her unique relationship to the planetary and zodiacal environments. The key factor for determining this relationship is, of course, her birth data, but the means of applying this key is provided by the sidereal time system of measurement. Sidereal time is a direct measure of the diurnal rotation of the Earth, and by local sidereal time we mean sidereal time as it is measured for a particular meridian or the observer's meridian – in the present case, the meridian of Janet's birthplace, Welwyn.

Calculating the angles of Janet's chart

Once we have calculated local sidereal time at Janet's birth, we can go a step further and calculate the angles of her chart, which we already know are the Asc.–Desc. axis and the MC–IC axis. Because the angles are determined by local sidereal time, we see that the angles are produced by the Earth's axial rotation. If we don't have a computer to do the task for us, we need to refer to the tables of houses for the necessary figures.

Calculating the planets' longitudes

We could not calculate the exact positions of the planets at Janet's moment of birth without having access to the 1948 Ephemeris. We know from the ephemeris the exact positions for noon on her birthdate, 23 May but, as she was born 9 hours and 25 minutes (in GMT) after noon, we must calculate how far each planet has travelled in longitude in that time interval and make the appropriate adjustment.

From the above brief observations we can see how each of us at our moment of birth is integrated with our cosmic environment.

Index

extreme psychological disorders, 326
mental type, 156
physiological actions, 335, 339
planet affinity, 128, 156
symbol, 2, 125
temperament, 156
planets
angular, 165, 169–70, 171–2, 179, 233
apogee, 191
deification of, xiii, 9–10, 126
ecliptic, 49, 52
inferior, 72, 189, 190
interpretation formula, 237
longitudes, 357
outer, 200
perigee, 191
perturbations, 67
physiological correlations, chapter 28 (327–40)
psychological role, xiii, chapter 11 (93–124)
progressions, transits, chapter 29 (341–9)
rhythms, chapter 8 (66–74)
sign affinities, 127, 128, 146
signs, 131, 232
superior, 72, 73, 189, 190, 191
symbols, 2
see also functional needs
Pluto
aspects: planets, angles, 178, 206, 212, 216, 220, 223, 225, 227, 228, 229
extreme psychological disorders, 324
functional need, 97, 120–24, 281
interpretation formula, 237–8, 255
latitude, 49
outer planet, 200
physiological actions, 335
progression, transit, 348
sign affinity, 128
superior planet, 72
survival needs, 122
symbol, 2
polar elevation, 45, 47

polarities, *see* signs
pole star, 68
precession of equinoxes, 68
prime vertical, 45, 47
progressions, chapter 29 (341–9)
psyche
activity, 100
basic structure, 80, 83, 84–5, 91
cells, 16
cosmos, 15
definition, 33
dynamic nature, 268
macrocosm, microcosm, 15
potentialities, xii, 96, 268, 282
satisfaction, 196
wholeness, 96, 273
psychiatrists, psychologists, 18, 80, 81, 257
astrology, prejudice against, 24, 82
confusion among, 81–3, 85
lacking astrological knowledge, 80–81, 257, 259, 272
value of astrology to, xiv, 26
psychology
astrology, xi, 8–9 81, 82
definition, 82
lacking coherent structure, 26, 80–83
psychopathic behaviour (definition), 316
psychotic behaviour (definition), 316

quadrature, 190
quadruplicities, *see* signs

reproductive system, 330
respiratory system, 329
retrograde motion, 72–4
right ascension
celestial longitude, 48
definition, 48
equator, 48
First Point of Aries, 48
measurement in, 48
meridians of, 47

Sagittarius
attitude, 154